"The stories that she has collected with such diligence, and presents with such clarity and skill, begin in the Soviet Union and end in Israel and the United States, the two main destinations of those who left Communism. The motives of those about whom she writes are set out clearly, as are their experiences. One of the strengths of this book is its portrayal of individuals: their personal stories, struggles, dilemmas and achievements. Each story is different, and each has lessons in it to illuminate and to inspire."
—**Sir Martin Gilbert**, historian

"By tracing the lives of several families and individuals over some two decades, Edith Rogovin Frankel illustrates the complexities of immigration generally and skillfully explores several dimensions of the experiences of Soviet Jewish immigrants in Israel and the United States. The twists and turns of Soviet Jewish lives are portrayed well by someone who has a deep understanding of their cultures, old and new."
—**Zvi Gitelman**, professor of political science and Tisch Professor of Judaic Studies at the University of Michigan

"*Old Lives and New: Soviet Immigrants in Israel and America* paints an incredibly sweeping and human portrait of Soviet Jewry over the past century. This immigrant group, which emerged out of the ruins of Communism, is captured through a series of individuals who tell the story from World War II and up through the trials and tribulations of immigrating and settling outside the Soviet Union at the end of the 20th century. The best history does more than give us facts and figures; it tells us how people lived. Edith Rogovin Frankel's work does that and more, interweaving the stories of a number of Soviet Jewish families in a way that makes a whole community come to life."
—**Gal Beckerman**, author of *When They Come for Us We'll be Gone: The Epic Struggle to Save Soviet Jewry*

"Dr. Edith Rogovin Frankel has written a highly original and absorbing account of numerous interviews she conducted with emigrants (mainly Jews) from the Soviet Union. She spoke to them the first time shortly after they arrived in Israel and the United States in the late 1970s . . . and a second time twenty-five years later. There are poignant descriptions of the difficult lives of Jews in the Soviet Union who sought to observe the religious traditions of Judaism, and then there are moving descriptions of the difficulties in adjusting to conditions in new cultures, and of the joys of those émigrés—a high percentage—who succeeded, both professionally and socially. . . . The book tells an inspiring story that deserves a wide readership."
—**Abraham Ascher**, Distinguished Professor Emeritus, Graduate Center, City University of New York

Old Lives and New

Soviet Immigrants in Israel and America

Edith Rogovin Frankel

Edith Frankel

Hamilton Books
A member of
The Rowman & Littlefield Publishing Group
Lanham • Boulder • New York • Toronto • Plymouth, UK

Copyright © 2012 by
Edith Rogovin Frankel

Hamilton Books
4501 Forbes Boulevard
Suite 200
Lanham, Maryland 20706
Hamilton Books Acquisitions Department (301) 459-3366

10 Thornbury Road
Plymouth PL6 7PP
United Kingdom

Library of Congress Control Number: 2011941556
ISBN: 978-0-7618-5784-6 (paperback : alk. paper)
eISBN: 978-0-7618-5785-3

For my daughters Leora and Rachel, their husbands,
Ilan and Jonathan, and my grandchildren:
Ariel, Eviatar, Dora, Daniel, Jordan, Keren, and Amitai Jonathan
with great love

And to the memory of my grandparents,
the first modern-day immigrants in my family,
who made their way from the Russian Empire
to the American shores over a hundred years ago:
Molly and Abraham Sider
Dora and Jacob Rogovin

Contents

Some Words of Thanks

Old Lives and New is far more than an objective report on the intricacies of emigration and the complications of the immigration process. It involves the personal testimony of dozens of people who left the Soviet Union in the 1970s and made their way either to Israel or the United States, summing up their own experiences, their observations and comments, their aspirations and the reality of what they found in their new country of residence. It is only through their generous sharing of information in extensive interviews that this work could transmit to the reader the full essence of the immigration experience. And it is for this reason that I wish to single out for thanks, first and foremost, the men and women who were kind enough and candid enough to provide the moving testimony in this book.

Writing *Old Lives and New* was a tremendous adventure. It involved selecting good potential interviewees—though it must be said that probably every single emigrant from the Soviet Union had at least one good personal story—talking to them at length and often with a follow-up interview, and then, twenty-five years later, tracking them down again, not necessarily an easy job. An old and dear friend, Virginia Kurtzman, put her hands on some useful information and without her and her daughter, Leigh Mauer, two of my original group would never have been located again for the second interview in the twenty-first century. Two more good friends, Enid Wurtman and Linda Baruch, located two more interviewees for me after I had searched fruitlessly to find them. Another friend, Tanya Akhonin Sochurek, hosted me in Florida, where we followed maps and vague instructions to discover the location for one of my follow-up interviews. And Yosef Zisels, who miraculously turned up just when I was trying to locate Yan and gave me his number, certainly deserves my gratitude. The ability of all of them to help me was both serendipitous and extraordinarily lucky.

Special thanks, as always, go to my unflappable agent, Phyllis Westberg, who had faith in this project and was most encouraging in her search for a publisher. I also want to express my appreciation to my editor, Laura Espinoza, whose patient and tactful approach helped us to solve so many small problems amicably.

I was also fortunate to receive generous grants from three institutions making it possible for me to have the tapes transcribed in their original language for later perusal. Most of the interviews were carried out in Russian, some in Hebrew and only a few in English, so the transcriptions were of major value. For this I have to thank the Israel Academy of Sciences, the American Council of Learned Societies, and the Memorial Foundation for Jewish Culture. Their help was inestimable. Help with transcripts was also provided by the Oral History section of the Institute of Contemporary Jewish Affairs at the Hebrew University of Jerusalem. Thanks, too, to Dr. Dov Levine.

A number of people struggled to decipher the tapes and type the transcriptions from various languages. This is of necessity a partial list. The main transcriber, back in the 1980s, was Esther Lomovsky, who did a marvelous job of transcribing most of the interviews of the first round, as well as other interviews that I had made for another project. Dafna Bareket typed up some of the later interviews.

My two wonderful daughters were helpful, each in her own way. Leora gave me some thoughts about how to conceptualize the project, given the amount of raw material that I had and the main theme that I wanted to explore. Rachel helped in a number of ways, including handling some of the later Hebrew and English interviews, and providing support and advice in innumerable ways. My son-in-law Jonathan Heller provided back-up support to me of a technical nature—something of a mystery to me and second nature to him.

The immigration process is common to us all: if we were not personally involved in it, then our parents, grandparents, or great-grandparents probably were. It can be a very painful experience and the outcome depends largely on how successfully the transplant took. Very often the new homeland is regarded with great affection and gratitude. But it is not unusual—depending upon the specific case—that in the long run, the person who migrated ends up unsure of where he or she really belongs and if there is any place on earth that they can truly call home. All too often it is only the next generation that can feel a true identity with the new country of residence. It is this process—leaving the old home and taking up residence in the new one—that fascinated me. I hope that through the stories of these particular individuals an understanding of migration on a personal scale can be achieved.

As in all of my endeavors, my husband, Jonathan Frankel, encouraged me. Although he did not live to see the completed work, he did read the first several chapters of this book and loved them. I think that he took as much pleasure—and found as much excitement—in my interviews as I did.

As in the case of books of this kind, some of the names and other attributes of the men and women who provided their stories have been changed in the text in order to provide privacy. In order to enable the reader to keep track of the various real life characters who come and go throughout the book, a list in the back indicates where each person appears.

Last, but certainly not least, I want to thank Joseph Grossman for his role in the completion of this work. Joe has steadfastly encouraged me and enthusiastically urged me to forge ahead even when it wasn't clear that the book would ever see the light of day, never doubting for a moment that it would reach a successful conclusion. He has been a true beam of light in the forest of the night.

Introduction

This is the story of people—some very specific individuals—who left their native land, their friends and families, their work and familiar surroundings, and started to create a new life in a strange country. They will be followed in time from their original lives in their home country, through the decisions to leave and where to go, right up to the present, twenty-five years later.

In today's world, migration is a constant theme, whether it is a political or economic or cultural or racial issue. Great numbers of people have moved out of Africa or Asia and into Europe, out of Eastern Europe and into Western Europe, out of South and Central America and into the United States. In some cases these migrants are welcomed and their skills gladly exploited in the receiving country. In many more instances, they are rejected, limited in their numbers, forced to work illegally in unacceptable conditions or with substandard wages. Walls are erected in some areas of the world to prevent the free passage of travel; electric fences have been set up in other places for the same purpose. Even the high seas are patrolled to avoid boatloads of migrants from docking in unwelcoming ports. With time—and the growth of populations—the problem has intensified. The rich, vast fertile regions that were once available, drawing the adventurous or the desperate, are no longer open to settlement. And in the towns, too many people are competing for the same jobs, even lowly ones.

The migrants in this book, however, do not fit into this generalized category. With disproportionately high professional qualifications, they could offer their new lands a wide spectrum of skills. Their principal problem was not that of finding a country to welcome them, but of receiving permission to emigrate from their country of origin. Early in the nineteen seventies, the Soviet Union, for reasons of its own, began a policy of limited permitted emigration. This was not for all citizens, but for very specific categories; in the case of our present study, for Jews and their families. During that decade, over two hundred thousand Jews—or people considered Jews for purposes of emigration—were allowed to leave the USSR. The destination of most of them was Israel and the second largest recipient country at that time was the United States.

Those who took the decision to leave had varied motivations. Some—particularly individuals from the western parts of the Soviet Union and the Baltic republics, which had all been absorbed into the U.S.S.R. at the beginning of the Second World War—were galvanized by a feeling of Zionism that had been nurtured during their childhoods in eastern Poland and the independent Baltic states. For the most part, they would doubtless head for Israel. Others feared an economic downturn either for themselves or their children and felt that the situation—particularly for Jews—would only become worse with time. So a large number of emigrants basically did it for their children and their children's future. Some of these people were leaving because of perceived antisemitism, a lack of equal opportunity for Jews and preferential treatment in jobs and education given to the natives of the Republics within the Soviet Union at the expense of the Jewish population. For others—probably smaller in number—there was a felt need to leave a country where there was so little freedom of expression and to search for a democratic milieu elsewhere. Yet again, there were Jews who wished to practice their religion openly and fully, something that was impossible to realize inside the Union of Soviet Socialist Republics.

As the decade wore on, many people simply felt the urge to leave because so many others had already done so; they feared that if they didn't act immediately, they might lose the opportunity to emigrate at all. They were concerned that with a smaller number of Jews remaining inside the Soviet Union they could conceivably receive worse treatment. Once a large number of them had already abandoned the ship, they might even be regarded as untrustworthy, given the willingness of their coreligionists (or co-nationals) to leave for countries that were not regarded as friendly allies. When the gates actually did start to close, in the early eighties, there were large numbers of would-be emigrants who found themselves locked in.

It had been Bolshevik policy, from the beginning, to try to stifle the separateness of the Jews. Religion, needless to say, was considered the "opiate of the people" and, whether Christianity or Judaism, was to be discouraged as much as possible. Large numbers of churches and synagogues were closed, some even destroyed. Further, neither Stalin nor Lenin had seen the Jews as fitting into their definition of a nation. Lenin suggested that they are actually a caste, a hereditary group that fulfills certain economic functions. These functions, however, would not be needed in the new socialist state that was being founded after the October revolution. The Bolsheviks intended that the Jews would gradually blend into the surrounding Russian population, would assimilate linguistically, culturally, and economically, and gradually cease to be differentiated from their neighbors. They had had no geographic territory that was their own within the Russian empire, having been forced to live, by and large, within the Pale of Settlement, where they formed only a small fraction of the total population of that vast area on the western fringes of the country.

After the destruction of the tsar and his regime, the Jews would have to become proletarianized, of course, abandoning their small craft and trading enterprises to become salaried or wage-earners like everyone else. There was even an attempt to settle Jews on the land—just as the nineteenth century tsars had tried—so that they could earn their living by tilling the soil. Indeed, this policy of the economic transformation of the Jews succeeded by the end of the nineteen twenties, although not all Jews became factory workers or farmers. Many—disproportionate to their place in the general population, it must be said—eventually found their place as engineers and teachers, mathematicians and writers, white collar workers and doctors.

Ironically, what did continue to keep them apart from the rest of the Russian or Ukrainian or Georgian population was not their religion or language, but the fifth line in the internal passport, or identity papers, that every Soviet citizen had to carry from the age of sixteen. On that line—*natsionalnost* (or nationality)—they had to identify themselves as Jews (*evrei*), for lack of a better grouping. They were not, by Soviet definition, Russians. Nor were they Armenians or Belorussians or Ukrainians. So, *faute de mieux*, in spite of all the previous Bolshevik ideology, they remained Jews by nationality. This may have been the single most potent factor in maintaining their Jewish identity.

There were, of course, other factors. It is difficult to estimate the level of importance of the various influences, but beyond the categorization of Jews in their passports, both historical events and family proved to be significant in reinforcing feelings of Jewish identity. Even though the Jews of the new Soviet Union had been cut off from their historic cultural and religious roots with the destruction of their community organizations, the regime's discouragement of attending synagogue services, and the prohibition of the study of Hebrew, many did, amazingly, continue to feel their ties to the Jewish community. It is true that in a period when religious practice was frowned upon, very few Jews actually maintained their religion to the letter of the law. Those who did were largely of two kinds of background: people who had received serious religious training during their youth in pre-revolutionary Russia or in Poland or one of the independent Baltic countries during the interwar period and more traditional Jews who lived in outlying areas of the Soviet Union, where such practices might be carried on far from the eagle eye of Moscow—the non-Ashkenazic Georgian Jews or Mountain Jews, for example.

But for the vast majority of Soviet Jews, there were nevertheless remnants of the religion or culture or language that survived in spite of everything. There were a number of contributing factors at play here. Early on, the rich Jewish background which most had experienced was still within living memory. Later, when the Second World War began, the Jews of the Soviet Union were forced to recognize that their Jewishness set them apart from the rest of the population and made them a special prey to Hitler's genocidal policy. While many Jews were caught and killed as the German army marched across the Western portion of the Soviet Union in the first months of the invasion, many others were out of harm's way or managed to escape to relative safety in the eastern reaches of Russia and Central Asia.

Following the war, Soviet Jews were shocked and saddened at the way the Nazi onslaught was generalized by the Soviet authorities to a "fascist" attack on "the Soviet people," with no special mention or understanding of the specific Holocaust aspect of the war years. This, too, reinforced their feeling of Jewish separateness.

Beyond that, parents and particularly grandparents had a significant influence on the maintenance of Jewish identity. This could be in small ways—the use of Yiddish in the home, making sure that there was matzah for Passover, even if the whole seder was not celebrated; marking the beginning of the Jewish new year or fasting at Yom Kippur—or in major ways, such as telling their grandchildren about their people's history, teaching them Hebrew, imbuing them with pride that they were Jews, even within a Soviet, atheistic context.

Furthermore, confrontations with various forms of antisemitism, including sometimes being taunted in childhood by their peers, reinforced their feeling of Jewish identity. Not everyone had problems of these kinds, but even the fear that such a thing could happen was enough.

It should be noted that there was another significant group that was emigrating from the Soviet Union during the nineteen seventies. These were the Soviet Germans. Like the Jews, who had originally entered Poland at the invitation of the King during the thirteenth and fourteenth centuries, the Germans had come to the Russian empire, beginning at the end of the eighteenth century, with the encouragement of the tsarina Catherine the Great. She had hoped that the industrious, efficient, hard-working ethos of the German farmers would influence the lazier, heavy-drinking Russian peasants. The Germans were offered advantageous conditions, land, freedom from taxation and the military draft. They started to pour into the Russian empire, setting up villages up and down the Volga River and in the fertile lands of New Russia to the north of the Black Sea, throughout the ensuing century. The ethnic

Germans retained their language, religion and their homogeneity to a large extent and established prosperous farms. During the Second World War they were treated with great suspicion by Stalin and eventually were brutally uprooted and shipped east under severe conditions. They were never permitted, even decades after the war, to return to their native areas along the Volga. It was this group that, along with the Jews, was permitted to emigrate from the Soviet Union beginning in the nineteen seventies, though in their case the destination was West Germany, a sort of "repatriation." Their emigration patterns—the increasing and decreasing flow over the next twenty years according to the vicissitudes of internal and external Soviet policy—matched those of the Jews.

THE INTERVIEWS

The characters in this book are real. There is no invention, no imagination in presenting them. Some of their names have been changed. Aside from an occasional correction in style or grammar, quoted statements are precisely what was said. Who are these people?

In the late nineteen seventies and early eighties, when the exodus from the Soviet Union had reached its peak, I set out to interview some of those who had made the great step. Some of them were living in Israel at the time and others in the United States. Most of those interviewed were Jewish, but not all. However, they had all left the Soviet Union with the Jewish emigration. The legal basis on which all of them had left was that of family reunification, though in many cases this was merely an excuse to get out, not a legitimate desire to be with a family member abroad. With very few exceptions, the interviews were conducted in Russian. They were tape recorded and later transcribed. Some of the interviewees led me to others. In certain cases, I interviewed both husband and wife, or a parent and child.

After collecting this wealth of material, I put it aside, while considering how best to use it. As it happened, other projects arose and the interviews remained safely on the shelf. My decision of what to do with them only came about a long time after. Looking over the transcripts a few years ago, I realized that I had a treasure trove of fascinating human stories and experiences. It was at that point that I decided to seek out the original people whom I had talked to and interview them again, now after twenty-five years.

Hunting down all of the original people was not that easy. As a generalization, one can say that there was far more movement, shifting of domicile, in the United States than in Israel. In some cases, someone who originally arrived in Israel had moved to America, though not the opposite. As might have been expected, a small number—four—had passed away during the interim. One married couple had no children and with their passing came the end of the story. I managed to find the daughter of one of the men who had died and she was able to fill me in on the remarkable details of the following decade and a half of his life. One woman ended up in a retirement home in Seattle and her daughter unfortunately seems to have disappeared without a trace. So in this case there are some loose threads.

Because the book is based on interviews, the language often reflects the way people spoke to me. There is thus a variety of words for the same place, for example. Jews always referred to the city as Kovno, while Lithuanians call it Kaunas. Similarly, Vilna and Vilnius are both names for the same city. Sometimes the same person would use different terms in a conversation. I did not try to keep geographical names consistent, for that reason.

This is a study of people who went through the vicissitudes of migration, just as many of our parents or grandparents or great grandparents did. They followed a familiar path that so many—whether from China or from Somalia, from Poland or from Mexico—have trodden before. They had to acculturate to their new community, learn another language, find a way to make a living, adjust to the demands and standards of a country very different from their home one. Thus, while they did not have the primary difficulty of finding a country willing to accept them—the most that happened was that they had to wait for an entry visa for a few months in Italy—the people interviewed, to varying extents, went through a difficult, often prolonged, time once they were in their new homes. One does not abandon one's old life easily. It is all too facile to imagine that immigrants, or refugees, fall gratefully into the arms of their new countrymen, happy to have found a haven at last. One must not ignore the human aspect of the process of migration. While the end result—successful acculturation and economic security—can be seen as the main object of immigration, there is usually a price to pay.

This is not a statistical survey. It traces the lives of real people in detail and thus while every story bears similarities, each experience is also unique. Can we learn from their experiences? Was there a "better" or "worse" way to handle emigration? Was one destination preferable to an alternate one? Could happiness have been more likely to be found in one place or another? No conclusions of these kinds have been drawn. Every case—just as every human being—is different from all others and trying to estimate a correct formula for happiness would bring us more into the realm of fiction than fact.

Part One

ORIGINS

Chapter One

The War

BACKGROUND

Talk to a person from the former Soviet Union who was born before 1945, and the Second World War looms large. Even for the next generation—people born in the sixties and after—World War Two is a significant part of family history. Everyone was affected by the war, those who were Jewish and those who were not. The tremendous loss of life from the war years, the destruction and chaos, the disastrous effects that went on for many years after the war had ended—this was the heavy toll that citizens of the Soviet Union had to pay. Beyond that, the Jews suffered the additional horror of the Nazi genocidal program unleashed on any territory where they gained control.

Life had not been easy before the onslaught of war. Soviet citizens endured increasing hardships throughout the nineteen thirties: collectivization; artificial famine; the tremendous pressure of rapid industrialization; the arbitrary arrests that came with the purges in the second half of the decade; a rule of internal terror. With the end of the relative diversity of the 1920s, people found their personal liberty increasingly limited by censorship, controlled information and a lack of personal mobility. Not only were political parties other than the Communist Party outlawed, private organizations banned, but also a policy against organized religion caused the closing of many churches and synagogues and reduced the number of people who openly adhered to their religion.

For Jews it became patently clear as the first decade after the Bolshevik revolution progressed that bright young people who wanted to succeed in their education and their careers would do well to avoid the traditions and culture of their parents and grandparents. But if they were willing to fit into the system, there were almost unlimited opportunities to rise up through the ranks, for Jews as much as for others. In the post-tsarist era, Jews were no longer being kept down by *numerus clausus* in education or by restrictions on domicile or profession. They were, though, forced to exchange the gains of the individual for the losses of the community.

By the 1930s, it was clear that the post World War I settlement had failed and that Europe was becoming dangerously unstable. Not only was there a severe economic depression, but Germany, which, as the main loser, had been suppressed politically and militarily, was, by the mid-thirties, on the rise, arming and expanding. Inside the Soviet Union, by the end of the thirties, the great purge had been unleashed on the military and almost the entire top echelons of the various services had been removed, summarily tried and either executed or shipped off to labor camps in the east. A whole new officer corps, inexperienced in war and lacking in the higher military training of the famed Frunze Academy, was put in place. This was at the very time that Germany was menacing Czechoslovakia and continuing to develop its military strength and preparedness. By the summer of 1939, Stalin approved of discussions between the German and Soviet foreign ministers, which culminated in late August in the Moltov-Ribbentrop Pact, a treaty of benevolent neutrality. From now on, Germany and the Soviet Union would tacitly ignore the other's incursions into foreign territory. Delineated in a secret addendum to the treaty was the partitioning of Poland between the two powers.

The war began almost immediately, with England and France declaring war when Nazi Germany invaded Poland from the west on September 1, 1939. The Soviet Union followed suit two and a half weeks later from the east, dividing the country between them. From this point on, Stalin assumed that the USSR could stand aside while others fought. His country could continue to develop its armed and industrial might without interference, safely relying on the pact.

It was thus to the astonishment of the Soviet leadership—despite intelligence reports—that the armies of the Third Reich invaded the country nearly two years later, on June 22, 1941. Early in the morning, German planes began to fly over Soviet territory and infantry and armored divisions started to cross the border in what was known as Operation Barbarossa. The invasion took place nearly 129 years to the day after Napoleon had led the Grande Armée across the Neman River into the Russian Empire. But his unsuccessful stay had been for only a few months. The Germans were to be on Soviet territory for years.

While everyone in the Soviet Union was touched by the war, even those who had not yet been born, untold numbers found that the war had a seismic influence on their lives. Among them were some of the individuals whose lives we shall be following throughout the book.

ZAKHARIA

By 1941, at age nearly 13, Zakharia had experienced considerable changes in his life. In 1933, his father, part of a German Jewish family that had a far-flung leather-working business, had moved with his immediate family to Kovno (called Kaunas by the Lithuanians), the capital of independent, inter-war Lithuania, to run his part of the business there. He and his wife had two sons, Alexander, born in 1923, and Zakharia, born in 1928. Zakharia was sent to a Jewish school (where he first learned Yiddish) and, from third grade studied in Hebrew. When the Bolsheviks came in 1940 the school switched back to Yiddish, as Hebrew was a language associated with religion and Zionism, and thus considered unacceptable for study in the Soviet Union. In the ensuing years the child also learned Lithuanian and, later, Russian. The family kept up certain Jewish practices: bar mitzvahs, Passover seders, occasional Saturday prayers at the synagogue. The family name plate is still on one of the seats in the synagogue in Kovno today.

Business was good: the whole world was preparing for war. There was a need for shoes for soldiers, coats for officers, all made of leather. The prices kept going up. His father realized that their personal situation was precarious and gradually made plans to take the family to Palestine. Large sums of money had to be accumulated in pounds sterling for their immigration certificates and this was arranged with a London bank. "I imagine that the person receiving the goods my father sent was also a Jew. And he would transfer a little money from each shipment so that we would be able to leave." But business was so good it was hard to give it up and move and in the late nineteen thirties Zakaharia's father kept putting off the decision from one week to the next. "And if we have been in the Diaspora for 2000 years, what's another two weeks?" This went on until the Bolsheviks came, and then it was too late. Zakharia's father later likened his experience to that of a monkey in one of Rudyard Kipling's stories of India. Because it was such a rare monkey, the local Indians tried in every way possible to catch one, alive. But the monkey was very clever and managed to keep out of their reach until, finally, the men devised a clever trap. Knowing that the monkey loved pineapple, they designed a cage with a juicy slice of pineapple inside. The bars of the cage were spaced widely enough so that the monkey would be able to reach in. However, once it was holding the pineapple, the monkey could not withdraw its hand—not without dropping the desired piece of fruit. He wanted the fruit, and he wanted to escape, but he could not have both and was thus captured. And I, said Zakharia's father, I am like that monkey and now we are caught.

At the end of the school year of 1941, Zakharia received a holiday voucher for a camp for the Young Pioneers, the children's organization of the Communist Party. His older brother, Alexander, was seventeen and already a first-year medical student; he remained in Kovno with their parents.

The camp was in Druskininkai, some 150 kilometers south along the Neman River from Kaunas and there were about three hundred children there, some eighty of them Jews. In the early hours of the morning of June 22nd, the German invasion began and they quickly took over vast swathes of territory. No enemy action, though, was in the area of the camp. The German army had not yet crossed the Neman in that area and was still to the north. That same morning, the children at Zakharia's camp were told that war had started but they were not to worry: the Red Army was doing well. They were put on a train to be returned to their parents, but it couldn't reach Kaunas or even Vilna because of enemy action and eventually the train headed east towards Minsk and then on to Smolensk, keeping just ahead of the German advance. After a day or two they were finally given some food and milk. They traveled for an entire month, ending up in a town in the northern Urals.

Eventually they were put into a children's home and spent the war years together, all the children and the Komsomol youth leaders from the camp. At one point they were deep in the countryside, and were expected to grow some of their own food. In fact, they were half starving. Most of the children came down with scurvy. They were also suffering from cold: they had left Lithuania in the summer and didn't have the right clothing for a Siberian winter. By the spring of 1942 they were moved to better conditions, with an improvement in the food—though there was never enough,—and a school. As Lithuania was under German occupation, none of the children received mail from their parents.

ISAAC

Unlike Zakharia, who found himself caught up in the panic from the first days of war, Isaac—growing up in Odessa—was not in immediate danger. By the beginning of August, the Germans had cut off Odessa from the great land mass, but even then the Russians managed to keep their Black Sea port open for a considerable amount of time. Only in the middle of October did the enemy take full control of the area. In the meantime about half the city's population—the Russians put the number at some 350,000 civilians—had escaped or been evacuated.

In Isaac's case, the whole family could not manage to get out. His father was hospitalized, and so it was his mother and aunt who took their four children on September 18, 1941, to the docks and boarded a ship, the *Dnieper,* east to the Black Sea port of Novorossisk. From there they took a train heading north. Isaac, at thirteen, was the oldest child, while the youngest, his aunt's child, was only three. When the train stopped at Povorino, Isaac was told to get off the train and get some milk for his little cousin. While they were in the station, the Germans started bombing the area and so the train immediately started up, leaving Isaac standing alone on the platform. For the duration of the war, Isaac wandered around, never near the place (in Siberia) that his family had been heading for. First there was a cattle train to the Sea of Azov, then another train to Alma Ata in Tajikistan. He was in Tashkent for a time; then he worked in a textile factory in Ashkhabad. He stayed in villages, lived in tents, camped out in a railway station, ended up in the mountains near the Iranian border; worked in an oil field near Krasnovodsk. Back in Odessa, he had had a big family—a grandmother, another aunt, cousins, his father in the hospital—and they were all killed. He was completely alone in the world from age thirteen until sixteen.

CLARA

By coincidence, Clara, the little girl who would become Isaac's wife in 1953, also escaped from wartime Odessa on the *Dnieper* in September, 1941, though not necessarily on the same sailing. Clara was six years old. She traveled with her mother, her paternal grandmother and her father's sister. From Novorossisk they made their way by train to Karaganda, in Kazakhstan, thousands of miles from the Black Sea. There they lived in a basement room. At night they could hear wolves howling; at times, the wolves even came up to their windows.

Clara's father wasn't with them as he was in the army. The only one in their family group who worked was her aunt. She was 16 at the start of the war and found a kitchen job in a *stolovaia*, a workers' canteen. One of her jobs was peeling potatoes and she would bring home the potato skins, which Clara's mother would wash and cook. These formed a very important part of their diet.

The room they lived in had a large Russian stove in it, which, as was customary, stood in the corner. On top was a ledge, which was always warm, and Clara's grandmother, as the oldest in the family, was given that as the best place to sleep. During the period of the war Clara had no schooling and when she got back to Odessa in 1945 at age ten, she could hardly read or write. Whatever she did know had been taught to her by her grandmother.

MARK

Mark was born in Minsk in 1938. In the summer of 1941, his aunt—his mother's sister, Frieda—took the little boy to the countryside where his maternal grandparents were living in Shchors, in Chernigov Province in the Ukraine.

It was a trip of some 250 miles. There he would have a pleasant stay with his grandparents where it was green and there was plenty of fresh air and a nearby river. Frieda returned to Minsk. His parents would join Mark and his maternal grandparents when they had their vacation. But this never happened. About ten days after he got there, the war started. His father was mobilized. By the 28th of June, Minsk had been taken. His mother found it impossible to get out of the city and eventually ended up in the ghetto. She was killed in one of the S.S. "actions" there in 1942. His father, Vulf, was killed at the front. Vulf's parents were killed in the ghetto as was most of the family. Of his two sisters, one, Tanya, was killed in the Minsk ghetto when she was 20. Berta, the younger sister, was sixteen at the beginning of the war and joined the partisans. She somehow managed to survive.

Mark and his grandparents were evacuated to Siberia, to the Ural mountains, during the war. His aunt Frieda had somehow managed to get out of Minsk at the last minute and so she joined her parents with her own son. Thus they all fled to the east and stayed together until the end of the war.

So Mark ended up being brought up by his grandparents. His grandfather was a blacksmith, a very good one. His skills helped the family scrape together a living during the near-starvation years. While the family was Jewish on both sides, Mark was not brought up with much Jewish tradition. However, his grandmother did bake matzah for Passover and they tried to keep track of when Jewish holidays were coming. He was in a loving home while growing up. As he lost all contact with his parents at age three, he has almost no recollection of them at all, just a few fleeting images.

SERAFIMA

A beautiful, rather delicate person, Serafima was born just after the Bolshevik revolution, in 1918. Her parents had been poor village Jews who moved to St. Petersburg before her birth. Her father was a joiner and found work in the big city, though they never did very well. Serafima was the youngest of five children and the only one to survive into the 1980s.

She was a musical child and studied the piano at a music school. "[In Leningrad] the culture was extraordinary and it was possible to study—in my time, as I grew up, everyone could study whatever they wanted." By "her time" Serafima meant, the 1930s. The tsarist *numerus clausus* for Jewish students did not exist after the February 1917 revolution and the world of education was open to them without limit. This period after the fall of the Romanov dynasty was the first time, historically, that Jews could live within the borders of heartland Russia without special permission or limitation.

She was on vacation, a twenty-two year old, when she met a young engineer, originally from Fedosia on the Crimean coast. They fell in love and married and their first daughter was born before the war. But life suddenly became excruciatingly complicated for Serafima. They were in Leningrad on June 22, 1941. Her husband took their little daughter and arrived safely in Ufa in Bashkiria, where he had a job in an aircraft factory. Serafima remained in Leningrad. Residents of Leningrad were called upon to do their utmost for their beleaguered city and Serafima trained to be a nurse and spent much of the war tending the wounded in her native city. She was, as she put it, "at the front."

Hitler had put aside thoughts of capturing and occupying Leningrad and, instead, ordered his troops to surround and blockade it. While Leningraders were saved from the savage hardships of street to street fighting, they nonetheless suffered greatly during the more than two years of the blockade. There were bombings. Food was strictly rationed—it was very difficult to get food into the city at all—and thousands of people died every month from hunger and the disease brought on by severe malnutrition and cold. During the summer months, a certain amount of food and supplies was delivered by boat. In the winter a road was laid on the icy surface of Lake Ladoga so trucks could bring in supplies. The route—the city's lifeline—was extremely hazardous, subject to enemy bombings. It was plagued by worries about the thickness of the ice, and blizzards often prevented traffic from moving for days on end. In all, with the toll of the hunger and the bombings, about a million people died in Leningrad during the war.

Serafima remained in the besieged city, working as a nurse, experiencing bombardments—including the bombing of her own house—and trying to stay alive. From the ruins of her house, she escaped with a little suitcase and some photographs. By now none of her documents had survived. She couldn't even prove that she was her husband's wife.

At one point, everything went quiet: "I thought that the war had ended! It turned out that I had simply gone deaf. For a long long time I couldn't hear." She somehow managed to join her husband and daughter, but in 1944 she returned to Leningrad, alone. Her husband wasn't allowed to come back with her. "Stalin didn't allow people from aircraft factories to leave. So he stayed there." This was to remain the unfortunate state of their lives.

AARON

Aaron was born in a small town, not far from Kiev, in 1924—a typical *shtetl*, a place with a sizable Jewish population, where the market place was filled with the sounds of Yiddish and where Jewish children attended a *heder* (a Jewish school in which the boys were taught from the earliest stages how to read in Hebrew and were started on the path of Jewish education). His was a very Jewish home; Yiddish was the household language and the language they spoke to their neighbors up to the Second World War; his parents were religious and, even in the worst times, his father always ate only kosher food. Before the war this wasn't much of a problem: there was always a *shochet* (ritual slaughterer) in their little town and in the bazaar there were chickens to be bought. All their kitchenware was kosher. "In our house, there were five or six neighboring families, all Jews. And the houses close by were also Jewish. Until the war. Until the war."

Aaron's father, who made a modest living doing manual labor, prayed at the synagogue regularly and, until the 1930s, took his children as well. But after that they went less often because it was clearly not a good practice under Soviet rule. Soon after the revolution, the Bolsheviks launched a series of anti-religious campaigns in general and specifically shut down the Jewish community framework—the *kehillah*—and with it, all the many organizations that the Jews maintained for their spiritual and material well-being: Jewish clinics, charitable institutions, mikvehs, a whole system of schooling, While his older brothers had studied in a *heder,* there wasn't one by the time that Aaron should have gone, so any Jewish study was done at home. He studied the *Chumash* (the Bible) well, but never got to the more advanced level of the commentaries of the medieval scholar, Rashi. By 1935 it was considered unwise to study these subjects at all, even at home.

From the beginning of Soviet power, Aaron's father was categorically against living a non-religious life. He would not let his older sons go to school because that would involve their studying—and writing—on the Sabbath. He probably thought that the situation was temporary. But by the 1930s, he realized that the regime was there to stay and so all five children were eventually sent to the state schools.

Two of Aaron's brothers were drafted before the war. When the war came, Aaron, his parents, his younger sister and younger brother were all evacuated to Central Asia. This was a piece of enormous luck for their family, as the fate of any Jews remaining within the area of Kiev after the middle of September, 1941 was certain: they would be killed without mercy. His father and sister remained in Central Asia during the war; his mother died in 1943.

Aaron himself was drafted in 1942 at age eighteen, and served in one of the most terrible and decisive struggles of the war. This was the battle for the Kursk salient, fought in the summer of 1943. Both Hitler and Stalin saw this as a possible key turning point in the war following the Battle of Stalingrad and both sides poured men and tanks and planes into the area in the hope of a major victory. New Tiger and Panther tanks, fresh out of German factories, were hurried to the front. On their side, the Soviets built up a huge troop concentration, fortifying the area with gun emplacements and miles and miles of trenches. In this mayhem, this place of slaughter, Aaron—a quiet and modest young man—found himself battling for survival. As his unit neared Kharkov, he was wounded in the head. He lost consciousness for four days and remained unable to move for two weeks. For six months he lay in a hospital far removed, in Krasnoyarsk, deep in Siberia, and then returned to duty. Although he remained in the army, he could no longer serve at the front. He continued his military service until 1947, long after the end of the war.

Aaron's oldest brother, David, was also injured and became an invalid. He joined the family in Central Asia during the war. Another of Aaron's brothers was wounded four times. The fifth time, he was killed. Even close to forty years later, Aaron cried telling this, the pain as fresh as when he first heard of his brother's death.

Gradually, with the decisive victories at Stalingrad and Kursk, the Soviet army started to push back the enemy and by 1944 large parts of Soviet territory were being liberated as the fighting moved to the western areas. Soviet citizens who had managed to stay out of harm's way by escaping to the Urals or Central Asia began the long trip home as they heard about the Soviet liberation of their home towns. For some, there were happy reunions; for others, a sad confirmation of what they had feared.

In 1944, with the war still in progress, Isaac ran into some people who had lived on his street in Odessa. They were in Krasnovodsk, on the Caspian Sea, where the sixteen year old had been living and working. This family, having heard that Odessa was back in Soviet hands, took Isaac with them to Baku, as part of their family. He somehow lost them there, but by now he was a resourceful lad and managed to get on troop trains, eventually reaching Odessa. He found a job at a shipyard and lived in a workers' dormitory where he was fed and housed.

Sometime in 1945, he was given a pair of American shoes, sent to Russia during the war. As they were too big for him, he took them to the market to sell. Also at the market at that same moment were his mother and aunt who had recently returned with the children from their evacuation. Isaac's mother immediately recognized him and there was an extraordinary reunion among all the boxes and barrels and stalls of the market place. Until then, mother and son had had no idea whether the other was alive.

Isaac happily moved back in with his mother and brother. They had retrieved their old apartment, which was in a basement. Even after all his years of independence it was good to be in a family again. He and his brother, who is two years younger, became very close and have remained so.

By the summer of 1944, the Soviet army had entered Lithuania. The children in Zakharia's camp followed the progress of the army with great interest. They had been living in such primitive conditions—no electricity, no radio, many thousands of miles away from home—that they really had no idea of what had been going on. Their teachers handed out good paper and envelopes—something rare under those conditions—to the children and told them, Jewish or Lithuanian, to write to their parents at their last known address. "The Lithuanian children, almost all of them, received answers," says Zakharia. Many of them were tearful replies saying that by then they had thought that their child was not among the living, and here they were, alive and well. Packages—mostly with food—started arriving from home. "And we Jewish children got our letters back, with the envelope noting that the person to whom it was written no longer lived at that address." When he received his letter back, Zakharia decided to write to his Lithuanian pediatrician, whose name he remembered. He asked what could have happened to his parents. Not remembering where the doctor's office was, the boy sent his letter, without the street name, to "the best children's doctor in Kaunas." The envelope reached the doctor, who wrote back a warm letter that he remembered his patient, but that his parents weren't in Kaunas now. "I don't know what happened; we have to hope."

Then, in October 1944, all the children were put on a train and sent back to the Lithuanian republic. It was a terrifically long trip, crossing much of war-torn Russia on primitive trains. When they finally reached Vilna station they found that there was a large demonstrative reception there, vaunting Soviet power. Thanks to Soviet success, the signs proclaimed, here were the children, protected during the war, being returned home. They had brought all the parents of the Lithuanian children to greet them. There was an orchestra, flowers. "We arrived and the parents and children threw themselves into each other's arms. Three and a half years since they'd last seen them!"

"And we, we stayed on the train and enviously looked upon the scene through the window. It was terrible."

This went on for two or three hours. Then everyone went home. The children who had remained on the train were all Jewish except, perhaps, four Lithuanians. The smaller children were to be sent to orphanages run by monks and nuns. Sisters and brothers were separated. Zakharia was in the oldest group: he was already sixteen. There were some thirty boys and girls of his age. They were photographed, quickly given internal passports and ration cards and could then leave, on their own. Some of them, having no one to go to, headed for the synagogue. Zakharia took a train to Kovno. He was certain, with a child's faith, that once he got to his home town, everything would be all right. He went there alone.

He got off the train carrying his suitcase, a wooden one that he had made himself, that had underwear and other clothing that he had been given. There was no bus and he walked all the way to the building that had once been home. The door was opened by a woman whom he recognized: she used to live in the basement. She and her family had moved into his family's five-room apartment after his parents had been taken away. She brought him in, sat him down and gave him something to eat and drink. She cried, crossed herself, and started to tell him what had happened to his parents.

She told him that his parents had been taken to the ghetto in Kovno and given a room, or part of a room there. They took what they could of value, but had to leave a lot because they had so little space. His mother gave most of what remained to their servant, Anelia: dishes, furniture, piano, whatever she wanted. When the apartment was more or less empty, the family in the basement moved upstairs. She offered to vacate the apartment if he wanted it back. At some point, he noticed that the fork he was eating with was his family's. She noticed him looking and said that it was his, that the credenza had been left by his parents, that he should take whatever he wanted. He couldn't. He could barely deal with his unwieldy suitcase as it was. He sat with her for about two hours; they both cried while she told him the story of his parents' fate.

And then he asked where Anelia lived. She had not only been the servant but had half brought him up for the first five years of his life. She greeted him very warmly. He stayed overnight with her and her husband, became ill and ended up remaining for two or three weeks. Anelia showed him a list of what she had received from his parents' home. After some of the items there was a V showing that she had selected that object and sold it in order to obtain food that she would bring to his parents in the ghetto: bread, butter. When the war started, it had been summer, but when winter came Anelia somehow got his mother's coat to her in the ghetto, so that she could keep warm that winter. As far as Zakharia could ascertain, his parents were in the ghetto until 1943. Then they were sent to Latvia, to a concentration camp where they worked. From what he understood, and it could not be verified, his father ended up in a different camp and was killed quite soon. His glasses had been broken and, being short-sighted, he didn't notice an SS man coming toward him and therefore didn't take off his hat. So he was shot.

Zakharia's brother, too, was killed early on, during the period of the ghetto. This is something that Zakharia is quite certain about because years later he ran into someone at the university who was shocked to see him alive. He looked very much like his brother and this man had actually witnessed Alexander being killed.

Anelia urged Zakharia to go back to school right away and finish his studies. He started to study, finding himself not just the only Jew in his class, but the only Jew in the school. And what a strange person he seemed to them: a Jew, but out of Russia, who spoke Lithuanian. "When they seated me on a bench, no one wanted to sit with me. I sat alone. And more than that: I came in one morning . . . and on my bench was written 'ghetto.'" Zakharia didn't pay attention and continued his studies. When another Jewish boy arrived, they sat together. During a two-hour math exam, both of them finished in fifteen minutes. After that everyone was eager to sit next to them. To keep himself alive, he started tutoring a non-Jewish boy who was at school with him and received food at his home in exchange. But after a few weeks he realized that the family barely had food enough for themselves, and certainly no surplus to feed to him.

In despair he went to the rabbi. There was already a small Jewish community reconstituted there and Zakharia had visited the synagogue on his first day back in Kaunas to give in his name, in case somebody turned up looking for him. This time he told the rabbi that he was living with non-Jews, good hearted but impoverished, and that his immediate problem was that he had to eat, today. The rabbi couldn't help him. From the synagogue, Zakharia went straight to the Komsomol, the Communist Youth Organization, to see if they could help him to find a job, any job. He knew a young man in the office there, a twenty-year old who recalled that Zakharia knew German. Within a short time, two soldiers came along in a jeep and asked, "Where's the guy who knows German?" As he got into the jeep, Zakharia asked where they were going and they answered that they were from an office where they ask questions, but don't give answers.

He was taken to the SMERSH (counterintelligence) headquarters. At the camp, there were prisoners of war, but none of the Soviet personnel knew any German. At the head of the unit was Lieutenant Colonel Lifshits. He was very impressed upon hearing Zakharia's story and saw to it that he was given good food, clothing and a salary. Zakharia tells of an interesting incident during the time that he was translating the interrogation of a German prisoner of war. He realized that the prisoner was lying because, although he claimed to come from Bavaria he, in fact, had a Hamburg accent. After that, Zakharia was very much appreciated in his unit and was even taken to the front early in 1945 to work there.

Although Lifshits pressed Zakharia to remain in the service and go through training for the secret police, the NKVD, it would have been impossible, even had he actually wanted to: he and his parents were foreign-born so he would have been ineligible. He left the service in August, 1945.

One day, Zakharia and two other boys went to the synagogue in Vilna and the gabbai said to them, "Look boys. You've got nothing, no house, no family, no profession, nothing. You are starting your lives now . . . Where would you rather start your lives; in Vilna or in Jerusalem? . . . Then go. You have to get to Bialystok." That meant crossing the frontier into Poland. He told them that in the synagogue in Bialystok, on the right side, was an office of the Joint. "If you get there, they'll take care of everything." By the Joint, the gabbai meant the American Jewish Joint Distribution Committee, which was the international Jewish organization whose name was best known in the Soviet Union. In fact, rather than the Joint, it may well have been the Jewish Agency that had an office in Bialystok at that time.

The boys had German bicycles and took them onto a train going towards the Polish border, and got off at Grodno, still inside Soviet territory. They spent the night in the forest and the next day set out for Bialystok some one hundred twenty kilometers (about seventy-five miles) away. "We rode. The traffic on the road, back and forth, was farmers with their carts, soldiers in trucks, and people walking and bicycling. No one stopped us. We got to a few road blocks and passed them. We rode and rode and rode." But at one road block, one of the boys, Moishele, encountered a soldier coming toward him. Afraid that the soldier would arrest him, he lifted his bike and threw it at the soldier, fleeing into the woods. The soldier started to shoot. "And I threw down my bike and fled into the forest on the other side." He didn't look to see what happened to the third boy, Melech. "I ran into the woods. I could still hear the shooting. I was very frightened." He knew that if he were caught he would certainly be killed.

Zakharia didn't know where to go, except away from the shooting. He crossed a railway line and simply followed the tracks. He lost his sense of direction and had no idea if he was in Poland or still in Belorussia. In the end, he hopped on a train at random; it took him to Vilna, "and that was very sad."

That was the first time that Zakharia attempted to get to Jerusalem. He wouldn't try again for another twenty-five years.

Chapter Two

Post War and Post Stalin

BACKGROUND

In the aftermath of the war, the Soviet people found themselves in a contradictory situation. On the one hand, there was no doubt that the Red Army—and the nation—had achieved a glorious victory. The enormous German onslaught had, finally, been stopped and then reversed. The sheer doggedness and heroism of the army and people in all walks of life had defeated an astoundingly professional and mechanized machine. On the other hand, the country lay in ruins. Besides the staggering loss of life, the entire industrial and agricultural infrastructure in areas that had been occupied had been destroyed. There was a catastrophic housing shortage. For a country celebrating a great victory, the population was facing a bleak period of years and years of hardship in trying to rebuild their lives.

Besides the extremely harsh economic climate, there were dark political clouds shadowing the country in the last years of Stalin's life. A hostile foreign policy was inaugurated against the West, which was condemned as capitalist, exploitative and imperialist. In Winston Churchill's memorable term, an iron curtain had descended, dividing eastern from western Europe. The USSR wrapped itself in the mantle of the socialist bloc, keeping strict control of all those nations that had fallen under Soviet domination. Purges were renewed. The need for increasing vigilance against enemies within was expressed in countless articles and speeches toward the end of Stalin's life. For people who had gone through such vicissitudes, who had suffered and given so much, there seemed to be no end in sight.

A campaign against "rootless cosmopolitans"—with the Jews as the clear target—was launched late in the 1940s. This was the first such anti-Jewish onslaught launched publicly by the Soviet regime. During this same period, various poets and writers—the core of the leading Yiddish-language cultural intelligentsia of the Soviet Union—were quietly arrested and imprisoned. In the summer of 1952, these men were summarily tried and executed. And then, in September, 1952, in what came to be known as the Doctors Plot, a group of doctors connected with the prestigious Kremlin hospital was arrested, accused of murdering top members of the Soviet elite. When the arrest was announced in the middle of January, 1953, most of the names were clearly Jewish. They were referred to as murderers in white coats. A campaign against Jewish doctors, and by implication, against Jews generally was clearly building up.

The end of the campaign came fortuitously: on March 5, 1953, Stalin died. Within a few weeks the accusations were officially dropped and an announcement was then made that the doctors had been released from prison. A new era had begun, this time—after a period of unstable collective leadership— under the leadership of Nikita Sergeevich Khrushchev.

Here, at last, was a break with the Stalinist terror tactics and institutionalized paranoia of the past two decades or more. A breath of fresh air pervaded the Soviet Union in the mid-nineteen fifties. Stringent economic policies were moderated. A certain degree of freer expression was palpable in the newspapers and journals of the day. Arbitrary arrests were reduced. Many victims of the earlier purges were let out of the hellish prisons and camps of the Gulag, permitted to move back to the center of the country, and reunite with their families.

In February 1956, disclosures were made in Khrushchev's so-called Secret Speech to the top membership of the Communist Party which, shockingly at that time, made critical comments about Stalin and Stalinism. A wave of anti-Stalinism now swept over Eastern Europe, resulting, among other developments, in the Hungarian uprising of October. This period, called the Thaw, after the title of a novel by Ilya Ehrenburg, inaugurated a new era and, while there were setbacks and difficult times ahead, there was never a reversion to the policies of Joseph Stalin.

The memories, still all too fresh, of the Nazi invasion and the destruction of the Jewish people in the conquered regions; the incredibly harsh conditions of everyday existence; the resurgence of state terrorism; and the overtly anti-Jewish policies of the late Stalinist regime, together planted the idea in some minds that somehow there had to be a way to a better life. Perhaps the country could be radically reformed? Or perhaps it might be possible one day to leave the Soviet Union altogether?

ANATOLII

It should not have been surprising that, in the end, Anatolii would do something daring, as well as quixotic. He was almost fated to. He grew up in a family of Zionists and rabbis. His father, a doctor, had been an ardent Zionist and, in his younger days, a member of the Tseirei Zion party. After his arrest in the 1920s for Zionist activity, he abandoned participation in all political involvement and stuck to his professional work. This was a prudent decision, as Soviet policy, starting from the early 1920s, harassed and gradually closed down all Zionist organizations. The hundreds of thousands of Zionists of the former Russian Empire could no longer hold any meetings or express support for settlement in the Land of Israel, at that time under British rule. This policy was continued throughout the existence of the Soviet Union.

For all his caution, Anatolii's father was arrested again in the late thirties, but spent a relatively short time, somewhat over a year, in prison. His mother was also arrested, as the wife of an "enemy of the people," but likewise eventually freed. During this time Anatolii, who was born in 1935, was looked after by one aunt and then another. "They told me that my parents were at a resort . . . but I somehow felt uneasy. I couldn't understand exactly . . . but [I knew] that something bad was happening." When his mother came home, four-year-old Anatolii didn't recognize her. His grandfather, too, was arrested: he had been the gabbai (the president) in the synagogue. He wasn't so lucky: he died in jail, probably during the interrogation, when harsh methods were used. While Anatolii's father survived the ordeal, he came out of prison with his health permanently undermined and was constantly sick. He died relatively young, in 1952.

As a result of the campaign against rootless cosmopolitans, and on the eve of the Doctors Plot, the family spent the winter at the end of 1952 waiting for the knock on the door. They felt that arrest, again, was imminent. His father burned all photographs, documents, any letters that might implicate someone in the family.

Anatolii's father, despite his frequent illnesses, did try to inculcate some feeling for his Jewish heritage in his son and even tried to teach him a little Hebrew. ". . . but I was exceptionally ungifted as a student [of Hebrew] and in the beginning I simply didn't understand why it was necessary." Anatolii did, however, somehow find a real interest in his Jewish roots and in Zionism and in 1951, he and his friend Alek began their "notorious criminal activity."

It was then, during a very dark period of Stalinism, that Anatolii wrote a leaflet, by hand, and threw it into the mailbox of someone with a Jewish name. This person, without any deep thought, gave it to the KGB, along with a patriotic letter absolving himself of any guilt in being the recipient of such a letter. He obviously didn't want anyone to think that he would welcome such a communication. The leaflet—and others that followed—focused on the situation in the country, charging that there was too much chauvinism, nationalistic policy, and anti-semitism. They called for pressure aimed at opening the doors and allowing people to leave the Soviet Union. Among other things, they called for the rehabilitation of prisoners.

The friends continued to distribute leaflets occasionally over the next few years. Starting in 1953, they typed their leaflets on an unregistered typewriter that they felt couldn't be traced. Anatolii thinks that the KGB finally traced the leaflets through the handwriting used in their initial effort, though it took a long time. "Then, in 1956, we put out another few leaflets and they immediately arrested us."

As Anatolii puts it in his dry way, if you had to be arrested, this was the best time for it. Theirs was the first arrest of this kind after the 20th Party Congress. They had never expected to make a real impact, but they had hoped to open eyes, make people think. Most of all, they wanted to express themselves, and had no other means to do so. "We were simply suffocating. . ." They were sentenced to six years in a labor camp and were released after four and a half years, in September, 1960.

While he returned to activist circles after his release from prison, Anatolii did not take the lead. He was studying at the university. But the seeds had been planted and he would take advantage of the opportunity to leave the Soviet Union as soon as it was offered.

CLARA

The poverty and hardship endured by so many Soviet citizens following the Second World War was staggering. When Clara and her mother returned to Odessa, they found that someone else had taken their apartment and they never regained possession of it. That went for all of the things inside the apartment—furniture, dishes, linens—nothing was ever returned. Instead, they were given a miserable place near the outhouse in the courtyard. Clara's father had returned from the war, having lost part of an arm, and all they had to live on was his small pension.

Fortunately for the family, Clara's mother was very resourceful and this kept them all alive. There were soldiers' barracks near their courtyard and they used to hang around near the gate, not permitted to leave the area. So Clara's mother reckoned that there were certain supplies that these men would like to buy but wouldn't have easy access to. She would buy a sack of nuts and divide it up into little packets that could then be sold. She also sold bottled water. With so many soldiers, Clara's mother assumed that they would want to keep in touch with their families, so she obtained paper, pencils and envelopes which Clara would then sell to them. If they didn't have the money, the soldiers would trade the goods that they wanted for food, which they had access to on their base. In this way, her mother was able to provide food for her family. Even so, when Clara was a little older, she was hospitalized a number of times, as a result of the early malnutrition that she had suffered during and following the war.

TANIA

Tania was sixty years old at the time of her interviews in the late fall of 1979. She was quite a short woman, with bright, alert eyes, a small well-formed nose and delicate mouth, fine graying brunette hair. Although not so old, she was already frail, a woman who had had to look after her health with care for the past thirty years. She presented an air of faded beauty, spoke articulately and displayed the intellectual background that she came from.

She was born in Riga, just after the revolution, when Latvia was coming into its own independence. Hers was a bourgeois intellectual family. Her father was an engineer, who also had shares in the company he worked for— something that would not sit well with the Bolsheviks after the Soviet take-over of the Baltic states in 1940. Her mother was well-educated, had studied music at the conservatory and, like many Riga Jews then, spoke both German and Russian well. Her father had been brought up and educated in Yiddish, learning Russian by himself. At home, Russian was the spoken language and Tania's only language until she was five. At that point she was put into a German-speaking primary school and the rest of her primary and secondary education was in German.

While their home was comparatively assimilated, it was definitely Jewish in culture. There was no *kashrut*, but they did mark the holidays. "We celebrated . . . Pesach, always celebrated, . . . but with bread: there were both, matzahs and bread, on the table." She rarely went to synagogue, and neither did her father, except for Kol Nidre, sometimes taking his children. "He liked it, I think, because of the music, also because he was a Jew. He was a Jew, through and through." He was "in the movement of 1905," never a communist, but an old-fashioned social democrat. Tania was referring here to the revolution of 1905, when many young Jews became galvanized in the general struggle to establish Russia as a constitutional democracy, decrease the power of the tsar and, they hoped, achieve the complete political and social emancipation of the Jews.

"He always told me: keep away from politics." Tania, however, did dabble in politics as a girl and, under the influence of a male cousin, joined an organization of socialist youth during the period of growing fascist activity in Latvia. Toward the end of the thirties, Tania decided to go to England, where she would join her soon to be husband, Joe, who was living and studying in London. This was in the summer of 1939. She went so far as to obtain a passport for travel abroad. Her father was against her going, as were others. They all told her to wait a bit: the war wasn't about to start. However, once the war did break out, in September, it was impossible to leave, even though Latvia was not yet officially involved. By then, of course, her parents regretted that they hadn't let her go earlier. In July 1940, came the Soviet occupation of Latvia when her father lost everything. The Soviets treated the bourgeois families in the Baltic states that they occupied just as they had treated those in the Russian lands after the Bolshevik revolution: these were enemies of the people, exploiters, and had to be expropriated.

During this period of sovietization, Tania became active in the Young Communist League in Riga. Being a member was probably a good move for Tania at the time, though by then she was not an ardent supporter by any means. Fortunately, no punishment was meted out to her father and he even managed to get a job with the Latvian regional government (the Council of People's Commissars), through the many communist friends that he had. They had all been revolutionaries together in 1905. Thanks to Tania's Party job and her father's work at the Sovnarkom, they all managed to get out of Riga in time, before the German army took over, though they were so rushed that "we couldn't even put on our coats. Nothing." This was the story of many: they were lucky just to get to safety. "We left everything. We had a whole apartment, full of things, stuffed with I-don't-know-what. We didn't even lock the door. We closed it and ran away." The family spent the war years in Alma Ata, in Soviet Kazakhstan.

During the war, Tania's husband returned from England to the Soviet Union of his own volition. He was a convinced communist and was anxious to be there to fight against fascism. He joined the army at once, a Soviet Latvian division. However, in the atmosphere of Stalinist Russia, a man who had spent extended periods of time abroad was suspect and it would be just a matter of time before he was arrested. After the war, both she and Joe were at the university, initially in Moscow. He was then given a job in Riga with the radio and, with it, a good apartment. They went there together. Joe's arrest came in 1953. While Tania was still officially married to him then, they were living apart and had spent little time together over the past years. He was called to Moscow and not heard from again for a very long time. He simply left his flat and disappeared. "You see, at that time people were arrested not normally with an arraignment, a warrant; it was a secret. They took away people secretly." Eventually she learned that he had been arrested. By the time his trial came up, Stalin was already dead.

The cynicism of the authorities was amazing. When Tania was called in to the secret police to be questioned, she told them she was certain that Joe hadn't been a secret agent. But the MGB asked her, "'Why, then, if he was not a spy, did he come back from London?' Can you imagine such a foolish question?" Tania got off lightly: she was expelled from the Party.

Not long after Stalin's death, Joe was released from prison. He immediately asked to be taken back into the Communist Party. "For him, it was the only possibility to live. Otherwise it was impossible to exist." Tania, clearly, was attracted to men who were committed idealists, though not always with the same ideal.

It was during these tumultuous years that Tania first met Peretz, who would, much later, become her second husband. Both of them were in Moscow towards the end of the war and met somehow. Later, when she was already living back in Riga, Peretz turned up there. "I lived in one flat with Joe. But it wasn't a very good life, from the very beginning. And Peretz, with whom I wasn't really friendly yet, lived in the second flat, where he could look into our windows from his window. . . That's how we made friends then." By the time Peretz was arrested in 1946, he and Tania were already close.

PERETZ

Peretz came from Riga as well, but his middle-class family was quite different from Tania's. At home, the family spoke German. He knew Latvian, but not well. The household help tended to speak Russian. This was all typical of Riga in the early twentieth century. His was a religious home, kosher. But while his father made Kiddush (benediction over the wine on the Sabbath), he didn't go to synagogue much.

Peretz, too, went to a German school, a private one. In his class of thirty or thirty-five boys, about "let's say, ninety-eight percent were Jewish." From age twelve or thirteen, Peretz was an ardent Zionist. This would become the guiding influence and motivation of his life.

Peretz had a technical education in high school. He became a draftsman, working in the heating section of a department linked to the aviation industry. He ended up in the planning institute of the Ministry of Aviation. This was all before the war. With the German invasion, his family too managed to get to Central Asia, ending up some fifty miles from the Persian border. During this period Peretz survived both appendicitis and, later, typhus. When he got his call-up papers for the army, he was glad: at least he would have something to eat. This proved to be an illusion. He was drafted into a Latvian Division of the Soviet armed forces and fought at the front; and by 1942 he was injured and eventually ended up in Moscow.

There were two Latvian Divisions established during the war, and in the larger one, the 201st, seventeen percent of the soldiers in it were Jews in the early years of the war. The Soviets also set up a Lithuanian Division, of which Jews composed nearly a third of the personnel. These were remarkable proportions, given the tiny fraction of the general population constituted by the Jews. There are impressive figures for heroism as well: Jews in the Soviet military in general earned citations for bravery far far beyond their percentage in the population.

Following his army release, Peretz studied physics at the university in Moscow. Even there, life was very hard. When he came to the student hostel, he had nothing, not even sheets for the bed. The classroom was so cold that they had to sit in their overcoats. At some point he became religious to at least some extent and got into serious trouble when he was checked on a train and a prayer book and *teffilin* were found in his pocket. These were clearly spy materials with a secret code, the officials thought, and he was actually brought in for investigation and was lucky to be let out after only a month.

Eventually, he got permission to return to Riga. In 1945 or 1946, Peretz became obsessed with the idea of getting to Palestine. There was an arrangement immediately after the war that holders of Polish passports from the western parts of pre-war Poland would be allowed to return home in an "exchange." It was considered an exchange because Soviet citizens would likewise be permitted to return to their native country from Poland under this agreement. Many people took advantage of this to get out of the Soviet Union. For the Jews who did it, Poland would most likely be a stepping stone to further travel, either to the West or, for many, to Palestine, where they could make new lives in what would become the Jewish homeland. Peretz, of course, was not from Poland, but this did not daunt him. "It was no problem to get papers, because . . . Vilna was a Polish town [in the interwar period]. . ." So all that had to be done was to go to the city archive and claim to be Polish, explain that you'd been displaced, had no documents, and receive a "new" set of documents proving your origins. He kept working on ways in which he could get out of the Soviet Union and, finally, during the summer of 1946, tried to arrange to go with his uncle and a woman they knew. He made a few trips to Vilna to see to details, though he never took the step towards leaving; but the woman was picked up under suspicion and eventually told the secret police about the plan. As a result, Peretz was arrested on August 18, 1946. The trial was held the following February.

Peretz was found guilty and sentenced to ten years' imprisonment. At first he worked in a labor camp near Riga, but afterwards he was sent north to the area of Pechora, where he worked on the highway. After this his luck changed and he was transferred to a special camp near Moscow where a scientific unit had been established. Prisoners of various backgrounds—physicists, mathematicians, linguists—had been brought from labor camps all over the Soviet Union to work on various projects. Peretz worked in the acoustics lab. Here, although they were still imprisoned, they lived in much better conditions and, for the first time in years, he ate decently. This was the *sharashka* made famous by Alexander Solzhenitsyn in his novel *The First Circle.* It was here that Peretz and Solzhenitsyn met and became friends. One of the characters in the novel is, in fact, a blend of Peretz and one of the other scientists incarcerated there. And, as in the book, Peretz did indeed get shipped off at the end, as a punishment, to the harsh camp at Vorkuta.

Peretz was let out in 1954, before the full ten years was up. He had worked overtime and earned an earlier release, without having to undergo internal exile as well. "When you work in the north and then you exceed one hundred per cent of the norm, then you get compensated. One day counts for one and a half . . . So you earned a little time." He emerged into a new climate in the Soviet Union and, after visiting one of his *sharashka* mates in Moscow (Rubin, in the novel, who in reality is Lev Kopelev), made his way to Riga. The world had changed since his arrest in 1946. Stalin was dead; this was the period of the thaw. The State of Israel had been established in 1948. In spite of the nearly ten years of soul-destroying incarceration, Peretz never stopped being the plucky, resilient man who had grown up in the Zionist movement in Riga. He still wanted to emigrate, to make his way to Israel, and thought of ways to do it. But it was a difficult time for him. He was tired after his long years of imprisonment. His father had died in the meantime and his mother was all alone, so it was an inopportune moment. The time would come.

Peretz and Tania got married some time after his release. There was no hope of having children. Tania had been told, in her early thirties, that her blood pressure was disastrously high and she was more or less ordered to remain at home, even in bed. This she would not agree to, but she did understand that she did not have the option of becoming pregnant, certainly not given the state of medicine in the Soviet Union in the nineteen fifties. So they remained a devoted pair, together in the world, and alone, but quite different in their attitudes and aspirations.

LEV

Lev grew up with two passions: Zionism and art. His father was the proud scion of a well-established religious family that traces its genealogy from the end of the 14th century. Lev's grandfather was a rabbi and was a first cousin of Nachman Syrkin, the well-known Zionist ideologist and leader. Lev's father was a scientist who did not bring up his two sons in a religious way, but personally retained the education and inclinations of his religious childhood. Lev remembers that every night, his father would close the door of his room in the communal apartment where they lived, take a copy of the Old Testament [*Tanakh*] from where it was kept out of sight, read a chapter, then hide it again and go to sleep. This went on for his whole life. That's how Lev remembers him. What did count in his children's training, though, was a feeling for their family and its roots. "Unlike many antisemites, I know my forebears and I know every one of their antecedents." The other strong component in the family was a feeling for Zionism. The boys grew up imbued with the spirit of the Zionist ideology.

He knew that he was a Jew quite early, because of the teasing of the other boys outside when he was four or five. Lev and his brother started asking what a Jew was, what it meant. "I remember our first discussion, when I ran in from the courtyard and said that I didn't want to be a Jew. What is 'Jew' and why am I one? I'm not a Jew, I started to shout. Then my father . . . said, 'No, you are a Jew and there's nothing to be ashamed of. On the contrary, you have to be proud of it. And he started to tell me, to show me books. We had a Tanakh in the house and we also had the Psalms of David . . ."

With the exception of two and a half years during the evacuation at the beginning of the Second World War, Lev spent his entire life in Moscow. Born in 1929, he was still a child during the war. The atmosphere in the home of his youth as well as the family that he and his wife established was intellectual and strongly Jewish, without being religious.

Art, his second passion, began very early. He loved color. He remembers his delight when he first saw a rainbow, at age three. He feels that his first teacher was his nanny, a sort of family retainer who had brought up generations of children in his family, a provincial Russian woman, uneducated. It was she who must have put a pencil into his hand the first time. "She modeled . . . little birds and chicks out of clay and gave them to me to paint. I think that I probably got my first skills from her at the age of two." His first word, he says, was the usual Mama, but his second word was the word for "color," or "blossom" which, in Russian, is quite a difficult sound for a child to pronounce.

Eventually, Lev became a student at a superb art academy, the prestigious Stroganov Institute, the oldest such institution in Russia, where he studied with outstanding teachers. He also studied in Samarkand, in Bukhara and in Tashkent, absorbing influences from the art of Central Asia into his own style. Lev became a successful artist, and, while he painted many fine works, his main creative endeavor has been in monumental art, large works in public places, full of vigor and color. He reached a high level of success, traveling all over the Soviet Union for his various commissions.

Apart from a few years when he joined the Komsomol, Lev stayed away from things political. Indeed, even as a youth he had not joined the Communist youth organization, which nearly everyone was in, and only joined when he was taking senior courses at the institute. He speaks of this with wry humor. "And when I studied in the senior courses at the institute, I entered the Komsomol, I suppose with a frankly completely careerist aim . . . This is the only deed in my life when I tried to make a career! Of course, I say this as a joke." But although he was never a member of the Communist Party, he nevertheless reached the pinnacles of artistic hierarchy in the Soviet Union, ultimately becoming a member of the presidium of the Moscow Artists Fund during the last four years of his life there. This is highly indicative of the appreciation in which he was held as an artist. In general, people in the arts, whether in literature, music or the fine arts, did not attain high organizational positions unless they were Party members.

In general, Lev was satisfied with his life. He had had the best of training in a leading institute. His native language was Russian and he had no desire to switch to another. He had high recognition as a leading creator of monumental art within his country. And yet, at some point, the decision would come to leave.

VALENTINA

Valentina's story is very different. Not only did she have no pride in her parentage, she didn't really even fully know about her family until she was in her teens. Her parents were very young when they fell in love and, at the time her mother became pregnant, war was raging in Europe, though Russia was not yet involved. Her father, a twenty-one year old officer, knew that his wife was expecting a baby and when they managed to see one another near his army camp shortly before she gave birth, he asked that if it were a boy, he be named Yurii and if a girl, that she be called Valentina. He was very pleased at the prospect of a baby.

He was killed in August, 1941, just two months after the German invasion. On September 13, 1941, his little daughter was born in the old Russian town of Pugachev, near the Volga River, where his wife's family lived. His wife was just twenty-one. The baby was named Valentina, according to his request, and was given to her mother's parents to bring up. For the first eight years of her life, she lived with her maternal grandparents and considered them her mother and father. They were simple, hard-working Russian people, Christians. Her grandfather built traditional Russian stoves out of stone. Her own mother was trying to adjust to her new situation and married again, perhaps more than once, and was largely out of her daughter's life. She never had any more children.

Unexpectedly, when Valentina was eight, her grandmother told her that she would be going to meet her mother and live with her and her husband. While she had seen pictures of her mother, they were actually strangers. Valya traveled by train and boat to the island of Sakhalin, off the eastern coast of Russia. While she lived there for several years, she and her mother never really developed a good relationship. For Valentina, this was an unhappy time.

Then, one day, when she was fourteen, her mother told her that there was another set of grandparents alive, people whom Valya had never met. These were her father's parents. They had invited their granddaughter to come to them in Belaia Tserkov, in Ukraine, and live there, completing her education under their care. In fact, just after her birth and her father's death, these grandparents had suggested to her mother that they bring up the baby, but she had refused at that time.

Valentina's second set of grandparents were Jews. In all her years in Pugachev, Valya had never met Jews, nor did she understand any differentiation between Russians and other people. Her paternal grandparents came from a classic Jewish past. Brought up in the Pale of Settlement, they had, by dint of hard work and a good education, made a success of their lives in the post-revolutionary period. Her grandfather, who came to be a great influence on her life, was a noted bio-chemist. He had been a professor in Moscow, but decided at some point in the 1950s to move back to his beloved home town of Belaia Tserkov, take a job at the local agricultural institute, and build a house. He and his wife, a pediatrician, had had two sons but both had been drafted into the Red Army and both were killed in the war. They had already taken upon themselves to bring up their grandson (their older son's son) and were now happy to have Valya join the family.

For Valya, it meant entering a new world, one which she gradually became used to and flourished in. Her grandfather was a loving man whom she adored. "My grandfather," she says, "was like a roof over my head." He was highly respected in Belaia Tserkov. He made an excellent living by Soviet standards. They had built themselves a comfortable, two-storeyed house on a street that ran along the bank of the Ros River. It was a verdant and cozy town. That period with her grandparents in Belaia Tserkov was the best of times. "It was . . . as if I'd been under his wings, protective wings . . . seven years. I always said it was the best years of my life."

When Soviet children reached the age of sixteen, they had to appear at an office to receive their internal passports. In these documents were registered their name, birth date and other particulars, including the famous, or infamous, line five where a person was identified by "nationality." Nationality was determined by historic descent, not by geographic domicile. While most people were "Russian" or "Ukrainian" or "Georgian"—nationalities tied to the ethnic origins of their family—"Jewish" was also considered a national group, and in this case was unrelated to whether the person's family had originated in Ukraine or Belorussia, in Bukhara or the Caucasus. For most Soviet citizens, the question of nationality was not a matter of choice. You took the nationality of your parents. But in the case of people of mixed parentage, then you could choose either nationality as your own. Valentina had a Russian mother and a Jewish father, so the decision was hers as to which she would identify with. Her grandfather escorted her to the office and was thrilled when she decided to put herself down as Jewish. Such were her strong feelings for him.

In fact, while her grandfather was a proud Jew, the household was not religious in any way. Valentina does remember seeing matzah at Passover, though they didn't have a seder. She was only aware of Jewish holidays because of a festive meal. She was also aware that her grandfather listened to special broadcasts, presumably from Israel or about it. He knew both Yiddish and Hebrew. While an atheist, he loved Jews. Indeed, "until his last moment, he dreamed of leaving. . . [he said] 'You know, I don't need anything, not the house not what's in it . . . I'm ready to take [my wife] and my granddaughter and slither away to Israel.'" But he died in the early nineteen sixties, long before the great emigration began.

ESTHER

Esther is a feisty little woman. She was when she was in her late fifties at the time of the first interview. She still is now that she is in her eighties. She is a fighter and comes from a family where nothing was taken for granted and no one agreed to anything unless they believed it was right.

Her parents were both imprisoned when she was a small child; so were her grandparents, for varied reasons. Indeed, the situation became so severe in her family that at one point when Esther, as a little girl, came down with scarlet fever there was some question as to who would look after her: almost everyone was in prison.

Her father, Moisei, was a mechanical engineer, who eventually taught theoretical mechanics at the Belorussian State University in Minsk. He knew Hebrew from the *heder*, considered himself a Zionist, and was certainly never a member of the Communist Party. One day his boss at the university told him that there was to be a general meeting of his colleagues and that he should stand up and denounce some people who were about to be tried, and demand the death sentence for what in those days were called "enemies of the people." This was in 1931 when it was already quite clear that one couldn't express doubt about the innocence of such ill-fated defendants. But Esther's father said, "How can I demand the death sentence? There hasn't been a trial. When there's a trial the court will say whether they're guilty or not." People were shocked at his refusal. It was unheard of. In the Soviet Union, people could sense, could feel in every part of their being, what was permitted and what not. As Moisei used to say, in Russia "any old woman is a diplomat." Shortly after, her father was arrested and treated as a saboteur. He was very lucky that this was in the early thirties; otherwise there would have been a much more severe punishment. As it was, he was imprisoned for over six months and then sent off for a year of exile, where he worked as an engineer in a factory, under guard.

When the Second World War began, Esther was sixteen. She, together with her family, fled from Minsk. "On the third day of the war, Minsk was burning; we went missing . . . I, together with Papa and Mama, walked out of town. But grandpa—my mother's father—and [my other] grandpa, my father's father, and grandma—papa's mother—and my aunt and her husband, remained and were killed by the Germans." The family made their way to Saratov, and later to Novosibirsk where her father found work and she continued her studies. The family never returned to Minsk, although her father was invited to take up a job there after the war. Esther was anxious to go back to Minsk, but her father said, "How can I set foot on that soil; maybe their [his dear ones'] blood is at every step."

So the family remained in Novosibirsk, with all the housing problems that they had to face, and Esther finished her studies in the Russian language and literature faculty in the pedagogical institute there. She was very excited about the developments in Palestine, still within the British Mandate, and tried to work out how she could get there. "I wanted to go to Palestine to fight. Really. I dreamed of going to Palestine to fight. I looked for the way, but there wasn't any. And then, suddenly, by chance, I met Iuzek, my future husband."

They met at a new year's eve party on the last night of 1945. Esther was sitting on a sofa, reading a book of Polish poetry and Iuzek came over to her and they talked. After that he visited her family a few times and had long talks with Esther's father. He seemed like such a good person, a nice Jewish young man. He was a Zionist, as they were. He had been born in Poland and ended up in the Soviet Union as so many Jews had in the period between 1939 and 1941 when Russia was dragged into the war. Indeed, had he not found himself in the Soviet Union he surely would have suffered the fate of most of Poland's Jews: either dying in one of the ghettos or being sent to a concentration camp for an equally horrible fate.

But here he was in Novosibirsk and he hoped soon to be back in Poland. He would make use of the exchange instituted for the return of Polish citizens to Poland and he really had been, unlike Peretz, a citizen of interwar Poland. It was part of the agreement that a returning Polish citizen would be allowed to bring a spouse.

This was the basis of Esther's plan. She would marry Iuzek in a fictitious marriage and, together, they would be allowed to be part of the exchange and move to Poland. They would then divorce and she—and he too—would proceed to Palestine. Marriage was just a means for her to get out of the Soviet Union. By April they were married in a civil ceremony in a registry office and went immediately to put in a request as a couple to go to Poland. Esther was twenty-one; Iuzek was eight years older. It took a long time, but in the end when the reply came; it was negative. The reason was that their marriage had not been recorded in 1945 or before. They had met and married just a little bit too late.

Iuzek (the shortened Polish form of Joseph) could have gone to Poland alone; he had the right. But by this time he didn't want to leave Esther. He told her, "No, I'm not going without you. We will get what we want together." Their real marriage—when they decided that they would truly be husband and wife and live together—was in July 1946. "We all sat at Papa and Mama's and drank tea, and that was the wedding." They subsequently tried to leave at least twice more, without success.

Life in Novosibirsk was tough. Living conditions were unbearable, not just for Esther's family but for the population as a whole. In her case, there were five people living in one room: Esther's parents, her brother (recently released from the army), Iuzek, Esther, and, from 1947, their baby, Iz'ka, whose full name was Israel. They shared a communal kitchen and had the misfortune of having a very unpleasant neighbor in the apartment, a communist who held them in contempt and eventually got them evicted. Esther and Iuzek were desperate to get out.

In 1948, they cautiously framed a letter of request for permission to leave, a very careful letter, so that there would be no hint of "nationalism." They explained that they wanted to go over and fight for the Jews in Palestine, making it clear that they only wanted to fight as volunteers and then return. In the letter they reminded the reader of such supporters of freedom as Mickiewicz working for Polish independence and Byron fighting for the Greeks. The plan was not as far-fetched as it might seem: during the first year of Israel's existence Stalinist Russia gave its support to the struggling nation, even directing arms its way through its surrogate, Czechoslovakia.

The letter was sent to the Jewish Anti-Fascist Committee, which had been founded in 1942 as an official Soviet Jewish body devoted to supporting the country's war effort. Among its leaders were some of the best-known Jews in the Soviet Jewish cultural world and it was headed by the beloved Yiddish actor, Shlomo Mikhoels. This organization continued to exist for a few years after the end of the Second World War and became a focal point for Jews of the Soviet Union, a committee that they could appeal to in their need after the wartime horrors. It replaced all the long-defunct *kehillot*, the Jewish municipal community structures, that had been outlawed shortly after the Bolshevik revolution. Great numbers of letters were addressed to the JAFC during these years with requests of various kinds: there was no one else to turn to. And so it was to them that Esther and Iuzek sent theirs.

Esther's mother cried when they sent the letter. "You're dead," she said. They knew that there was a great risk in doing this in 1948: they felt that they were throwing themselves from the fifth floor. But they also felt that they had no choice: "We knew that we were risking our lives, we knew that. We knew, but we thought, these are our boys . . . there was a siege on Jerusalem, there was a blockade . . . We knew what was going on there . . . the Irgun . . . Stern, Lehi [Jewish organizations fighting first against the British and then against the Arab forces] . . . we knew all that and we were suffering with it and we thought: they're risking their lives. And we? Are we afraid to risk our lives? . . . That's how we saw it."

It actually took two years for their action to catch up with them. August 10, 1950, was a fateful day. Esther had just decided that she was fed up with her teaching job and decided to resign. She was at home doing housework and went downstairs to throw out the dishwater. With the primitive plumbing system she had to walk some distance in order to do this. On her way back, she spotted Iuzek, who seemed to have come home from work unusually early. In a ruse, he had been phoned by what he thought was the draft office and told to bring in his internal passport. In fact, it was the secret police, who were on the point of arresting him. Esther called out to him to wait: she wanted to tell him that she had quit her job, but he said he was in a hurry and just waved and ran off. She didn't see him again for five years. He was sentenced to ten years and sent off to a camp in the Baikal region, a place of horrific conditions and extreme climate. Esther doesn't know why she wasn't arrested too. She remained at home with her parents and her little boy and waited. Thanks to Stalin's death, Iuzek was released early, in 1955, but the severe rigors of camp life had undermined his health, and he died in his early forties in 1959, never having seen the land of his fathers.

Chapter Three

The Formation of
Hopes and Plans

BACKGROUND

When Nikita Sergeevich Khrushchev went to the Crimea in October, 1964 for a brief break from his duties as head of the Communist Party, it was completely unexpected—by him, by the Soviet population and by experts in the West—that when he returned to Moscow he would have lost all his power. During that short time, Leonid Brezhnev and Alexei Kosygin had convened delegates from all over the country for a special meeting at the Kremlin of the Party's Presidium and Central Committee and by the end of it, Brezhnev was the new head of the Communist Party, Kosygin was the Prime Minister, and Khrushchev was a private citizen.

The decision to leave him a free man marked a significant difference from the past: Khrushchev simply went into retirement, like any failed politician in the West, and was seen over the next years strolling in Moscow, making comments to inquisitive interviewers. The fate of previous high Party and KGB officials who lost their positions was execution, imprisonment or, if they were lucky, internal exile.

Something new had been happening in the Soviet Union: since Stalin's death in 1953, expectations had been rising. There was a pervasive feeling that things would improve, economically and in the intellectual and civic spirit of the state. The beginning, of course, had come with the de-Stalinization initiated by Khrushchev. Without a question, the atmosphere had become more relaxed. Materially, life had improved somewhat. Camps had been emptied of many of their political prisoners. Tourists started arriving from abroad and some privileged Russians managed to take organized trips out of the country.

Not everything had improved: for Jews there was a clear feeling that the Khrushchev regime had not been friendly to its Jewish population. This had been seen, for example, in a further reduction in the number of operating synagogues and in the difficulty to obtain matzah at Passover. On the other hand, there had been a small publication of a new edition in Yiddish of some Sholem Aleichem stories; a new *siddur*, the Jewish prayer book, had come out; and permission had been given to open a small yeshivah in the principal synagogue in Moscow. By the end of the 1950s, some twenty young men were studying there.

It was clearly a period of mixed development with some positive trends emerging, if not enough. Even if broader ideas were finding their way into print, the country still did not enjoy freedom of expression. The stamp of the Glavlit, the official censorship body, still had to appear on every publication.

With the change of political leadership in 1964, Soviet intellectuals hoped that the pace of change would increase and that they would see more improvements in the legal and intellectual atmosphere of the country. Expectations ran high. But then, soon after the start of the Brezhnev regime, two men were arrested and later tried for what they had written. These were the writers Andrei Sinyavskii and Iulii Daniel. Their trial attracted great attention, both inside the U.S.S.R. and abroad. They were given harsh prison sentences. The Soviet intelligentsia was incensed at what seemed to be a backward step on the road to liberalization. Other such acts followed. In 1968, for example, the Soviet army marched into Czechoslovakia to put down a maverick regime. As people protested, more arrests were made inside the Soviet Union; there were more trials and more prisoners were sent to labor camps. From a sense of optimism and hope, the atmosphere in the 1960s turned into one of disappointment and dissidence.

There was still strong control of the written word through censorship. But life within that kind of system begets its own solutions and opinion began to be expressed on an impressive scale through the phenomenon of *samizdat*. These were the days before the photo-copier and certainly before the computer and printer. Mimeograph machines were to be found only in offices and were kept under careful control. The solution was to be inventive and dedicated if you wanted your message read. Essays, poems, short stories were typed up on onion skin paper in multiple carbon copies and distributed to friends or like-minded individuals. They, in turn, would pass on what they had read to others. Sometimes a recipient of *samizdat* material would think so highly of it that he or she would sit down and re-type the whole text with carbon copies so that even more readers could be reached. An article written in Moscow could find its way to Leningrad or Kiev or Novosibirsk. Ideas flowed.

When the government pursued an unpopular policy—such as the arrest of Sinyavskii and Daniel for their writings or the invasion of Czechoslovakia—there would be an outcry of public opinion—on a small but vociferous scale—through *samizdat*, petitions, letters and even tiny demonstrations that would be quickly disbanded. Dissident activity flourished, although there were serious attempts to control it and punish the activists. Not only were political prisoners again being sent to prison and camps; the regime also saw to it that some suspects were incarcerated in psychiatric institutions.

In the beginning, many like-minded Jews joined in with the general dissident activities, often taking leadership positions, whether it was to demand constitutional rights, to protect writers from persecution, or to oppose Soviet foreign policy. But gradually, many came to the idea that although they sympathized with these aims, they did not feel that their fate should necessarily be entwined with that of the Russians, a people with its own history and culture, often antithetical to that of the Jews.

In the second half of the nineteen sixties a key development in the Middle East changed the contours of Israel and ultimately affected the fate of Soviet Jews: the Six Day War. Israel faced six hostile states in June 1967, some of which were client states of the Soviet Union. At the end of the sixth day of war, Israel had vanquished its hostile neighbors and now held vast tracts of Jordanian, Syrian and Egyptian territory. In retaliation for the embarrassment caused them by the war, the Soviets and the member states of their bloc— with the exception of Rumania—broke all diplomatic ties with Israel and this would remain the state of relations for over twenty years.

For a significant number of Jews the experience of the period from 1964 until 1967 would lead to a decisive break in their lives. On the one hand they had been exposed to new ways of thinking by the dissident movement. Paralyzing fear of the totalitarian state was being eroded. On the other hand, the Six Day War had awakened in them a pride in being Jews and they started thinking along radically different lines. If the situation here in the Soviet Union was static and if there was a strong feeling of belonging to the Jewish nation, why not think in terms of leaving? A comment by President Kosygin at a press conference while on a visit to Paris in December 1966 encouraged this trend: he suggested that Soviet Jews had the right to enjoy the possibility of family reunion. "As regards reunion of families, if any families wish to come together or wish to leave the Soviet Union, for them the road is open and no problem exists here." First reported in the Parisian daily *Le Figaro*, it was then published in the Soviet government newspaper *Izvestiia* the next day. Many a Jew clipped the report of this interview and kept it for future reference. Perhaps there was really hope.

The atmosphere of the sixties had a profound impact on the way people saw themselves and their future. Change was in the air. The uplifting desire for a better life and the forbidden attempts to join together with others to achieve their goals proved a heady mixture. The combination of optimism and disappointment so typical of the early Brezhnev years resulted in acts of unexpected personal courage. People took chances that they never would have taken ten years before. They made decisions that would change their lives forever.

MARK

Having lost his parents during the war, Mark grew up in Shchors, with his maternal grandparents. It was an uncomplicated childhood: he was dearly loved by his grandmother and grandfather whom he regarded, as closely as could be expected, as his mother and father. His grandfather died in 1954, just a year before Mark finished high school.

He had done well in school and the family felt that he should go on to study in Minsk, the city where he was born, where his parents had lived. In Minsk he had his aunt Frieda, the same aunt who had originally taken the little boy to Shchors in the early summer of 1941 to visit her parents, Mark's grandparents. They had maintained a warm relationship throughout his childhood.

In school, Mark had been blissfully unaware of any differentiation between national groups in the Soviet Union. Many of his friends were Russians—that is, not Jews. They all hung out together. It was only after he left school that he realized that grownups felt differently. Over the next years he would perceive various attitudes that would eventually convince him that Jews were not receiving equal treatment. As Mark put it:

> I saw . . . that during my lifetime it was not becoming better for Jews in the Soviet Union, but with every year the situation of the Jews was becoming worse and worse. . . Well, after I finished school, where they told us all the time that we were all equal before the law, that the door of opportunity was open to all of us equally, that we were all children of the same state; well, right after school I saw that it was certainly not so.

Mark's experience was not unique. He encountered numerous cases of what he saw as unfair treatment because he was Jewish: putting in an application for a job and being told the next day that it had already been taken, for example. He needed documents for his study in Minsk and his grandmother sent them to him. However, they never arrived. When he went to check what had happened to them at the post office, he was given a large file and told to go through it. He found the envelope with his papers, but he couldn't help noticing that all of the surnames in the file of undelivered documents were Jewish.

In spite of this, Mark became a mechanical engineer, although he had to work during the day and study at night. He observed that Russian friends of his seemed to progress within the field faster than he did. He had no doubt why. He continued to live in Minsk where not only Frieda lived, but also an aunt on his father's side whom he was very close to as well.

He made up his mind that he would only marry a Jewish girl. He didn't want a divided home, a "domestic ghetto." He was lucky to find the right girl there in Minsk, a bright, pretty Jewish girl called Bronislava, or Bronia for short.

BRONIA

Bronia was born in the summer of 1946, and so she escaped the traumatic threat, fear, and evacuation of children during the Second World War. Her parents had married in 1939 and her older sister was born before the war, while she and her twin brother were post-war babies, growing up in Minsk. Her father, a butcher by profession, was the assistant manager of a grocery store; her mother worked in a super market. Between her mother's and her father's work, there was no problem having decent food in their household, something which could not be said in those days of most other Soviet citizens, who often had to stand in line for hours to put together some kind of meal. But gradually the situation became worse and even they had trouble bringing home good products.

The home of Bronia's mother had been religious before the war. Bronia's grandmother, in fact, had never abandoned the traditional way of life and maintained the Jewish holidays until her last day. She ate only kosher food, maintained separate utensils for meat and milk, had special dishes for Passover just for herself and tried to keep to the letter of the law. Born in 1876, her grandmother lived until the age of 96, so when Bronia got married, she and her husband moved in with her parents and grandmother. Bronia's own immediate family did not maintain Jewish traditions in the same way. Her twin brother, for example, did not have a bar mitzvah. But this would have been a very difficult thing to arrange in the Soviet Union even if they had felt that they should. In the late 1950s, when he turned thirteen, a religious service of this kind would have been officially frowned upon; and in any case, the number of synagogues still extant was being cut down.

Bronia's mother had ceased to practice religious rituals: during the war it had been impossible for her to eat only kosher food. She tried to make up for this later, once they were back home, but not with the dedication of the grandmother. Though Bronia's mother was far from religion and Bronia knew very little, not even what a bar mitzvah was, still, when Bronia's grandmother died, the two of them sat down and sewed a shroud for her, so that she would be buried in the Jewish tradition. Someone came from the synagogue to prepare the body for burial. Unfortunately, there was no longer a Jewish cemetery in Minsk: after the war the authorities had come in with bulldozers and leveled it.

After high school, Bronia went to a pedagogical institute and studied to be a librarian. She found work as a librarian in a large public library for eight years and later she took a job with an agricultural college. Still later, when she was in search of a new position she found it very difficult to find one. There were two ways she could look for a job, either through an employment bureau or from posted notices. In both cases, there were clearly openings for someone with the right qualifications. While she had those qualifications, she kept getting refusals, statements, for instance, that the job was already taken (once the interviewer had had a look at her papers) and she was convinced that it was all because of line five in her internal passport, the line that asks for "nationality," for which the answer in her case was *evreika*, Jewish.

Bronia married at age twenty, in 1966. Mark's grandmother, too, was still alive at the time of the wedding. She died at 83, a few years later. Like so many Soviet couples, they moved in with her parents and both worked full time to make ends meet. She and Mark had their first daughter in December 1970. They named her Tanya, in memory of Mark's father's sister of the same name, who had been killed in the Minsk ghetto at age twenty.

AARON

Following his release from the army in 1947, Aaron returned to Kiev and immediately went back to work. Before the war he had held a position as a chief accountant and he returned to a similar job now. But his home town lay in ruins, a result of the early bombing of the city in 1941 followed later by combat. Kiev had been smashed: the beautiful curving street in the middle of town, the Khreshchatik was destroyed; so were Krasnoarmeiskaia Street and many others. Housing had been flattened and people were desperate for a place to live, something to eat. Early in the war the authorities had succeeded in moving much manufacturing equipment out of the city to the Urals so that it would not fall into enemy hands and could contribute to the Soviet war effort. Now industry had to be re-started. A massive effort had to be made.

In 1948, Aaron met the girl who would become his wife. Bella was just finishing medical school. Evacuated with her father during the war, she had started to study medicine in Omsk, where they had found refuge. She completed her studies in Kiev when the faculty of medicine re-opened there. A quiet girl, Aaron found her very pretty and was delighted with her family: her father was a *shochet*, a Jewish ritual slaughterer, and religious. Aaron's family lived in abysmal conditions and here was a family living in a decent place, a fine family which welcomed him. When they married, his father-in-law wrote out a marriage contract, a *ketubah*, for them and they had a traditional wedding under the customary canopy, a *khuppah*. This was very important to Aaron.

When Bella finished medical school she specialized as a cardiologist and was assigned to work as a young doctor in Siberia temporarily, so the young couple packed up and left Kiev, returning one year later. In 1953, Aaron started to work in a very responsible job as an accountant in the office where he would continue to work for the next twenty-one years. He and his wife had one child, a girl, born in 1950. The three of them lived in modest conditions in various workers' suburbs of Kiev until 1961 when, through his place of work, Aaron acquired an apartment in the city itself. This was something special, because it was an apartment of two rooms just for the three of them, without having to share. Although they never made an attempt to keep kosher—it was, as Aaron put it, unthinkable there—they maintained a Jewish life. On the anniversary of his mother's death, Aaron would say the mourner's prayer. He knew when the date fell according to the lunar calendar because it was during the week of Passover.

This was another problem faced by Soviet Jews. As all holidays occur according to the cycle of the moon, a special calendar is needed—or an astronomer has to be on hand. It is not enough to have the ordinary Gregorian calendar. These Jewish calendars were not printed during most of the Soviet period and therefore only those who made a special effort knew when particular celebrations should take place. One of the things often asked of tourists in the 1960s and later was to bring a pocket-size Jewish calendar, showing the phases of the moon and the correlating secular date.

During the week of Passover the family ate no bread. They would celebrate the seder at Bella's parents' home. Their daughter Frima recalls that when they arrived at the apartment, her grandfather would close the curtains so that no one could look in. He managed to provide matzah. He had a minyan, a prayer group of the requisite minimum of ten adult males, in an informal place where he could pray, not far from his home and he would go there for holidays and the Sabbath. He actually seldom went to the synagogue for a few reasons: "First, he lived very far; there was just [sic] one synagogue in Kiev, very far, and it was impossible to get there on a holiday. Of course he wouldn't ride on a holiday and the Sabbath." The synagogue was also under the watchful eye of the KGB and that was another good reason for staying away.

In 1957, Aaron's father—an old man by then—got permission to leave the Soviet Union and go to Israel. He and his second wife emigrated and spent their remaining years there. Aaron never saw them again. Bella's father died in 1972 in the Ukraine. Aaron was with his father-in-law during his last hours. The old man told him that he hoped that Aaron and the family would emigrate to Israel. Aaron saw this as his dying wish.

SIMON AND LIUBA

Simon and Liuba both grew up in Leningrad and both, with their separate families, were lucky to be evacuated from the city over Lake Ladoga and live to the east, away from the war, she in Samarkand and he in the Altai in Siberia. Liuba's father served in the Soviet army and was severely injured. In 1949 he died of his wounds, leaving his wife, his thirteen-year-old daughter Liuba, her brother and sister. Her brother had been taken into the army when he was only sixteen, in 1943 when, in desperation, the Soviets started to draft sixteen-year-olds. He wasn't released from the army until the 1950s. Having been in the army so long, he missed the opportunity to study. In all, his life was ruined by the war. He married after his release and moved away, so there was never a close connection. The rest of Liuba's family was brutally killed when the German army reached Belorussia, buried alive in a pit.

Simon, also born in 1936, grew up with both parents as well as a grandfather, who had a strong influence in his formative years. "[My grandfather] was a religious man. He served as an example to all of us. And, as life has shown, it was a good example." Even in the Altai mountains during the war his grandfather managed to maintain a kosher diet. While Simon was growing up they marked the High Holidays and at Passover; there was always matzah for the seder as long as his grandfather was alive.

> I'd like to say about my grandfather that although we ourselves felt it [that we were Jews], we were helped to feel it. Those around us emphasized that we were not like everyone else . . . It's a little difficult to explain: on the one hand we were citizens and obeyed the laws of the country. But on the other hand . . . . when everything is bad, then people look for culprits are and from time immemorial Jews have been very suitable victims for this. . . Here are Russians, Ukrainians—it's bad for you, so the culprit is the Jew . . . so if there's not enough bread, if there's a poor harvest, if it rains or if there's a drought—the Jew is guilty. And simple people believe this very easily. They won't look for those who are guilty in the Supreme Soviet or in the Communist Party; they'll look for the culprit in someone who lives nearby. . .

This doesn't mean that Simon had only Jewish friends when growing up. Even with all the antisemites around, there were still decent people. He grew up with a mixed circle of friends. Being the youngest in his class, he did not join the Komsomol when everyone else in his grade did and when he should have gone in the following year, he didn't. The issue was forgotten and he, in fact, never became a member.

Liuba and Simon feel that it was inevitable that they would have chosen Jewish partners to marry. In each of their families this was expected of them and they were comfortable with it. Liuba's sister also married a Jew. Liuba feared stories that she had heard of Jewish women who had married Russian (that is, non-Jewish) men who, in anger, sometimes called them by the pejorative *zhidovka*. Simon, too, couldn't imagine building a life with someone "different." They both became engineers and continued to live in Leningrad. In 1967 their son, Mikhail, was born.

Various events influenced their transformation into active Zionists. The first, and perhaps the most influential, was the concert in Leningrad given by the popular Israeli singer Geulah Gil in 1966. Both of them found it an overwhelming experience. She sang in Hebrew and in Yiddish. "It gave us," says Simon, "the ability to feel ourselves sitting among our own people, because most of the audience was Jewish." It was a powerful feeling, to be united with those sitting there together. Liuba was also deeply moved by the concert. After each song the audience gave a standing ovation, standing! "It was like a demonstration, a recognition that Israel is your country. . . . The Russians understood precisely what this meant: that people were not so much applauding the songs and the singer as applauding the country . . . which was not just visible somewhere on a map, but a country which lives, exists . . . and this was greetings to the Country . . . a tremendous ovation . . ." Another push, as Simon calls it, towards "forming my sense of national belonging," was the Six Day War, the following year. Not trusting the Soviet media, they listened to the Voice of Israel in Russian, to the Voice of America and to the BBC.

The tremendous source of pride given to Soviet Jews (and Jews in other lands) by the quick and quite astonishing victory of Israel over the neighboring countries is often given as a key factor that initiated or bolstered Zionist feelings and, in many cases, an urge to emigrate to Israel. Other factors include the concert mentioned by Liuba and Simon, a delegation from Israel to the International Youth Festival held in Moscow in 1957, and the publication of the book *Exodus* by Leon Uris. Copies of this book in English or in a Russian translation circulated all over the Soviet Union as *samizdat*.

It was perhaps not surprising, then, given his background, that Simon should have become an activist in a Jewish dissident organization. He made the acquaintance of Hillel Shur and through him became involved in an illegal Leningrad group that included Hillel Butman and other activists whose names would become well-known in the early 1970s. The aim of the group, says Simon, was to help Jews living in Russia to feel a sense of national dignity and, eventually, help them to leave for Israel. This preceded the beginning of the massive permitted Jewish emigration by a couple of years.

Although Simon was unaware of the plan, members of this group planned to hijack a plane from an airport near Leningrad and fly it out of the country. It was to be more than an escape; they wanted to show their desperation to the world. Among these men and women was a pilot. The group was caught on the tarmac before the hijacking took place, arrested and tried in a case that garnered world-wide attention. Some of the would-be hijackers were given the death sentence and such a huge international hue and cry was raised that the Soviets reduced the sentences to long prison terms. Simon, though not personally involved, was a member of the larger organization and he was investigated by the KGB at this time. He was taken in and questioned; their apartment was searched. The security police did find some Hebrew material there: poems of Bialik and a few other items. Surely it would only be a matter of time before Simon would again be arrested and this time imprisoned.

YAN

Born in 1947, Yan, an only child, grew up in Kiev. His father, who was a doctor, died when Yan was thirteen years old and a year and a half later his mother re-married. He lived "in a pretty good neighborhood," grew up in a middle class, intellectual environment and had a number of good friends, Russians, Ukrainians and Jews. Yan never thought about these differences in his youth. His parents were both Jewish, but it was only while his grandmother was alive that there was some Jewish atmosphere in the house. It was not of importance to him that he marry a Jewish girl, though in fact he did marry someone whose mother was Jewish. She was artistically very gifted and balanced his more scientific orientation. Natasha was only 19 when they met and he was 21. They married the next year, in 1969.

Jan, a good-looking, talented young man, studied engineering and managed to find a very interesting and challenging job while living in the Soviet Union. His work was very important to him. Though he had close friends who were involved in the campaign for human rights, he himself was less active than Natasha. She became involved in dissident activity after they met. While he did participate in meetings and discussions, despite his skepticism, he felt that it was hypocritical to urge human rights on a communist government. It was clear that when signing international human rights agreements, the Soviet

Union had no intention of abiding by them. "So to me it was just playing a game with them and destroying your own life and that of your children and your parents; [it] wasn't worth doing." They were all playing with fire and in the process, some of his friends would be arrested.

Yan was referring to the Helsinki Accords, to which the Soviet Union became a signatory in 1975. In the hope of improving relations with the West, the Soviet Union agreed to permit certain basic human rights—including the right to leave one's own country—and willingly, though not enthusiastically, promised to maintain a legal framework to enable citizens to enjoy those rights. Various protective measures, such as watchdog groups, were put in place to assure compliance. However, it can be said that there were no truly significant changes in Soviet practice until Mikhail Gorbachev came into power many years later.

Natasha and Yan lived fulfilled and busy lives in Kiev: art, work, friends, family, and a little son. Although they were not satisfied with the state of human rights in the Soviet Union, they were happy within their own small world in Kiev. When the opportunity became viable in the Soviet Union, did they consider leaving? Certainly not.

SERYOZHA

Seryozha's family was a study in contrasts. In his early twenties, his father, the son of a wealthy contractor under the last tsar, entered the Communist Party. That was in 1941 or 1942. At the time he was in the Soviet army, serving as a pilot. His joining the party was a fervent act of faith, not one of convenience. An ideological person, he had been involved in communist youth activities for years; this was the culmination of his enthusiasm. He remained a convinced member of the party until his son emigrated.

Seryozha's mother, on the other hand, was completely indifferent politically. She was a dentist and stayed away from political issues. Born in 1927, she had finished school with a gold medal during the war. A talented student, she was also a gifted pianist. While she was in dental school, she was simultaneously studying at the conservatory. She finished both at the same time.

Seryozha was an only child, born in 1953, and grew up in post-war Kiev. Both of his grandfathers had been involved in some way with manual labor. His father's father, whom he never knew, had been a builder in Kiev and had had permission to live in Kiev in the Russian Empire when a Jew had to have a special dispensation to do so. He had been a master builder, and had been presented with a gold medallion from tsar Nicholas II for his work. Indeed, among his buildings still standing is the "Brodskii" synagogue, although it no longer functions as originally intended.

Seryozha's maternal grandfather worked with his hands, but in his case he made furniture, repaired locks, understood electricity, was in general manually gifted. He was bigger than life. Seryozha tells how at age 78 this physically large, very strong man walked from one end of Kiev to the other carrying a 15 kilogram (33 ½ pound) sack of potatoes, which he then carried up to the fifth floor.

This grandfather did not get along well with his daughter's husband. "My grandfather was more an emotional person than reasonable." He was also anticommunist. All of his first cousins had been arrested by the Cheka (secret police) in 1923 and when he went to ask what had happened, was told that it was none of his business. He had looked after his five younger siblings very responsibly after his own father (Seryozha's great grandfather) was killed in a Petliura pogrom during the Civil War not long after the revolution. His little sister was asked in her class in a Yiddish-speaking school that still existed in the Soviet Union in the early 1920s who the greatest person on earth was. The expected answer should have been "Lenin." Instead she answered, *"Mein bruder Shmerl!"*

"I very much loved my grandfather and in practice everything in the house that was Jewish was from my grandfather. In spite of the fact that he said that he wasn't religious, every Purim he would come and read the *Megilat Ester.*" Because of his grandfather the whole family was aware of the holidays: there was always matzah for Passover, whatever the situation. Somehow he always managed to get hold of some. There wasn't an actual seder, possibly because of the difficult relationship between Seryozha's father and his grandfather.

In an official way, Seryozha became aware that he was Jewish when he went to school. But in some way, he had known for a long time. "But the truth is that when I was altogether small, before I went to school, it seemed to me, from my surroundings, that to be a Jew, this was not very good. And therefore, I, like every child, said that my grandfather was Jewish, my papa was Jewish, my mama was Jewish, but I was Russian." For Seryozha's father being Jewish was a matter of indifference. But his grandfather tried to show him in various ways that being a Jew was not such a bad thing. "And grandpa succeeded to the extent that when I went to school I already came with a feeling of national dignity, as it were." He started to tell Seryozha about Jewish history. At the time, Bulgarian stories were very popular for children and his grandfather would say, "Why read Bulgarian fairytales? I'll tell you something better: Jewish stories!"

Seryozha, like his father, was a Marxist, at least as a young man. He belonged to the Communist Youth League, the Komsomol, until 1972. Most young people did. It was more or less required for anyone who intended to go on to a university, enter a career, get a decent job.

But Seryozha was an introspective person, one who liked to examine various philosophical ideas. At some point, when he was about 19, he met an enthusiast who convinced him to become a Tolstoyan, which he did, for a long time. He could see the value of Tolstoy's ideas: "Why does one live and suffer if there is no God, if there is no aim to our existence?" As a Tolstoyan, he became a vegetarian. The exploration of ideas, as we shall see, was of crucial importance for Seryozha.

All during this time, Seryozha was living in Kiev, whose Jewish community had suffered on such a cruel and massive scale during the Second World War. In September 1941, with the army of the Third Reich now in full control of the city, SS troops rounded up the remaining Jews still in Kiev—over thirty-three thousand—forced them to walk to a ravine (Babi Yar) on the outskirts of town and, row by row, they were shot down, shoved over and buried where they fell. Men, women, children were all treated mercilessly, so that Babi Yar eventually became emblematic of the murderous policy of the Germans. It would also—in the late 1950s and early 60s—become a matter of internal conflict regarding Soviet policy, when it was decided to convert the area of the ravine of Babi Yar—now well within the enlarged city of Kiev—into a sports stadium. How could they profane such a sacred place? Why wasn't there an appropriate memorial on the grounds? Why was no mention made of the fact that it was Jews who had been particularly singled out for death in the fall of 1941; they had not been shot en masse as "Soviet citizens" despite the official statements to the contrary. Thus Babi Yar continued to be a source of pain and controversy.

It was not until he was twenty years old that Seryozha actually visited the site. "Then, completely by chance, I came across Babi Yar. Just like that. I went to look." A girl he knew from school—they had shared the same desk—told him that it was the anniversary of Babi Yar and he decided to go with her. He had only heard about it from her and went simply because he thought it would be interesting. At around the same time, Seryozha got himself a Bible and started reading it. After his first visit, he returned other times to honor the dead in that hallowed place.

His grandfather and mother were worried about Seryozha frequenting the area and tried to talk him out of it. As a matter of fact, his grandfather had been going to visit the site all along and, at the request of Seryozha's parents, hadn't told his grandson. But now when he went he would sometimes see Seryozha there.

In the early 1970s, Seryozha also got involved in dissident activity. During the winter of 1971–72, a group of Jews had demonstratively gone to the synagogue. He had gone with them but, by chance, he wasn't arrested. A number of them were, however, and spent fifteen days in jail. When they got out, the group wrote a letter complaining that what they had done had been completely legal according to the Soviet constitution. Seryozha didn't compose the letter, but he typed and signed it. He immediately lost his job. The head of the institute where Seryozha was working as a draftsman was Jewish and, like so many Jews in Kiev, listened to Israel radio, which reported the incident at the synagogue and the subsequent letter. Seryozha's name was listed among the signatories and when he heard it, the director turned white and shouted that because of Seryozha, his own son would lose his chance of getting into the institute. He demanded that Seryozha promise that he would never do anything like that again or he would have to leave. Seryozha left.

Seryozha was involved in both Jewish-oriented and general human rights activities. He and Yan later ended up in the same group of like-minded individuals, having first met at a musical evening at friends'. They were listening to a performance of the Passion of St. Matthew, reading the text along with the music. The group carried on the same discussions and dissident activities as others of their kind. Eventually some of the members of this group were arrested and some of them became very well-known defenders of human rights in the Soviet Union.

During this period, Seryozha began reading *samizdat* materials, both general and Jewish. He read works of Buber and Solzhenitsyn; *We,* a futuristic satire by the 1920s writer Zamiatin; collections of *samizdat* works such as *Iz pod glyb,* and the underground dissident newsletter, *The Chronicle of Current Events.* The *Chronicle* was a unique "publication." No one knew exactly who put it together or where it originated. It contained facts, facts about dissidents of all kinds, about petitions and demonstrations, facts about people who had been arrested and about what was happening to people in the camps. If someone were ill or died in imprisonment, the *Chronicle* might be the only source of information about it. If someone was arrested, the information might reach the outside world in the pages of the *Chronicle.* Instructions were given in each issue of the *Chronicle* on how to relay news to the editors: just give the information to the person who passed the *Chronicle* on to you, he will pass it to the one who gave it to him and so on until it gets back to the editors and then they will publicize it in the next issue.

Seryozha's tastes were broad: literary and philosophical, Jewish and human rights. He was, however, playing with fire. *Samizdat* materials were illegal, not to be found in your home or discovered on your person. People tended to read them quickly and pass them on: it was like playing hot potato. One day when he was out of Kiev, the KGB called in his father. Seryozha himself was brought in for questioning a number of times. The first time, he was kept there for eight hours but refused to cooperate. He was threatened: they would bring in his sick mother. Seryozha felt that they probably wouldn't, but he did warn his mother. When they eventually called her in, she refused to go, saying that she wasn't well. But his father was afraid and went with them.

Around this time, Seryozha got married. His wife was much better prepared for these problems than his parents. She knew how to answer. They were married in 1976.

ZHENIA

Zhenia grew up in Yalta, in Crimea, a beautiful part of the Soviet Union dipping into the Black Sea. It is a place that she has always been very attached to, where she and her mother and younger sister had a happy life.

Zhenia's family first came to Crimea a couple of generations back. Her grandmother, who was the daughter of a Russian Orthodox priest, came there at the turn of the twentieth century, a devoted young teacher. Not a member of the Communist Party, she came to Yalta as a member of the intelligentsia whose aim was to bring enlightenment to ordinary people. In the early years after the revolution, she was working in a village and was shot at by someone trying to get her out of the area. She survived this danger, but later died of tuberculosis, leaving three young children, the oldest of whom was Zhenia's mother, with her second husband, a Latvian who had been a strong supporter of the Bolsheviks.

In the early years of Soviet rule, a disproportionate number of Latvians and Jews had been active in helping the Bolsheviks consolidate power. They were involved, along with Russians and other national groups, in taking over disputed areas and enforcing Soviet policies. In the case of Zhenia's adoptive grandfather, he found himself fleeing when Stalin in the late 1930s started to crush the Latvians who had once been his allies. The children found refuge with an aunt. In the end their stepfather was arrested, sent to a labor camp and ended up living in Kazakhstan. Many many years later Zhenia's mother succeeded in locating her stepfather, still alive in Central Asia.

Zhenia's mother had her own marital problems. Her husband was drafted into the army during World War II as a young man and only released after he had served for seven years. By this time, life had passed him by: it was too late to begin his studies and he simply became a driver. Zhenia's mother parted from him in 1962. Zhenia, born in 1951, had little contact with her father after that.

Her father, born in the mid-1920s, had a brother, Radek, who was killed on May 9, 1945, that is, on the last day of the Second World War as celebrated in the Soviet Union. It had been the fashion in Soviet Russia to name children after socialist heroes or ideological concepts, and his brother was clearly named for an early Bolshevik, Karl Radek. Zhenia finds this very amusing. "Thank Goodness," she says, "that it wasn't Karl Marx or Stalin or Lenin. Later they were naming kids Mirnyi Atom (Peaceful Atom) and Traktor and Lampochka (Light Bulb)!"

Zhenia's mother had started working in the school system when she was just seventeen years old. She had teaching jobs at various levels of responsibility, rising eventually to the position of teaching teachers. It is a profession that she has loved and prospered in.

With an ideologically enthusiastic mother who belonged to the Communist Party, it was no wonder that Zhenia not only entered the Komsomol, but was an active member. She was an organizer for her class and, for three years, for the school. Through her work, she came in contact with the Komsomsol organization in the city of Yalta. However, disillusion set in when she reached the upper levels of the organization. It was there that she saw that the higher officials were receiving privileges that no one else had. This was not the communist spirit that she had seen in her mother at home. She was greatly distressed: "And I suddenly saw such filth; it was such a nightmare, that they were using their position! Where were their ideals? . . . I went to Komsomol meetings and said, 'Write about this to the newspapers! Support the Komsomol organization!' . . . I told the truth and they laughed."

Zhenia wanted to hand in her membership card. Luckily for her she had a wonderful teacher who told her not to do that until she was finished with high school. She warned the girl that the authorities would make it very hard for her if she rebelled and might even not let her graduate. Zhenia took her advice and remained in the Komsomol. Her own mother assured her that the despicable behavior of the Komsomol officials constituted the acts of individuals and that they weren't always like that. Without her mother's backing or that of her sister who was too young to understand what was going on, Zhenia turned to a male cousin, with whom she was very close. But he was a practical fellow and, even if he supported her, said: "Go ahead—shout it in the street. What good will it do?"

Zhenia herself, while academically gifted, was not interested in teaching, though it had become the chosen field of two generations of women in her family. The only higher education she could have obtained in Crimea would have been at a teachers' institute, so she chose to go to the university in Chernovtsy, which was relatively close. Friends had told her that it was a lovely town, and Zhenia, when she arrived there, discovered this to be true. It really was a beautiful city. She studied Russian language and literature there.

When she went to the university, she decided to avoid any kind of Komsomol activity. While she was automatically appointed to some organizational position (because of her past experience), she refrained from real involvement and eventually explained that she'd come to study and couldn't do other things. So although she retained her card she ceased to be active.

But another development was taking place. By her third year at the university in Chernovtsy, in 1971, Zhenia was introduced to materials in *samizdat*. At this time she was about twenty years old. She became friendly with people, many older than herself, who took an active role in securing and distributing *samizdat*. Some of them were fellow students in her courses, others were teachers. People were afraid to talk at the university, but in these self-selected circles one could talk. "Everyone shared their convictions. And I not only absorbed this knowledge myself, I actively introduced it to my mother and sister! I started to bring materials home."

The *samizdat* that she read in the beginning was literature, starting with Solzhenitsyn. Then she went on to other writers and literary critics. These were not revolutionary texts that had been written especially for distribution in *samizdat*: they were simply works that could not be published in the Soviet Union because of censorship restrictions. Some were recently written; others had been published in the past but could no longer appear in print in the U.S.S.R. "Then an ordinary question arose: but why couldn't they publish it? Why—because some monster will come crashing down if someone says a word sideways? Nu, why don't they publish? . . . You won't find Akhmatova. Tsvetaeva you won't find. Pasternak: they just brought out one little volume . . ."

Whenever Zhenia came home to Yalta on vacation she brought *samizdat* with her. Her mother read what she brought but "actively resisted." She firmly stood on her principles in opposition to what she had been given to her by her daughter. "She didn't want to listen; she didn't want to talk. She said what all the papers said: 'Errors of the past; perhaps a small amount of what was said really happened'" and so on. But Zhenia kept bringing material home and her mother read everything. She never mentioned any of this to the Party. Zhenia even brought a whole bundle of the *Chronicle of Current Events* to Yalta when she came on vacation. She found that many of her friends there wanted to read it.

Eventually, things closed in on Zhenia. A friend innocently asked her to give regards to someone in Chernovtsy. Zhenia, not realizing that he was under KGB surveillance, went to see him and, when he asked if she had anything for him, said that she'd brought the *Chronicle*. Shortly after, she was summoned to the university and was greeted by a KGB officer. From what he showed her it was clear that they knew she had been distributing the *Chronicle*. She was taken to headquarters, where she played dumb, but to no avail. They wanted names. They had checked into her family history and knew a lot about her and threatened to ruin her sister's chances of getting into a college and have her mother thrown out of the Party.

Zhenia's adviser had been urging her to go on to graduate study, but after the KGB conversation everything turned to ashes. As she wasn't "loyal" she could not get an "Excellent" on her diploma. She received a lower grade and realized that she would not go on to an academic career. Disappointed, she returned to Yalta and found a job in a museum. Two years later, she met the man who would become her husband. He was already an active dissident, had signed various petitions, been called into the KGB himself. When she married Seryozha she moved with him to Kiev and they continued their activities there.

Did it bother her that he was a Jew? "The question didn't exist in our family." She herself had no connection with Christianity. She was nothing. For her the matter of religion did not exist. Seryozha himself, though consciously Jewish, was not religious, so there was no conflict. She certainly never envisaged herself going to Israel.

Part Two

AWAKENINGS AND DECISIONS

Chapter Four

The Decision to Leave—and Where

BACKGROUND

The year 1971 produced a dramatic change in the history of the Russian Jews. Suddenly and inexplicably thousands and thousands of Jews were being permitted to leave the Soviet Union. Nothing like this had ever been seen before. There had been a small trickle of Jews leaving in the few previous years—largely older people. But why, at this point, did the regime change its policy and let large numbers of Jews leave? And why would the Jews take the opportunity to do so?

The truth is that in terms of education and career, the Jews had not done badly in the Soviet Union. From the moment of its inception, the Soviet Union had permitted Jews to live wherever they wanted (there was no longer a Pale of Settlement), to study in institutions of higher education in impressive numbers, and to enter a wide range of careers (until the early 1940s, when some fields—the upper ranks of the army, the diplomatic corps, for example—began to be closed to them). A look at the statistics of Jewish participation in the scientific, legal, pedagogical, and communications fields shows clearly the very high percentage of Jews.

By the 1970s, however, the trend could be seen to be changing for a variety of reasons. In some cases, it had become policy to encourage natives of the eponymous republics to get a better education and try to fill many of the posts themselves. Thus, even if the number of Jews in a field remained static, their proportion would go down. In other cases, such as mathematics, there seems to have been an actual policy of keeping Jews out of the finest math faculty, the one at Moscow State University, and relegating them to lesser institutions in spite of their spectacular record over the past decades. However it may be,

59

Soviet Jews began to have a sense of discrimination starting in the 1940s and 50s. This feeling was reinforced by other phenomena.

It was impossible for the Jews to turn a blind eye on the official attitudes toward them. While they were, of course, grateful to the Soviet Union for winning the war against Germany and saving them from the inevitable slaughter of the Holocaust, they felt shortchanged in the state's policy of ignoring the fact that they had been a specially targeted population during the war. They didn't want the few memorial sites to be labeled "Soviet citizens fell here" rather than that these victims had for the most part been Jews. They could also still remember the attack on the Jewish cultural community as well as the Doctors Plot in the post-war years of Stalin's reign.

In the wake of the Six Day War, the Soviet Union severed its diplomatic relations with the State of Israel. Official propaganda then became increasingly critical of Israel and of "Zionism." A plethora of articles which attacked Israel and which confirmed the Soviet notion that "Zionism is Racism" appeared in the Soviet press. Books on the subject, some clearly antisemitic in tone, also appeared. Such publications in a country of official censorship could not be seen as accidental or devoid of significance. Many Jews felt that the Soviet Union was no longer home to them.

In the early 1970s, small groups of Jews started to engage in a variety of Zionist-related activities, such as circulating materials in *samizdat*, studying Hebrew clandestinely and meeting with like-minded people out in the woods or at synagogues. On June 15, 1970, a small group in Leningrad made a daring attempt to hijack a plane at Smolny airport. They were arrested before they even reached the plane and there followed a spate of further arrests, trials and a large-scale crack-down on Jewish activists.

Beginning in 1971, a major exodus of Jews began to flow out of the U.S.S.R., starting with over twelve thousand the first year. This was certainly a very impressive number of people to be permitted to leave the country legally and the annual figures increased over the decade. By the end of the 1970s, over two hundred twenty thousand Jews had emigrated from the Soviet Union. This was the largest Jewish emigration from the Russian state since the beginning of the twentieth century and was a remarkable phenomenon in many ways, both for the country being left behind and for the countries that received these immigrants.

The people who left initially were of two separate categories: Jews who had somehow retained their religious orientation, even within the distinctly anti-religious Soviet environment, and those who had strong Zionist inclinations. The latter, in the beginning, tended to be what were referred to as "Western" Jews—Jews who had for the most part spent the interwar years in independent Poland or the Baltic States. They had a strong influence on many of the "Core" Jews of the Soviet Union, those who had grown up with little connection to their religion and their culture. Eventually they, too, in increasing numbers became caught up in a desire to leave the land of their birth and seek a future elsewhere. As more Jews left, more felt that perhaps they, too, should leave before it was too late.

In the first years of the emigration, almost all of the Jews went directly to Vienna and then on to settle in Israel. This was their goal, their dream. As the decade progressed, more of the emigrants opted out of going to Israel and became what were called "drop-outs." They would travel as far as Vienna and from there to Italy, where they would wait, sometimes for months, until they managed to obtain a visa to the United States (or Canada or Australia or South Africa).

However, whatever their eventual destination, every Jew had to go through the same process inside the Soviet Union: they had to apply to leave for Israel for purposes of family reunification. This was a complicated process, both on the Soviet and Israeli sides. At the Soviet end, each would-be emigrant had first to receive an invitation (or *vyzov*) from a family member in Israel, with whom he or she would be "reunified." The Jewish Agency in Israel facilitated this procedure. If there were truly relatives in Israel, they would be contacted and would then go to the Agency to fill out the appropriate documents and have them notarized. If it was impossible to find one's own relatives, someone appropriate would be found—perhaps someone with the same family name—and that person would be asked to send the invitation. Nothing was actually stated about what the relationship was: the person would simply invite the Soviet Jewish family to come to Israel. This met the criterion of family reunion which—although largely a fiction—underlay Soviet emigration policy in this early period.

Once the *vyzov* had been received, the would-be emigrants had to go through a long process of obtaining documentation. The undertaking often involved very awkward and even unpleasant confrontations with one's fellow workers or neighbors. They needed a statement from their housing unit that they were tenants in good standing. They had to get a report from their place of work. They were required to fill in forms of various kinds. All of this was handed in to the OVIR office (Office of Visas and Registration) in their locality, which would then deal with the request and issue its decision. This might take a couple of months or half a year or longer. Or there might be no permission granted and then the person would end up being what was called a "refusenik." By this time, he might have lost his job and he would then have to seek another one as it was illegal to be without work, to be a "parasite" in the terminology of the Union of Soviet Socialist Republics. Some people lived in this limbo for years.

It was thus a matter of major consequence to decide to attempt to emigrate. Not only did you have to go through a difficult process: you also had to be sure that you wanted to leave the country of your birth, to leave your friends and family and the familiar landscape of your life. Anyone leaving in the nineteen seventies had to assume that he would never be able to return, that saying goodbye to loved ones was forever. You faced an uncertain future with little knowledge of the place you were heading for or the language you would use. You were limited to taking with you a very small amount of money and only specific personal belongings. It took a lot of courage to embark on such a journey.

If everything went well, you then had to obtain Israeli travel documents. Upon leaving the Soviet Union you lost your Soviet citizenship. These documents were available from Israel, but Israel had no embassy or consular services in the U.S.S.R. The Netherlands had agreed to take over any consular duties for Israel when relations between Tel Aviv and Moscow were broken in June, 1967, following the Six Day War. At that point it was probably not imagined what a busy role the Dutch would have over the next two decades. Thus Soviet Jews received their Israeli visas from the Netherlands embassy in Moscow. They saw nothing of Israelis until they reached Vienna or Israel itself.

Emigration is almost always difficult. The unknown is frightening. In the case of Jews leaving the Soviet Union, they had to fear not only what awaited them in the country towards which they were heading. They also had to fear the authorities in the country they were leaving, the pitfalls of the process and the possible hostility of their former colleagues and neighbors.

The period of the seventies saw large numbers of Jews trying to decide on their futures. Would things improve in the Soviet Union or remain mired in a system of intolerable control? If some Jews were leaving, would that make it difficult for those who remained behind? Would the Jews in Russia find themselves worse off by the end of the decade? Was it possible that the gates, now open, might be closed again? How could decisions be made rationally when there was so little information from abroad upon which to base one's opinion? Pressure from the world outside began to make itself felt, urging the Soviets to allow free emigration. But by the end of the seventies, the policies of détente had fallen apart; the political agreements the Soviets had hoped for were not reached, and the Soviet Union had invaded Afghanistan. Within a year, the rate of permitted emigration had dropped precipitously. People who hadn't left by 1980 might not manage to emigrate for a long time to come.

LIUBA AND SIMON

Liuba and Simon feel that their eventual emigration to Israel was inevitable, given their—particularly Simon's—background. Once Simon chose to participate in a Zionist group in Leningrad his fate, more or less, was sealed. Liuba had not been happy when he came home and said that he had spoken to Hillel Butman about joining. I'm not one of the brave, she said. However, in her heart of hearts, Liuba could not oppose it and did not stand in his way. She was simply worried about the implications of such a move.

Once Simon had been called in by the KGB for questioning in 1970, there was really not much choice. The KGB made it clear at some point that they considered Simon an undesirable person. While most people left of their own volition, there were certainly numerous examples of "encouragement," where the authorities decided that getting rid of activists was preferable to making them into martyrs and even increasing their power to influence others. Indeed, it is believed that one of the reasons for allowing large numbers of Jews to leave at all in the 1970s was the pressure-valve theory: get rid of the trouble makers, relieve the pressure, and things can return to normal.

As Simon put it, "You understand, after everything that happened with the plane, with the organization, not to speak of what had happened before this—such a revival of national striving to leave—it all came together in a need to go. Under these circumstances it was impossible to stay. Our bridges were burned." Simon continued, "I think that with all my upbringing, step by step there was a logical consistency and the final aim was to leave the country."

For Liuba the situation was somewhat different. While Simon knew that his family—his parents and his brother—would follow, Liuba knew that she would be leaving alone. So while she agreed that there was no choice, Liuba found it much more difficult to face the inevitable: she might never see her family again. At the beginning of December, 1971, less than a year after the start of the exodus, Liuba, Simon and their little boy left the Soviet Union.

BRONIA AND MARK

In this case, the idea was wholly Mark's. He felt that the situation was such that they had to leave the Soviet Union and find a better life. Bronia had very mixed feelings and tried to put off the decision.

For Mark, there were no parents to leave behind and that had never been a factor. His grandparents had already died. All he had were some aunts, to whom he was close, but not enough for this to be a barrier to departure. For Bronia it meant leaving her parents and her brother and sister. There was no question of their following: her parents were old and their son (her brother) was ill, so they would not consider leaving him. Bronia's parents also had brothers and sisters whom they would never leave. Her parents, in their loving way, urged the young couple to do whatever they felt was best for themselves and their children. Anyway, even if they should decided to join them in emigrating, how would Bronia and Mark be able to help them? They would just be starting out themselves and would not have the financial means to support others.

Mark felt that his Jewishness weighed on him. He very much wanted to live in a place where he and his family would not be judged by their origins, but by their intrinsic worth.

They spent a great deal of time talking about their possible emigration. They had friends who had already left, but for Bronia, this was a very personal burden because of her close ties with her family. At the time, they had a baby and she urged him to wait until she was at least a year old before they proceeded. He agreed to do so, but was anxious to start the process.

There was also a question of where they should go. Bronia had a first cousin, from Chernovtsy, who had gone to Israel, but they couldn't locate her. So Israel was never really an option for them. Mark had some good friends in Denver and another in Boston. "We had, of course, a difficult trip [ahead] because when a person doesn't know everything, he is afraid. . . Therefore wherever you are looking, what counts is where your good friends or relatives are."

In the end, Mark and Bronia were very lucky. When their younger daughter was just over a year old they handed in their documents. They left the Soviet Union on October 12, 1979. A short time later the gates of the exodus would begin to close.

TANIA AND PERETZ

There was never a question of who wanted to leave the Soviet Union or what the destination would be. According to Tania: "In my case, Peretz decided to leave Russia. I objected to it. I stood firm for several years. He didn't go because of me . . . the thing is, he had had his wish, his desire, to go to Israel, even Palestine before Israel."

This was true. Peretz had made a furtive attempt to leave for the Holy Land even before the establishment of the State of Israel. He had paid the penalty for this. But he had never lost the aspiration and was waiting for the day when he could have the chance to realize his dream.

Tania had defended her thesis on Byron in Latvian translation at the university in 1969. By then she was earning a decent salary and together with Peretz, who also had a job though earning less, they lived comparatively well. She had worked hard to get where she was in the academic world. Doctorates in the Soviet Union are received later in life, when the candidate already has long experience in the field. Peretz and Tania had their own, separate, beautiful apartment in a suburb of Riga near lush forest land. He had managed to parlay their former flat and his late mother's room (the only part of the old family apartment that she had managed to retain) into this fine place. Their lives, finally, had settled down into a degree of comfort.

For Tania, going abroad would probably mean a reduction in her academic status or, perhaps, no job at all. Peretz, too, would have to find himself work, but he didn't mind: his work in Riga wasn't really interesting. As Tania comments, "No, what was interesting was when he was in prison. That was marvelous, he says. It was, as you say, a golden cage."

"Peretz always wanted to come to Israel and he gradually changed me . . . You know how it is, he's a very overbearing person," she said laughing. "So that gradually I also became a Zionist. Because, first of all, I was completely disillusioned with communism, you see. That is the first point. Otherwise, I wouldn't have listened to him, of course." Although he was champing at the bit, Peretz decided to leave Tania in peace and quiet while she was preparing to defend her thesis. She wanted to continue to work until she reached pensionable age which, for women, was fifty-five. She was sure that if they decided to put in a request to emigrate, she would immediately lose her job and she didn't want this to happen.

In the early 1970s, Peretz frequently saw people off at the Riga train station. These were old friends, many of whom had been secret Zionists. Tania sometimes accompanied him and each time he would say, "When are we going to go?" One day Peretz came home from seeing someone off and said that they had to leave. "And I was so upset; we quarreled so much. He left the house without a goodbye, without anything. He said he's going by himself." He came home that evening. At some point Tania felt that she had to decide. She couldn't even manage to heat their flat alone. She was ill, having suffered from high blood pressure for a long time, and was very dependent on her husband. She had turned fifty-five. This was what Peretz had been waiting for. The push was on. Tania took ill and was in the hospital, so she didn't even return to the university for the new semester. She resigned because of illness and took up her pension. Just after the Yom Kippur war, in the autumn of 1973, they handed in their papers. Permission was granted in less than two months. "That's all that I wanted to tell you. Peretz *dragged* me out."

AARON

Although Aaron did not technically follow a religious way of life, he never-theless had a strong spiritual affinity for Judaism and this became the main motivation for his desire to go to Israel. It was not the glorious victory of the Six Day War. Of course, he knew about it. It was not the fact that his father had left for Israel, although that held some significance. (By the time people were leaving in large numbers, his father was no longer alive.) It was not to facilitate his daughter getting an advanced degree: she would sooner or later have obtained one in Kiev. Looking back on that period, he was certain: "I want to repeat again that I consider that there came a period when I simply felt in my soul that I had to leave, and I consider that only from the religious point of view." He felt very strongly that it was not to make life easier or better but that the real cause for his wanting to go to Israel was an internal, religious sense that this must happen.

This strong motivation was felt by his daughter as well. The two of them were in a partnership of sorts to move things forward toward emigration. They both knew, said Frima, "that it was impossible to live as Jews in the Soviet Union." Bella, Aaron's wife, found herself caught in the middle be-tween her daughter and husband on the one hand and her family on the other. She found it very difficult to consider staying in Kiev to be near her brother and sister and extended family and friends while her husband and daughter went off without her. She found it equally untenable to think of leaving these beloved people behind, probably never to see them again.

Aaron planned his strategy carefully. He needed his wife's agreement so that they would all leave together and he wanted to retain his job during the period that he would be waiting for permission to leave. He realized that with his present job he could not even consider leaving: it was quite a high position and connected with a large number of people. So he would have to slip out of that accounting job and transfer to a less high profile one before he could start the process. In order to do this without arousing suspicion, he relied on the fact that he was a bona fide war invalid. He claimed that the job had become too much for him and that he wanted to lower his work load. He was then given lighter work—for which he was also paid less—with less responsibility. With this matter settled, Aaron then felt that he could proceed with the process of emigration.

For the next step, Aaron worked in cahoots with his daughter, Frima. In March, Bella had gone alone on a rest cure at a sanatorium out of town. Aaron and Frima knew what the situation would be at the health resort and that she would be in an awkward position if she had to carry on a lengthy phone conversation or argument. They phoned her to tell her that they were requesting "an invitation to the south." They realized that there would be no private phone in her room and that she would be called to the lobby to speak on a public telephone. "She understood what that meant, but she couldn't talk. There were a lot of people around and she just wanted us to leave her alone. So she mumbled, 'good, O.K.'" The poor woman didn't want to make a fuss in a crowded lobby. After their brief conversation, Aaron sent a letter to his relative in Israel asking for an invitation, the required *vyzov.*

When Bella returned to Kiev, she was faced with a trying situation, though not a *fait accompli.* Her husband and daughter offered every argument they could think of to convince her to agree to emigrate. The only thing that carried real weight with her was that her father, on his death bed, had told Aaron that he wanted them to go to Israel. He hadn't said it of anyone else in the family, just them. This was what finally clinched it.

In June 1974, they handed in their documents and waited for a few months until permission was given. From the moment the request went in Bella was told to leave her position as a doctor. Frima, who was a teacher, was not permitted to work any longer either. Indeed, there was a sort of mock trial at her school when it became known that she was planning to leave for Israel. It was unpleasant, but not worse than that. But Aaron, who had prepared the way well, continued in his job until shortly before they left. He could have stayed until the end, but he needed the last ten days to make arrangements before their departure date.

Frima did not say good-by to anyone. "Maybe now I'm sorrier about that. I had a few good friends and it's too bad that I didn't part from them. We left; we knew that it was a complete break. We wouldn't come back; there would be no connection . . . not even with relatives." Years later they heard so many terrible stories about people who started out just as they had but had had difficult tangles with the authorities, ending in serious complications. It was different for her family: "We simply wanted to immigrate to Israel; that's all. That was all we wanted. Look, with us it was very easy, in retrospect, very, very easy. Emotionally it was quite hard. . . all that indecision."

ESTHER

Although Esther's husband, Iuzek, did actually get home, he was a changed man. His son, Izia, had been three years old when he was arrested; now he was eight. He recognized him when he found him playing outside the building when he arrived home after being released. Iuzek was only thirty-eight years old, but his health was that of an old man. He had contracted tuberculosis while in the camp. He had trouble breathing. He had heart problems. It was at least half a year before he could begin to work and as an ex-con it was hard to find a job. They didn't have anyplace to live.

Esther, for her part, had moved professionally from teaching to translating. She had taken correspondence courses in English and in 1956 she started working full time for a large industry, as a translator. Their lives seemed to be coming together again, finally. But then, in 1959, Iuzek became very ill, with cancer, and died quite soon, after just four years of freedom.

Thanks to Esther's father she finally managed to obtain her own apartment in 1964. For almost her whole life she had lived with her parents. Now she and her teen-age son had a two-room apartment, with their own kitchen.

She became friendly with a man who had been in the camps with Iuzek and who had now returned home to Novosibirsk with his wife and son. Misha invited Esther to join a little extra translating project together with another friend of his who later became her second husband. She and Volt married in 1967, when she was thirty-nine years old.

After Iuzek's death, Esther had more or less given up on any hope of leaving the Soviet Union. The first time she thought about it again was in 1969. She was at work at her regular job as translator at the construction bureau when her boss, a young Russian engineer with whom she was on excellent terms, said to her one day: "Esfira Moiseevna, you always stand up for Israel . . . So why don't you go to Israel?" Esther: "Gennadii Safronovich, if it were possible to go to Israel, I would already be there." He answered, "But it is possible. . . I just came back from Moscow . . . and I saw twenty-five Georgian families, Georgian Jews, who were leaving from the train station. I saw: they were going to Israel." "I said, 'Gennadii Sofronovich! If this is true, I'm also going.'"

She ran straight home, "like a madman," and told her papa, Volt and Izia. They all decided that if it was true, they were going, right away. "No one of us asked, no one was interested, how it was in Israel, where there's work, what's there . . . We didn't know and it wasn't important to us, not important."

A friend suggested that they contact a friend of a friend of his who had been in prison with him. The man's name was David Khavkin and he could tell them how they could manage to get to Israel. Her father suggested that if these were Georgians leaving, they should go there and find out how it was done. So she and Volt took their spring vacation that May first in Moscow and then in Georgia.

They flew into Moscow from Novosibirsk and phoned Khavkin, who told them to come over right away. They went directly to his apartment from the airport. On the wall was a picture of Moshe Dayan and a map of Israel. Going round and round on the record player, one after the other, were two records: Israeli songs and dissident songs. In order to talk without their conversation being overheard (there were often bugs in activists' homes), Khavkin took them out to the street where they would have some "privacy." He explained about having to acquire a *vyzov*. He warned them of the problems: they could be thrown out of work; how would they live in that case? The family might be split up with some allowed to emigrate and others forced to stay. He told them that they should consider all this and think it over if they wanted to request an invitation. Volt and Esther looked at each other and said "We don't have to think about it." So Khavkin wrote down their names and address in his notebook and also those of Volt's parents, and of Esther's father and son.

Khavkin told them that at this point no one was being arrested for such activity. They had been a few years ago and it might happen again in the future (as it did), but right now there wasn't much of a danger. "Khavkin told us: 'The situation is this: we are fighting to leave for Israel. The more of us, the better. At the moment there aren't many of us . . . It's not known how our struggle will end. . . .But if you have decided, I'll be very happy. We will welcome you . . . we'll all be like brothers in this fight. We hope that we will be able to break through the wall!' And how will we break through, I asked. In general all of this was like a fairy tale. . . But he said, 'We will write letters, open letters." I said, then they'll put us in jail right away. He said, 'Maybe they won't jail us right away. We will write to the UN, to all the organizations, to everyone.' He told us about the Declaration of the Rights of Man, which had been signed by the U.S.S.R., about the right to leave your own country and return to it. (We weren't so interested in the second part, of course!) . . . We had caught fire . . . as if God had suddenly opened up the heavens to us!"

Then Khavkin asked them to come back to his apartment, where they met a number of people, including some who would be well-known later in the annals of emigration history, such as David Drabkin and Volodya Slepak. They made many close friends in the movement during the ensuing two years.

Upon their return to Novosibirsk, they turned their apartment into an open house, just as Khavkin had in Moscow. They had a few things to put out: a little flag of Israel that they had sketched and a picture of Yitzhak Rabin (who had been the architect of the victory in the Six Day War). People interested in Israel and possibly in emigrating there would stop by, meet one another and use their home as a center.

Esther's son Izia, a twenty-two year old student now living in Moscow, had started out as a dissident but then became an ardent Zionist. He, too, was interested in leaving. They received the six invitations sent from Israel very quickly, handed in their documents to the Soviet authorities, and waited for a decision. When the reply came it was only partially positive. Esther's eighty-year-old father would be allowed to leave, as could Volt's parents. (Esther is convinced that the authorities were really interested in getting hold of her father's apartment.) But they were told that a younger member of the family should accompany the older people. In the meantime, Volt's mother fell ill and so the couple could not go at that time. This meant that it was Izia and his eighty year old grandfather who left Novosibirsk together in December, 1969. They were among the first to leave, well before the first major wave in 1971. It would be two years until Esther and Volt would join her father and son in Israel.

LUNA

Luna and her family are salt of the earth. They have had no higher education. They are wage earners. Luna's family, at least, lived in the grinding poverty so typical of the large population of Odessa, enjoying none of the advantages associated with Party membership or good connections. They were, in many ways, typical Soviet citizens.

Luna was born in 1943, probably the result of a wartime furlough visit of her father to her mother then evacuated to the Republic of Georgia. He only saw his daughter when he got home after the war, wounded. He died when she was three and she has no recollection of him, nor are there any photographs. Luna's mother, young and alone, brought the little girl to her own parents, who lived, as Luna says, in a shtetl, the kind of place you read about in a Sholem Aleichem story. After her mother had settled down into a new marriage, she brought her back to live with them. When five-year-old Luna arrived in Odessa, to her mother's embarrassment, the little girl couldn't speak Russian, only Yiddish.

The new father, also Jewish, adopted her, gave her his last name, and brought her up as his own daughter. He and her mother did not have any further children. The three of them and her maternal grandmother lived in one room, about 170 square feet. The room had a sink in it, but no kitchen. Eventually her father built a kitchen into a kind of porch they had. There was no toilet, only an out house in the back yard, which had no running water. In the yard you could also hang out the laundry. They went to the public baths: "Once a week. That's all we could afford."

Luna's grandmother was orthodox and kept her own separate dishes. She never ate her daughter's cooking. "My grandmother, I . . . shared the same bed with her until the day she died." That was when Luna was almost twenty and in her second year of a technical college where she was learning about sewing and sewing machines. After graduating she got herself a job in a large factory, with about five hundred employees. Her task was making patterns, not actually sewing. Eventually Luna was a technology engineer at a fashion house. She designed the process for manufacturing particular fashion items for mass production. In the end she headed a workshop with 120 people working under her.

Even with her full-time job, the salary was never enough. "Neither mine nor my husband's, and my mother used to help me. I also did some sewing for people." This was strictly illegal. While there was a "gray economy" in the Soviet Union, the reality was that private business was not allowed and discovery could bring punishment. Luna thus had to hide the illegal work that she did from the neighbors. She made dresses. Customers would bring in their own patterns as well as the material, even zippers. Everything was expensive, but the finished product would be far more attractive than anything to be found in the shops. Financially, it was certainly worth her while: that was how they lived.

After marriage she continued to live at home with her parents, but now with her husband as well. At some point they got a larger apartment and the real luxury was that they could fit in their furniture in such a way that a table was placed between her parents' bed and their bed "so we couldn't see each other at night." They still didn't have their own bath or toilet. They lived like that for many years. Luckily, they got along well with her parents. "You learn to get along, you know; otherwise . . . a lot of marriages break up because of that." As time went on, they acquired a separate room in the apartment for themselves. The neighbor with whom they had shared the kitchen left for Israel in 1972 and they fought to add his room and kitchen to their flat. Her father started to build a bathroom with a tub. With all these arrangements— private room, indoor plumbing, a kitchen plus good jobs—it is amazing that at this point they should have started to think about leaving. Her father even expressed this: "What in the world makes you leave Russia right now when everything is going so well for you?"

Luna thinks that one reason they started thinking about it was "because there was an opportunity to leave, that's one thing. The other thing—after the Yom Kippur war antisemitism became really bad. . . You could have felt it everywhere." "It got so tough," she said, "it got so terrible that everybody was picking on you. It was such a shame to be a Jew then." There was so much propaganda in the Soviet press at that time with articles depicting Israel as an aggressive country, comparing the Zionists to Hitler. The public didn't even realize that it was Egypt that had attacked Israel in 1973.

The neighbor with whom they had shared the apartment had a lot to do with their beginning to think about emigration. He was a nice man, though not a friend. "That's the funny thing; soon we started to feel good about it. I knew I wanted to go." But Luna's husband, Sam, would not consider going anyplace as long as his mother was alive. "My husband didn't want to leave under any circumstances because he loved his mother . . . So I just had to wait. And as soon as she died, he said, this is it. There's nothing left here." That was in 1973.

Luna had married a man from a well-connected Odessa Jewish family, one of five children. (Such large families in those days were highly unusual.) Luna describes them as "old school," who had their sons circumcised. His father held a high government position, though he was not a Party member. He had taken part in the 1917 revolution. Because he was worried that he would lose his post, he was initially very negative about his son leaving. Indeed, he denounced them publicly, saying he had nothing to do with them. He disowned his son, saying that he hadn't raised him that way. Sam's two brothers also held high positions and it could have been a problem for them that he was leaving. So they didn't mention them on their applications, just one sister. The right hand, says Luna, doesn't know what the left hand is doing in the USSR and they didn't check the records.

In the Soviet Union if someone wanted to emigrate, their parents—even if the applicant was in his forties—had to give permission. A friend of Luna's suggested that Sam's father should write a letter that although he didn't approve, he didn't object to their leaving. He agreed to do that. Four months later, Sam, Luna and their son received their exit visas. It was 1975.

Two weeks after the three of them had left, the teacher of Luna's twelve-year-old son came to their apartment to see what was the matter with him, as he had been absent from school for so long. To avoid any conflict, Luna's mother told the teacher that they had moved to Kiev. But the teacher didn't believe her. She said, "I bet they're in Israel." "And believe it or not," says Luna, "she—she's a Russian woman and she's a member of the Communist Party—she says, 'I think they did a smart thing.'"

ZAKHARIA

Zakharia, when asked about when he started to consider emigrating from the Soviet Union, says that he had always thought about it. He is, after all, the boy who tried to escape from the USSR on a bicycle right after the war.

In the early 1950s, after his studies were completed, Zakharia had entered what would be a lifetime profession in the media. He became a member of the Communist Party in 1952, when he was the editor of a rural newspaper. It would have been very difficult to prosper in the world of communications without Party membership. In 1958, he bought his first radio. It had short-wave reception. He even managed to hear Yiddish programs on it.

In 1959, he married Bella, whom he had known for many years. She was older than he and had been married previously: her family had been deported to Siberia after the Soviet takeover of Lithuania during the Second World War. So that was where they spent the war years. In fact, her father had been in a labor camp for ten years. During the time in Siberia, Bella had married a boy from a similar family background and they had a child. Life was very dangerous there in 1945–46. They could kill you for a pair of shoes. One day her husband went out and didn't return. He was never heard from again. Bella was alone with her child and her mother. Her father didn't return from imprisonment until 1955.

Zakharia and Bella settled down to a productive life, enjoying a decent middle- or upper-middle class life in their own two-room apartment with a private bathroom and kitchen—a good standard for the Soviet Union. Bella was a German teacher and Zakharia worked as a political commentator for radio and television. But when their son would ask for something special—a watch, a bicycle—Zakharia would answer, "When we're living on the Carmel I'll get it for you!" It didn't seem that there would be much of a chance for people with academic degrees to get permission to leave, but then in 1968 they heard that the singer, Nehama Lifshits, had been let out. There was hope. Both Zakharia and Bella were anxious to emigrate, but nevertheless when Zakharia made his first dissident move he didn't tell anyone, not even his wife. On February 15, 1968 Zakharia wrote the first letter that went out of the Soviet Union with a protest against antisemitism and a demand to leave for Israel. It was anonymous, but it was Zakharia who had written it, claiming that it was signed by twenty-six (un-named) intellectuals. In fact, there was no one else involved. He did tell someone in an underground Zionist organization about it, but that was all. He sent the letter out with an American tourist. It was subsequently read out on the radio, on the Voice of America, Kol Israel and the BBC. It was the first of its kind, and made quite a sensation. Up to then, it was unheard of to do such a thing in the Soviet Union. Bella realized that it was his work when she heard it on the radio, and said "That's your style."

Zakharia had excellent connections in the Central Committee of the Communist Party of Lithuania, also in the KGB. Many of them had been together during the war in the orphanage in Siberia. The First Secretary of the Communist Party, Snieckus, had been known to have said that as long as he was alive there would be no Jewish trials in Lithuania. They'd had enough with Ponar and the Ninth Fort (referring to the notorious Holocaust sites). The truth is, says Zakharia, while there were trials in Leningrad, in Riga and in Kishinev (following the hijacking incident), there wasn't a single one in Lithuania.

Later the Georgian Jews followed with a letter of their own, in the same style as Zakharia's. But their letter had signatures. This letter was a landmark case, as it was sent to Israel, which chose not to publicize it, fearing that the subsequent uproar would be bad for the Jewish cause in the Soviet Union. However, after the arrival of a second such letter, one hundred days later, Golda Meir decided to read it aloud in the Knesset and a public campaign for the exodus of Jews was taken up by Israel. By 1971 the eighteen families in the Georgian letter were on their way.

In order to leave, Zakharia had to resign from the Communist Party. It would be impossible to request an exit visa while still a member. In March 1971, he had received his invitation from a cousin of his father's who had been living in Israel for many years. There was an unpleasant procedure in the Party and great resentment that he might be alleging any antisemitism on the part of the authorities. He played the game and explained that he just wanted to leave for purposes of family reunion. Bella worked as a teacher until the end, but Zakharia immediately lost his job. In order to avoid charges of parasitism, he had to find work—any work—quickly and a well-placed friend found him something in a factory. During the ensuing period, Zakharia was politically active, went to a few demonstrations, was arrested once for "hooliganism." He even went to a sit-in at the MVD (the Ministry of Internal Affairs) in Moscow, together with his wife and other people, complaining that Soviet law wasn't being complied with in terms of allowing family re-unification. Lots of foreign correspondents were there and they did manage to see the deputy minister.

They received permission to leave on December 21, 1971. They had to run around, getting rid of their appliances, arranging their trip. As often happened, not all family members were allowed to leave together. In their case, Zakharia and Bella left first, in January, 1972 and her mother and son followed in March. Was it hard to leave the Soviet Union, to say goodbye? On the contrary, there was euphoria!

ISAAC AND SOPHIA

Isaac, who had lost sight of his mother at a train station and spent the war years wandering around on his own, eventually made his life back in his home town of Odessa. He found work as a welder in a factory that made ploughs and similar implements. He managed to make a decent living by Soviet standards and married Clara when she was just eighteen years old. Even at that age, Clara had health problems, something that has plagued her all her life.

The young couple moved in with her mother. "There's no such thing that you get married and get your own apartment," explains Isaac. "So either you live with your family or her family." This was already ten years after the end of the Second World War. They lived in one room in a basement apartment, twelve feet by twelve feet, plus a small kitchen. However, the kitchen had no running water. They also had no toilet. Downstairs in the courtyard there were two outhouses that served fifty people from three apartment buildings. There was no running water in them, just holes. According to Isaac, "I lived not badly. People lived worse. My brother lived worse." After marriage, his brother and his wife moved into a room in another awful basement, where there were mice and wet walls. Isaac's own mother lived in the same damp basement apartment, with sewage backing up, that he and his brother had shared with her for years. Later on, Isaac built an extension to his mother-in-law's place, added a room, put in gas and radiators. Until then they had had no heating system.

Living in these circumstances, Isaac and Clara had two little girls. Sophia, their older daughter, explained that to keep clean, "You would get the water from outside, heat it up [on the coal stove], and wash."

At some point, Clara's brother married a non-Jewish girl. He was ostracized by the family and his mother never allowed him or his child to enter her home. Being Jewish was all-important in both families. Nevertheless, his mother hadn't been able to disown her son completely and, while he couldn't come to her home, she would visit him in his. Clara's mother was widowed in 1964. She had a very close relationship with her granddaughter, Sophia. They used to talk to each other in Yiddish. Even after Clara and Isaac were living in their own apartment, Sophia, as a child, would go to her grandmother's place, across the street and spend a lot of time with her. Sophia saw her as her friend. "I would say that my whole personality . . . all the good things that I think that I have, I got from her. . . She was my best teacher."

Isaac engaged in a practice that was quite common in the Soviet Union. He illegally took on private jobs in search of extra income. This was strictly forbidden and could have resulted in a serious punishment had he been caught. What did he do? He would give a couple of bottles of cognac to the man delivering steel to the factory and would get a ton or two of extra steel. "Who cares? He receives and I receive." In a delivery of twenty tons of steel there would be one or two extra tons. With this Isaac would make things for private customers: water tanks, a fence, a garage, fans. Everybody, he says, took bribes, even doctors.

They started to think about leaving in 1971. Isaac didn't belong to any group; he didn't engage in any dissident activity. In fact, when they left, his daughter had never seen the inside of a synagogue, nor had he since before the Second World War. (His mother would walk to synagogue.) He did listen to radio broadcasts from abroad, once they had a radio that could receive them: the BBC in Russian and Kol Yisrael. He knew what was going on, the Leningrad hijacking, for example. He saw himself as a Zionist. It was Isaac's idea and Clara liked it. Some of their friends had already left, one family to Israel, the other to Australia. Clara had an aunt in Israel, so getting the invitation was no problem. It was very early in the period of emigration and they became the butt of a lot of criticism. Someone even drew a Star of David on their building.

Sophia's school made trouble when they heard that the family was leaving. She found it unbearable. Teachers wanted to adopt her and bring her up in the Soviet Union. Let her parents leave, they said, they are deserters. When Isaac and Clara went to the school for a meeting, they were told that they had sold out their country. While many Odessa Jews would eventually emigrate, Sophia was the first one in her school, so there was more of a reaction.

Both of the grandmothers said that they were doing the right thing in going and urged them to leave. But there were tears. They never saw their mothers again. Isaac had thought that his beloved younger brother would be following, but as luck would have it, it took him over nine years. Clara, Isaac and their daughters were heading for Israel, but their path would take some strange turns.

ANATOLII AND SVETLANA

After his release from prison in 1960, following his sentencing for writing "anti-Soviet" letters, Anatolii went back to the university, but no longer as a medical student. Unreasonable requirements were placed on him so that effectively he was not permitted to return to medical school. Within a year he was married to Sveta. She was from a Jewish family that, on one side, before the Bolshevik revolution, had been merchants of the First Guild, that is, were of sufficient economic importance that they were permitted to live in Kiev. Needless to say, none of that wealth remained after the revolution.

She was both a nurse and a music student. Her closest friend was the sister of one of the boys who had been imprisoned in the camps with Anatolii. It was she who introduced Anatolii and Sveta and she has remained her closest friend. Following her marriage, Svetlana switched from nursing to music and started to teach music professionally. She made a decent living doing this.

From quite early on, Svetlana had thought about leaving the Soviet Union. This started in 1968, when Poland expelled many of their Jews and, in the same year, the Soviet army marched into Czechoslovakia. She spoke to Anatolii about it then and they started thinking about how they could get permission to leave.

At the time, Anatolii was living in Kiev working as a translator, mainly of scientific articles, from English into Russian, having completed his degree in the department of philology. Sveta was teaching piano in a music school. By now, he was completely alienated from Soviet life and described his work as "completely solitary, that is to say, an ideal place for an internal emigrant . . . In practice, there was no need to associate with anyone, no need to go to any meetings, no need to participate in anything."

The first big group allowed out left in March, 1971. The couple feared what might happen if they didn't try to leave as well. What if the gates were to close? It was at this point that they really became activated and looked into receiving an invitation from someone in Israel. Upon receiving it, each one had to obtain a *kharakteristika*, a document that was a sort of resumé/ recommendation. Sveta went to the secretary of the party organization where she worked and asked if he was going to fire her. He asked her if she had already received permission to leave and when she said no, he said, "Then why should I fire you?" He suggested that she write out her own *kharakteristika*, which he would sign, and she wrote something very modest about herself. You shouldn't have done that, he said: it looks like we've had a bad employee working among us. He then rewrote it into a very good one. When the people at OVIR saw it, they asked, What is this, an application for getting into the communist party?! Clearly, each potential emigrant had a vastly different experience from others. Sveta managed to continue to work until the last moment. Anatolii, on the other hand, got no cooperation, was almost refused the *kharakteristika* from his place of work, and was immediately fired. It all depended on the individual.

Permission came through in only three weeks. The preference to head for Israel was more Anatolii's than Svetlana's. At the time he felt that one had to go to Israel, that it would even be dishonorable not to if the possibility was presented. Later, he was more broad-minded in considering the question.

EVA

Eva's father, Lev, was the monumental artist introduced in chapter two. She was only about twelve when her family started talking about a real possibility of leaving the Soviet Union for Israel. Actually, it was in the air in her family throughout her childhood. "I was always very conscious about the fact that I was Jewish and that everybody in my family was Jewish. It was a matter of special pride . . ." She described her background as "not a religious Jewish education but a nationalist one." Her father had been intent on a life in the Jewish homeland long before she was born. "My father, in fact, before he married my mother told her parents that whenever there was the possibility, he would take her to Israel. So actually . . . children in the family knew that the time will come and we will all leave."

Growing up in Moscow, Eva had a mixed group of friends. "But when I think about it (*then* I probably didn't think about it at all), I think I tended to mix with Jewish friends. And if not Jewish, I tended to mix with those who openly said that in their families 'antisemitism' is a curse word . . . But my best friend was Jewish." This friend was the only one who knew that Eva was leaving for Israel, when the time came.

Eva went to a very privileged school. Most of the children there had been abroad, though Eva, of course, had not. While the language of instruction was Russian, there was a bias toward English. She heard many stories from them about the wonderful life in the West, but she feared that, as a Jew, she would probably never be able to experience that.

The first that Eva heard that her parents were actually planning to leave was as soon as her uncle left, in 1970. Her mother was pregnant with her third child and they would leave only after the baby was born. There would be a wait, then, until everything was sorted out. Eva remembers that "the whole year I didn't study, because I felt, it doesn't matter; I'll leave anyway." Nevertheless, she had a strong attachment to Russian culture and had many friends. "I realized, of course, that it was going to disappear. It was never going to be like this again. It was very sad. But I suppose that one doesn't think about it, until the day comes. I remember that when my father told us that we had actually received permission I felt some sharp, sharp pain. Because I realized: that's it. But then the events went so quickly that I didn't really have time to think about it. Only when we landed here, suddenly: 'That's it.'" This was Eva talking, years later, in Jerusalem in very fluent English.

Lev had kept everything very quiet because he didn't want any trouble or criticism of his family during the waiting period. So his daughter had been told not to say anything to her friends. She felt that it was not good that she hadn't been able to say good-bye. "I spent eight years with them. I went with some of them to kindergarten, and I think that's the most terrible thing, that you can't say it to anybody, to the people who loved you and the people whom you loved." Her parents, though, had told their friends and many came to say good-bye to them and even to see them off at the airport.

Lev had told Eva specifically that she would not be able to take any letters or diaries with her. There were all sorts of rules about what one could remove from the country and, also, one didn't want to get others in trouble with what might be in the documents. "I had kept diaries for eight years. And I had to leave it with my best friend, because I couldn't burn it. And all my poetry; all the notes of the theater studio. It doesn't matter now, but it mattered to me then."

LEV

In many ways, Lev's decision to leave the Soviet Union had been a given from the beginning. Still, he could not deny the benefits he had received there. "As a Jew, as a citizen of the Soviet Union, as a private person with the passport of a Jew, I achieved, I received a great deal from the Soviet regime. I finished art school. I was given an excellent higher education in one of the best educational institutions in the world: the Stroganov College."

Nevertheless, there were good reasons for going. Antisemitism was a part of his life. "I personally experienced antisemitism present in numerous groups of the population, whether in childhood from the boys in the courtyard [calling me names]. . . in the institute, always in school, always in the army, always in all the layers of life I came in contact with antisemitism." Many of his friends said that they had never experienced antisemitism, but he finds that hard to believe. "I think that they didn't want to feel it."

Some time before leaving, Lev and his wife had a conversation with the assistant minister of Finance, whom he described as a respected, lovely woman. She asked them why they were leaving Russia. Lev's wife gave the following reply: "Tell me, are you Russian?" She replied that she was. "But we are Jews!" So? "The whole difference lies in this, that we are not Russians, that we are Jews, that we have our own country. Here we don't have our own language; you took it away from us. We don't have the ability to be loyal, patriotic, even patriotic to the Soviet regime, as a nation preserving its own language. Take any republic: they are also dissatisfied, and they don't value a lot of the good things that they received from Russia, but I understand them. It's better to be poor but in one's own home, than rich in someone else's. We Jews have been pushed against the wall; we are publicly humiliated every day, not permitted to be ourselves. . ."

In August 1972, over a year after the major Jewish exodus had begun, the Soviet Union enacted what was called a "diploma tax." Those who had received a higher education would be required to pay an exorbitant amount of money before they were permitted to leave the country. The justification for this tax was simple: the state had spent a lot of money educating its citizens and wanted to be compensated for the loss, when they left, of the skills thus acquired. The real reason for what was considered an outrageous demand on the part of the state was probably that the regime was beginning to realize what a huge amount of valuable talent was being lost as more and more Jews emigrated. The departure of a great number of scientists, doctors, musicians, engineers and so on was starting to be felt: hence the attempt to discourage the process from continuing. Outrage at this policy was expressed in various Western capitals and one result was the initiation in the United States of an amendment to the Trade Reform Act, which would link the granting of certain trade benefits for countries of the socialist bloc with the status of their emigration policies and practices. Various benefits, including Most Favored Nation status, would be offered to those states whose behavior coincided with the demands of the human rights standards of the West. While the Act was not finally passed and signed into law until January, 1975, the threat seems to have been sufficient to convince the Soviets that they should rescind their diploma tax, which they did, in March, 1973. But during the seven months that the tax was in place numerous Jews with a higher education were forced to pay outrageous sums for the "privilege" of leaving their country.

The emigration of Lev and his family fell just during the dates when the tax was in place. Lev described this requirement in his own idiosyncratic way: "I'm not a hateful person. On the contrary, I am grateful—they let me go. It was worth it to pay. There's a certain illness—nostalgia. Whoever received the injection, as I did, it cost him 14,000, as I paid, so that there wouldn't be any nostalgia! I have no nostalgia."

VALENTINA

Valentina, who had only discovered her Jewish heritage when she moved to her grandparents' wonderful house in Belaia Tserkov, hardly ever left that lovely green town. Originally interested in chemistry, like her grandfather, she eventually went to the local dental school, which had just opened, and finished her studies in 1962, after her marriage. As there was no full-time position available, she worked only part-time.

She met Roman when they were quite young. He had just completed three and a half years' compulsory service in the army and she was barely twenty. Having grown up in a Jewish household, he felt that it was preferable to marry a Jewish girl and was attracted to Valentina and to her family, living in their own house on the river bank. He was working during the day and studying through correspondence courses at night, while Valentina was a day student, close to completing her degree. After finishing his studies, Roman started to work as a dental technician.

After their marriage, like so many young Soviet couples, they moved in with her family. Their first child, Marina, was born in 1963, just a month and a half after the death of Valentina's beloved grandfather. Her grandmother, who had already been diagnosed with cancer, continued to live with them until she died. Then Valia and Roman and their daughter had the house to themselves. Their second child, a son, was born much later, in 1975.

It is not clear why they decided to leave, but there is no question that it was Roman who felt that they should and pressured Valia. Having lived in the same town since her early teens and hardly traveled, Valentina couldn't imagine living anywhere else. Both of them realized how complicated it would be to leave, to turn their backs on everything in their lives. They started talking about emigrating quite early, back in 1969 or 70. For a long time, she would not agree. They lived in such a small town; information on emigration and on the places to which they might move was hard to obtain. She was afraid to go into the unknown. On the other hand, she had no family to leave, other than her mother, with whom she had had a troubled relationship. She did have some friends.

What had convinced them, it seems, was the benefit that such a move would hold for their children. They were painfully aware of the uneasy Soviet policy towards Jews in education and employment in the late sixties and in the course of the seventies. But it took a long time for Valentina to come to the conclusion that they should attempt to leave. In the end, she felt that while her grandfather had been able to offer her tremendous advantages in life, she could not do the same thing there for her own children. She was concerned about their education, about putting them on their feet. So emigration would be for the children's future.

Roman started to feel desperate and finally came to Valia and said, "Either we leave or I'll hang myself." That decided it. At the end of 1977 Valentina quietly left her job. Ironically, after working part-time for eleven years, she had recently finally been given a full-time position. They didn't tell anyone that they were leaving the country, just that they were moving out of the city. Their impression was that most of the people who had been emigrating had come from big cities and so they were concerned that it might be harder for them to receive permission to leave a small town. They sold the house, which was very valuable, and were worried about where they would then live. But in the end, the whole process took only three and a half months. In April 1978 the whole family of four crossed the border. They had been lucky.

ZHENIA AND SERYOZHA

Once Zhenia was living in Kiev with her husband—in a tiny apartment they shared with her parents-in-law—she found work at a museum of folk architecture, something like the position that she had had in Yalta. But when they realized that she was pregnant, the museum gave her various tasks that she felt were demeaning and, in general, made her life a misery. When she went to her mother's in Yalta on maternity leave, she wrote to the museum that she wouldn't return.

In spite of the various difficulties of her life and her dissatisfaction with the political situation in the Soviet Union, Zhenia had no thought of leaving the country. "I, at that time, actively did not want to go. I did not want to go . . . because this is my country. This is my language. Everything here is mine . . .I love, I very much love Russia, but not as a patriot, but because I was born there, I know it all like no one else. I absorbed all the culture . . . Russian philology made me into a real Russian. And my break with it was very painful." Second, because she did not think that her specialty could be useful in another country.

Seryozha, on the other hand, had thought about it for a long time, but with parents and a wife who were not interested, he put the idea aside and tried to convince himself that it wasn't necessary to leave. But in his heart he wanted to go. "I already wanted to go to Israel not because I was afraid what might happen in the Soviet Union . . . but I wanted to go to Israel simply because I wanted to go to Israel." He was less influenced by a political Zionist feeling than a religious national feeling. "I wanted to go to Israel; I wanted to end up precisely in Jerusalem. I wanted to live in that holy city. Purely instinctively I understood that it would be good for me in this city—good in the moral sense."

In the mid-1970s the situation became more complicated. Seryozha was active with his circle of like-minded friends. He had never been a healthy person and had suffered from diabetes from early childhood. He had been called into the police, as had his parents, and his father started to worry when they threatened him that he would rot in the basement of the KGB headquarters. Things seemed to be falling apart when the final blow came: Seryozha was diagnosed with tuberculosis. Faced with a sick husband who was also in trouble with the authorities, Zhenia began to feel that she had no choice. On the one hand was her native land, her family and on the other hand, her husband and the question of his health and safety. Zhenia: "I started worrying that all my persistence would end up with someone's death. I only had an idea; but he had life. It was more important to save a person's life. And then the idea of leaving took hold of me." In December 1977 they decided definitely to leave. Where they would go was not even an issue for her:

Because for Seryozha leaving was at that time tied to the national question. He had suggested leaving a few times before. But it was very hard for me to decide to start again from nothing. To come and start life in an empty place. This was very difficult and, to me, terrible. Besides, all my national problems: I told him that here you are in the national minority, but there I will be in the minority. But if I had already decided to save my husband and leave, then for me the question of where to go wasn't there: to me it was absolutely all the same. Wherever they take me, there I'll be, as long as he is healthy.

She didn't particularly care where they would go: it was all the same to her—America, Germany, France. But for Seryozha it was only Israel. He worried about antisemitism. And furthermore he "had very reasonable objections. If you're leaving one *galut* [place of exile], then why go to another *galut*? Let's go to a place where they are waiting for us."

For Zhenia, there was the big problem of parting from her own beloved family. "We understood very well that once we left the Soviet Union we would not be able to return, even as tourists, for, say, twenty years." One of the people whom she hated to be parted from was her grandmother, her father's mother. To leave her there, "it was as if I was burying her." Like so many Russians of her generation, Zhenia was extraordinarily attached to her grandmother. She had grown up under her eyes and her grandmother took great pride in all of her achievements. And, after all, they were leaving for who knew what kind of country: "a terrible country that is shown on television as pitch-black hell: they're aggressors, they fight, there's always war . . . and with a child and a sick husband." They had a long talk and she explained to her grandmother about their problems, the KGB, a husband so sick that imprisonment would be a death penalty.

The next problem was her mother. It was clear that an arrangement must be made for her. Zhenia and Seryozha agreed not to hand in their documents until her mother came round. Zhenia enlisted the help of her younger sister in this. In February 1978 Zhenia went down to Yalta. She wanted to convince her mother to leave as well. "I had decided that I didn't have the right to go and leave them there. I would leave and they would quickly remove her from the Party and take her out of her educational work . . . and she didn't understand this. 'You want to leave? So long! And I'll be here.' And only because my sister began to work very actively on my behalf and said that she was also leaving . . ." Zhenia's twenty-three year old sister had indeed decided that there was no future for her in Russia. She felt that they should all leave together, and helped to convince their mother. At that point their mother quit the Party and there was a real blow-up at the meeting. The truth is that her faith in the Party had been weakening, with all the material that Zhenia had been channeling to her.

Zhenia and Seryozha got a *vyzov* for the whole family, their daughter, his parents, her mother and sister. In April, they all handed in their documents "but we waited until Seryozha was finished at the tuberculosis sanitorium." It was in August that the first permission came through: for her mother. Soon after, theirs came through as well. They didn't even have enough money to pay for everyone's departure, for the Soviet visa, which was expensive, and for the required renunciation of Soviet citizenship, which cost three hundred rubles. This was at a time when Seryozha was earning 110 rubles a month and Zhenia 80 rubles a month. Seryozha went to the Dutch Embassy in Mosocw because he had heard that they could get a small subsidy from them. They gave it to her mother. Zhenia's mother and sister took one suitcase each. They didn't have much, in general, because of their financial situation. They left a month earlier than Zhenia and Seryozha, in November, 1978. What was amazing to them is that they all received their permission so quickly, within a couple of months. Zhenia feels that this was because the KGB was so eager to be rid of them. She sensed that it was all connected with Babi Yar. The authorities were afraid that Seryozha would go to Babi Yar, for the annual memorial meeting. It very clear to them: either you get permission or you'll go to Babi Yar.

YAN

Yan was in a difficult position. He wasn't involved whole heartedly in dissident activity. He certainly wasn't a Zionist or connected with activists because they wanted to go to Israel. He was, however, in trouble with the KGB because of the company he kept. There was so much pressure in their lives that his wife, who is an artist, found that she couldn't paint for the three years before their departure.

Yan, for whom his work was everything—or at least a central part of his life—really didn't want to leave. He had a good job and felt that it was hardly possible that he would ever have another one like that again. But he realized that if they started to remove him from his job he would be motivated to put in an application to leave the Soviet Union. He had three meetings with KGB officials and at the last meeting "*they* told me (not OVIR) that I'd been given permission to leave." It was clear that he had the choice of leaving or being in trouble.

Yan commented on this phenomenon shortly after his emigration: "In principle, the KGB knows that people don't really like the Soviet regime . . . the majority. But they can't put up with open disloyalty." Yan was a victim of this policy. He and his wife and nine year old son reluctantly left friends and family because they had no choice. How did you feel when you left? "It's hard to say because I was terribly tired, simply unbelievably tired, because this parting in the Soviet Union was very much like a funeral, only you are burying yourself."

Chapter Five

Departures and Arrivals

BACKGROUND

The emigration pattern from the Soviet Union was remarkable. From fewer than twelve thousand Jews allowed to leave during the entire period from 1948 until 1970, in the year 1971 alone almost thirteen thousand Jews were given exit visas. The following year there was a huge jump, with almost 32,000 permits issued. The figures varied in the ensuing years, with the low point reached in 1975 and 1976 (though both years were higher than the emigration of 1971) and rising to the all-time high of 51,331 in 1979. That would remain the record number for almost a decade.

However, the character of the emigration—the direction in which Soviet Jews headed—would change in the course of the 1970s. In the beginning, the goal was to head for Israel in as direct a manner as possible. This made sense, as the principal émigrés in the early period were either devout Jews who wanted to live in the Holy Land (such as the Georgians who originally wrote the famous letters of request) or enthusiastic Zionists (largely from that group of "Western" Jews who had had a childhood steeped in Zionist ideology in inter-war Poland and the Baltic states) who wished to live nowhere else but in Israel. This largely held true until the middle of the decade.

But by 1974, the tide was turning. The Jews who were now leaving the Soviet Union had been seized by a desire to get out, but not necessarily by a need to live in Israel. A major factor in decisions was the flow of letters that went back and forth between those who had already emigrated, mainly to Israel in the early years, and their friends and family still living in the Soviet Union. These letters would affect the basic decision to leave the Soviet Union and might also be decisive in where the next emigrants would go, what area they might choose to settle in their new country.

In ever growing numbers, Soviet Jews decided to take their chances in the wide world, continuing their lives in the Diaspora. The vast majority of this group would end up in the United States, but many would go to Canada, South Africa, and to various European countries. These people, too, were forced by the Soviet regulations to apply to leave to join relatives in Israel for the family reunification scheme. This was a fiction understood on both the Israeli and the Soviet sides and everyone played the game. Later on, the Israelis, on various grounds, started to object to what came to be called the "drop-out" phenomenon. But the pattern continued throughout the 1970s and even during the 1980s when the number of permitted emigrants was far far lower. In 1979, the year of the highest emigration of the decade, out of over 51,000 people leaving the Soviet Union on the basis of family reunification in Israel, only about seventeen and a half thousand made their way there.

During this period, there were no direct flights between Moscow and Tel Aviv, so it was necessary that those with exit visas make their way by train or plane to Vienna. In Vienna they would be met—usually at the train station—by workers from the Jewish Agency, who would divide the passengers up into those who planned to go directly to Israel and those who were "dropping out." The Israel-bound emigrants would then be placed within a day or two on a flight to Israel. Some people even flew out on the very same day. Others were put up overnight in Vienna and taken for a tour of the city before their departure for Israel. For nearly all of them, this was the first time outside the Soviet Union, a first look at the western world. But they had very little time to enjoy it before being hustled along to the airport for the final flight.

The other group was put up in Vienna and, within a short time of their arrival, they made their way to an office building on the Brahmsplatz for a series of meetings. The Soviet emigrants would first visit the office of the Jewish Agency, where they would be questioned about whether they were absolutely certain that they did not want to go to Israel. There were few who changed their minds. After all, they had just spent the preceding months or year working out what they wanted to do. It was unlikely that a brief meeting at Brahmsplatz would change their decision. Following this, they would visit the office, in the same building, of the HIAS representative. The Hebrew Immigrant Aid Society had existed in the United States throughout the twentieth century. Its purpose was to ease the problems of the new Jewish immigrants arriving in the United States. Funded by the American Jewish community, the HIAS representatives made a desultory attempt to assure themselves that they were indeed dealing with bonafide Jews—such as showing them a tallis (prayer shawl) or some other item and asking the emigrant to identify it.

Among the Jewish emigrants there were Christians, or at least non-Jews. As spouses of Jews they were treated like everyone else. But practicing Christian groups, such as the Seventh Day Adventists, did not fit into that category. They had been told if they wanted to get out of Russia it would have to be as part of the Jewish quota. This was a fiction that was forced upon them by the Soviet regime. Thus there were Christian organizations, such as the Tolstoy Foundation, which were also there in the Brahmsplatz building in Vienna to help this smaller group of emigrants.

Assistance for those opting out of Israel included financing the trip to La-dispoli, a Mediterranean town not far from Rome, helping the emigrants to stay there until they managed to get a visa, transporting their goods, giving advice, and so on. Jewish emigrants in transit would stay in Ladispoli and make trips into Rome for meetings at consulates, checking on the progress of their applications, and earning a little money by selling objects that they had brought with them from the Soviet Union—samovars, matrioshki (dolls within dolls), icons and other typical Russian items. Many of them adopted dogs during their Italian stay and whenever they traveled into Rome, the dogs would wait for their masters' return by the bus stop in Ladispoli. Visitors there said that one of the sadder sights was the dogs waiting for their families day after day when they had actually already received their visas and left the country.

For families heading for Israel the path, in many ways, was initially smoother. They were flown there very quickly. They would be met at Ben Gurion Airport near Tel Aviv by an assortment of customs officials, immigration personnel, and social workers. Their relatives would often be waiting for them outside once they had finishing the processing. Immigrants would immediately be assigned a place to stay, often at what was called an "absorption center," where many immigrants would be housed in apartments or little bungalows and arrangements would be made for them to start their study of the Hebrew language in an "ulpan" as soon as possible. This system applied mainly to educated immigrants, who depended on knowledge of the language for the furtherance of their careers. After an initial stay at an absorption center, immigrants were given low-rent (or temporarily free) apartments. In most cases, whatever housing they were given—whether in an absorption center or in an apartment—was vastly better than anything that they had ever known back home in Russia. Every family had its own kitchen and bathroom! Who could have imagined this? It seemed like complete luxury. Needless to say, in the 1970s in Israel there was a certain amount of resentment on the part of some of the needier parts of the population who questioned why these Russian Jews should be given so much more preferential treatment than their own parents or grandparents when they had arrived in the nineteen forties or fifties. The new immigrants were permitted to import certain goods free of customs duty. Native-born Israelis were charged very high taxes on cars, almost doubling their price. This meant that any immigrant who possibly could, would buy a new car after his arrival. When would there ever be such a bargain again?

This is the parting of the ways. After a long history, side by side, enduring the war, the authoritarian system, the deprivation, the censorship, the struggle to leave, after all this, the emigrants who left the Soviet Union chose different destinations. People who chose one country sometimes ended up in another eventually. Even within families or between friends the paths diverged. From the moment of their departure from the Soviet Union, their experiences differed vastly. This is the point at which the break came.

ZHENIA

Zhenia describes a hellish trip out of Russia. They left in December 1978. As they were traveling with a small child—only a year and a half old—and it was freezing cold, they decided that they should fly to Vienna. But they were told that there were only flights from Kiev to Vienna in the summer. They begged to be permitted to leave from Moscow, explaining that Seryozha was a sick man, just out of the sanatorium and that he would have to have his injections en route. This would be very complicated on a train. A short plane trip would be much easier. But the authorities refused to allow this as the family was supposed to be leaving from Kiev. They ended up taking a train from Kiev to Chop, on the Ukrainian-Czechoslovak border, then changing trains.

Zhenia perceived what happened next as simple cruelty. By the time it was over, she was not sorry to leave her native land. Everything they had on them was examined thoroughly. They had three books, Pasternak, Mandelstam and a book on child nutrition. In the end, the officials returned everything to Zhenia and said that the train was about to leave, but great tension had been engendered by the process. They shouted, "Faster, faster, the train's leaving!"

"The train was standing still . . . 'The train is leaving!' And at the end, what we heard on our warmly beloved soil was 'Schnell!' It was so terrifying. I immediately was reminded of those evacuations that the parents talked about, how the Germans transported the Jews. And there stood a young border guard with an automatic weapon shouting at us, 'Schnell!'"

The continuation of the train journey had a nightmarish quality. Traveling through Czechoslovakia people had nothing to feed the children on the train. It was cold. They wanted to use the toilet, but Zhenia and Seryozha hadn't gotten coins for this in Chop. The attendant on the train suggested paying in dollars, but a dollar to get into the toilet seemed a huge extravagance. Finally the train stopped in Bratislava, in Czechoslovakia, for a few hours. At this point they exchanged a bottle of vodka for kroner and with this they could buy only one meal. They shared this with other children. For Seryozha, for whom it was important to eat regularly, they bought a roll.

When they arrived at the train station in Vienna, there were "Jewish Agency people who said to us, 'Do you want hot tea?' You can't imagine. Women were crying. They were crying simply because this was the first humane word in all the time we'd been traveling, since we left. It was something unbelievable."

"This was my first acquaintance with Israelis. They said that they'd been waiting for us! They give us hot tea! They talk with us. They don't shout at us. They don't demand anything of us! That was very good." But others at the train station were hysterical. There were "terrible scenes—half the family is going to Israel, half to the States. People are crying."

Zhenia and Seryozha waited in Vienna and flew out late on the third day. They hadn't had a chance to see anything of the city at all, probably for security reasons. Their bus was accompanied by police cars in front and in back. It was only when they got on the plane that people relaxed.

Their impression of Israel was positive in the first hours of their arrival. Because Zhenia pointed out to the officials on duty that she had a mother and sister living in Jerusalem, they were sent there. Her mother had been waiting for them at the airport, though they weren't allowed to see her until they had finished all the paper work. Her sister was waiting at the absorption center.

At the airport they had been given money. To their amazement, the next day they were again given some pocket money. In their little apartment they found supplies which had been put there for them: canned food, bread, food for the next day.

So, was your first impression good? "One hundred percent. It was unusually beautiful. We were stunned by the beauty. We arrived [in Jerusalem] at six o'clock in the morning. The sun was just rising over Jerusalem. We saw Jerusalem. There was a feeling that we were seeing Jerusalem for the first time, that we were greeted so wonderfully. I'm very happy that we were so well received because first impressions always are put aside for future reference." This was Zhenia talking two years after her arrival.

ANATOLII AND SVETLANA

By the time Anatolii and Svetlana were in a position to leave the Soviet Union, their daughter was nearly ten years old. It was very early in the decade of emigration: they left the Soviet Union on November 8, 1971, just after the

holiday commemorating the October (Bolshevik) Revolution. They made
their way to Vienna, where they were put up at Schönau, a practice that was
later stopped. Svetlana felt that it was a terrible place: mice, filth, and—worst
of all, she said—aggressive questioning of their aunt by the Jewish Agency.

Anatolii's main feeling in Vienna was one of relief. "I was very happy that,
at last, thank goodness, we had managed to get out, that at last we had reached
a place where we were relieved of so many worries. The main feeling was
relief; we were terribly tired after all our adventures."

Unexpectedly, when they arrived at the airport in Israel, Anatolii and his
family were sent down to Dimona, a small development town in the Negev.
There, too, was an absorption center and they were given a decent apartment.
But, as Anatolii put it, they were suffering from culture shock. For the two of
them Dimona had certainly been the wrong choice on the part of the Absorption
Ministry. Even with the comfortable arrangements, Anatolii says that it wasn't
very nice. "After green Kiev, suddenly to find one's self in a completely bare
desert—it was a shock." Some of the other immigrants there were highly problematic. Their behavior was shocking. Not all beginnings, it seems, are easy.

EVA

Eva left Moscow with her father, mother, younger sister and baby brother.
They flew in a small Soviet plane, with eighty-six passengers, sixty of whom
were Jews going to Israel. While some people flew on, the same night, her
family stayed in Vienna for twenty-four hours.

In Vienna they saw a lot of people from Bukhara and Georgia. "I didn't
know about their existence. I knew only the [intellectual] Jews of Mosocw
and Leningrad, like my family, like my father's friends. And these people,
tribes, they wore rags . . . They looked like a strange gypsy tribe. They didn't
speak any Russian. If they spoke it, it was a pidgin Russian. Their manners
were rude . . . They looked primitive to me. I was astonished. I was shocked.
I said, 'Who are those people?' My mother said, 'Those are Jews.'"

They all took a flight the next night in a jumbo jet, with three hundred
passengers. On the plane these same people she had seen in Vienna started to
pray. Eva had no idea what they were doing. An announcement came through
that they were approaching Tel Aviv. "But nobody understood anything.
They only picked up the word 'Tel Aviv,' so everyone went to look down
[below]. The plane almost turned over."

Entering the customs hall the family had to go through the immigration
procedures and be assigned to an absorption center. Luckily, the baby fell
asleep. Israeli soldier girls walked around giving out refreshments. "Chewing gum. Oh, chewing gum, what excitement! And Coca Cola!" Eva and her

sister sat through the very early hours of the morning waiting for their parents to finish. "I was looking through the airport window . . . and I couldn't see anything. And then when the dawn broke I saw the desert. It was grey and pink and I was frightened. Now I realize that it was just bare fields. But then I thought, 'That's it, it's Africa,'" Eva said, laughing. "'It's Asia! That old life is over and the new life begins, and you have to live with it.'" Eva felt frightened. "But then we went to the customs office and saw our family waving and blowing kisses . . ."

Before the sun had risen, they drove up through the mountains to the absorption center in Mevasseret Zion, just outside Jerusalem. It was a very new place then and there were no trees and nothing had yet been planted. "But there was a great view there; there were mountains, the Judean Mountains. And when I saw them and the sky I said, ah, that's beautiful; that's my place. That's just how I think the Bible land should look. It fit me very much somehow."

ISAAC

Isaac and Clara and their two daughters left Odessa and traveled by train from Lvov to Chop and from there on to Vienna. Their treatment by inspectors at the border town was like that of so many others: officials combing through their belongings, making life difficult for the emigrants, taking advantage of their situation. They were only in Vienna for a few hours before they took the plane to Tel Aviv, where Clara's aunt was waiting for them at the airport. They went to her house for a few days and then the Jewish Agency transferred them to Nazareth, where there was a whole block of new apartments. They must have been the first ones there; even the lights didn't work for a few days. The apartment was beautiful, more luxurious than anything they had ever had in their lives. They were given beds—iron bedsteads and mattresses—a little table, some chairs and some money.

Isaac himself did not even go to an *ulpan* to learn Hebrew. On his second day in Nazareth he already had a job and started to work. With a skill like welding he would never have trouble finding employment. The job was in Haifa and a company car brought him and the other workers from his area back and forth every day. It seemed to be a very good beginning in a new country.

SERAFIMA

Serafima, who had survived the Leningrad blockade and was half starved throughout her life, decided to leave the Soviet Union early in the period of exodus. She had become a widow quite young, in 1956, never having succeeded in getting her whole family—her husband, her older daughter, Tamara, and her twin daughters (born in 1944 in Ufa)—to come and live with her in Leningrad. As she made her living playing in an orchestra that was based there, it was unrealistic for her to try to make a new career in Bashkiria, where the others were centered. So her family life had continued to be complicated well after the end of the Second World War.

She didn't want to emigrate alone but it was difficult for all of them to leave because of husbands or jobs. In the end, Tamara, who was single, decided to come with her mother. They were faced, as were others, with the relatively high cost of emigration and realized that it would have anyway been impossible to cover the cost of documents and travel for everyone.

On October 17, 1973, a year and a half after they had first started thinking about leaving, Serafima and Tamara made their way to Vienna. Their intention was to go to Israel. Serafima had a nephew there who had helped them get the original invitations. In fact, he looked for them in vain in Israel afterwards. But there was a war on, the Yom Kippur War, and they were told in Vienna that Israel wasn't taking in immigrants at that moment—there were no flights—because of hostilities and that they should think about an alternative destination. It was in Vienna, after their arrival, that "for the first time we ate good rolls."

Tamara and Serafima were sent on to Italy to wait for an entry visa to somewhere. They now had their hearts set on Australia, where friends of Tamara's had gone, and they waited in Ladispoli, near Rome, for signs of progress in their application. They were only there for a month and twenty days when they received the offer of a visa from the United States. Tamara actually cried: she was afraid. Serafima tried to comfort her and said, "As far as I can remember, Papa always said that America always helped Israel and the Jews. You don't have to be afraid." Neither of them knew English. They were concerned that they'd have a hard time.

LUNA

They left Odessa in November, 1975, just after the big holiday of the anniversary of the Bolshevik Revolution. Luna and Sam's intention, when leaving Russia, was to try to get into the United States. "I never had doubts in my mind about going anywhere else," says Luna. But when they got to Vienna, a representative from the Jewish Agency spoke to them, "and he talked beautifully about Israel and everything. And my husband kind of softened up. He was almost ready to go to Israel. And then it was just me. I said, you see there's our son and it's probably like [jumping] out of the frying pan . . . into the fire. You see, it's like running out from Russia and jumping into Israel with all the mess and I think I'm not a fighter." Luna was concerned about her son, who would have been drafted into the army a few years later if they were to live in Israel. Sam was attracted to Israel because, "My husband, he's a fighter, you know. He's a man who will stand by the country." So although her husband had strong feelings for Israel—and, actually, Luna did too—they opted out of going there.

They ended up spending seven months in Rome, waiting. They had arrived at a bad time—just before the Christmas and New Year's holidays when everything slows down—so the process may have taken longer than usual. Though they were in Italy for months, they didn't enjoy the experience. "It was so tiring, you know, when people try to tell us enjoy it, enjoy it . . . You get everything . . . you don't have to fight . . . you don't have to work . . . but you know . . . you . . . live in a gypsy camp; you don't know what's ahead of you . . . you know only what is behind you. And you want to say, what the hell, you want to start a new life . . . and it felt terrible, so insecure. You don't know what to expect and you want to go there, you want to see what it is."

LIUBA AND SIMON

Liuba and Simon and their little boy traveled by train from Brest-Litovsk to Vienna and stayed overnight at Schönau for a couple of nights. This was the first time that they had ever been abroad. Simon's feeling was that on the one hand "we had broken out of a huge [prison] camp for the West. On the other hand was the impression that we had left, that we could never return. And the third feeling was that we should quickly get ourselves to the Land. It was very nice, very clean and beautiful in Vienna, but our striving had been just to Israel, not to Europe, and I remember that we waited for a plane that would take us so as to reach our destination quickly."

For Liuba, "Vienna was a big, beautiful city, very beautiful. That's what I remember. But the fact is that I was in a rather bad state, a purely inner, moral state. And therefore I didn't particularly observe Vienna . . ." She explained that altogether the trip out of the country was taken when she was in a very difficult mood, very heavy-hearted. "And therefore I didn't see Vienna. I'm awfully sorry!"

They arrived in Israel in a downpour in the late afternoon. "We were taken from Lod [the airport] to Carmiel, to the *ulpan*. The next morning we saw the town." Carmiel is a small town in the upper Galilee, well east of the Mediterranean. They had hoped for Haifa because they felt that in a large port city it would be easier to find jobs. Also, they knew that other Leningraders had already been settled in Haifa. But for the next five months they remained in Carmiel, learning Hebrew at an *ulpan,* an intensive language institution. This was not exactly what they had been dreaming of.

TANIA AND PERETZ

Like everything else in their lives, Peretz had a point of view, a goal, and fought to have his way, even when leaving the Soviet Union. Most of the emigrants left by train: that was the standard and Tania's own brother went by train. But because they could document the fact that Tania was not a healthy person, they managed to receive permission to go by air. They were to fly from Moscow to Vienna.

They packed very quickly and made their way to Moscow, where they stayed with a friend. They took no furniture, only clothing and linens. They couldn't even take all of their cutlery with them: some of it was confiscated by the inspectors.

While they were in Moscow, Peretz was running around from morning to night, trying to get on a flight to Amsterdam instead of to Vienna. He had his principles. He would not set foot in either Germany or Austria. Peretz was a very resourceful person. Having survived so many years in the camps, he could always find a way around the rule and this time was no exception. He discovered that, while he would not be allowed to change his Vienna ticket to one that would be good for Holland on the following day, there was no problem with leaving earlier than his fixed date. So Peretz switched their Vienna tickets to tickets to Amsterdam, from February 10th to February 7th, just adding some money for making the change.

In the meantime, that morning Peretz had given Tania a little money and told her to go out and buy something for herself, whatever she wanted. She should leave the country respectably outfitted. Tania went out shopping, looking for clothes or underwear or a bag. "And I couldn't get anything. I went a whole day through Moscow and there was nothing [in the shops]." When she got back to their friend's apartment she discovered that her husband had changed the tickets. He came home and said, "We're leaving." That same night. Tania didn't even have her things ready.

In haste, they left Moscow for the airport. When the clerk looked at their documents, he said, "Why are you going to Holland? You have to go to Vienna." That was the only route for emigrants that he was familiar with. Peretz gave the excuse that they had relatives in Holland who were waiting for them there. The man disappeared and they waited at the barrier with a long line of impatient travelers behind them. Everyone with them in the KLM line for Holland was furious. "And then he was away for ten minutes and I thought, everything is over . . . and Peretz was also trembling. And then he came back and said, 'You want to go to Holland? You go.' And we went."

Part Three

SETTLING DOWN

Jews have been associated with migration since the earliest of times. Abraham, credited with being the first Jew, was said to have wandered as a nomadic merchant over vast areas from Mesopotamia through the Fertile Crescent to the shores of the Mediterranean, where Israel now stands. That takes us back some four thousand years. Later, the Jews were expelled from the Biblical homeland, first by the Assyrians (the "ten lost tribes"), at the time of the destruction of the First Temple and, then again when the Second Temple was destroyed. The Babylonian Exile—the first of these cases—proved to be temporary as a coercive measure and in less than one hundred years a large number of Jews had returned to their homeland. But the second exile, brought about by the Roman conquest of the province of Judea, became the norm, extending over a period of almost two thousand years. Even during this long period of the Diaspora, Jews were rarely able to settle in their new homes on a fully permanent basis. For various reasons they found themselves uprooted and forced to move to another location, usually for considerations of safety.

In the Middle Ages, Jews fled areas in Central Europe where they were accused by their Christian neighbors of poisoning wells, ritual murder, Host desecration and introducing diseases. They were devastatingly attacked by Crusaders on the way to the Middle East. They were thrown out of England late in the 13th century, evicted from France over the course of the 14th century, and told that they had to convert to Christianity or leave Spain and Portugal in the 15th century. Reversing the migratory trend to Eastern Europe, in the seventeenth century they fled large areas of the Polish Kingdom in the wake of massacres by troops led by Bogdan Chmielnicki. Later, when pogroms started up in the early 1880s, they began to move out of parts of the Pale of Settlement which had been established in the Russian Empire, following the partitions of Poland.

By the end of the 19th century, East European Jewry demonstrated larger migratory patterns, leaving Europe altogether in search of safety or for economic improvement. At this time, thanks to modern means of transportation, they could head for the Western Hemisphere in one direction or towards the Land of Israel, situated within the Ottoman Empire, in another. By the twentieth century their wanderings took them all over the world, whether to Mexico or South Africa, to Argentina or Canada. The far-flung Diaspora concentrated in the United States, although there was a small but significant group that set up a Jewish settlement in Palestine. By the end of the Second World War, the Jewish population of America was the largest in the world, followed by that of the Soviet Union, France and Argentina. The new State of Israel gradually built up its own population through immigration and fertility, eventually overtaking all other countries in the world, except the United States, in its concentration of Jewish population.

The fact that migration has been part of the Jewish psyche since its early history in the post-Temple period of the Common Era has not made it any the easier for the people who experienced it. Jews did become highly adaptable linguistically and in other ways, but the uprooting could never have been a felicitous process for them, not the ones who actually made the move.

Both countries that became the focus of the Soviet Jewish migration in the 1970s had been founded on the principle of welcoming those from other lands. In the case of the United States, there was a general policy of opening the doors to others, though preference had traditionally been towards those coming from the British Isles and, following that, from Western Europe. The spirit of the larger concept of hospitality to the peoples of the world was enunciated in the famous poem by Emma Lazarus and placed on the base of the Statue of Liberty in New York harbor early in the twentieth century: "Give me your tired, your poor, your huddled masses yearning to breathe free . . ."

Israel, too, is a country—much younger, of course—whose existence is inextricably linked with immigration, in this case, the "ingathering of the exiles." Jews, who have been scattered over the face of the earth for thousands of years are urged to "come home." Through the Law of Return, one of the first pieces of legislation enacted by the new state, all Jews are informed that they can find refuge in Israel without discrimination. Thus, both countries seemed a natural destination for the Jews leaving the Soviet Union.

To some extent, there was a kind of self-selection in the immigration process. Soviet Jews who were ideologically committed to Zionism made their way to Israel. They had aspirations and expectations associated with the historical homeland of the Jewish people. That is what exerted a "pull" on them. Their satisfaction—or dissatisfaction—with their new place of abode was to some extent a function of their initial motivation.

Those who elected to leave the Soviet Union but chose the United States, Canada, Great Britain or even Germany tended to be more affected by the "push" factor: they knew that they wanted to get out of the Soviet Union for whatever reasons and that was the stronger element of motivation. Their expectations of their new home country were, often, less emotional and ideological.

Whether the people who immigrated either to Israel or to the United States would settle down in contentment was a highly individual phenomenon. It depended, in both cases, on a variety of factors including professional qualifications (or lack of them), initial expectations, ability to accommodate to a new situation, the atmosphere in the receiving community and, perhaps most of all, luck.

Chapter Six

Israel

BACKGROUND

The immigration of tens of thousands of Soviet Jews into Israel during the decade of the nineteen seventies had a great impact on the country. It was the first major influx since the fifties. In the late forties, there had been a flow of survivors of the Second World War and the Holocaust who made their way to the new state. In the fifties, Jews left Arab countries in large numbers and also came to Israel. The population continued to grow and gradually the balance between Ashkenazi—or European—Jews and those from Middle Eastern areas—North Africa, Yemen, Lebanon and Syria, Iraq, Iran—was evening out. It looked as if the majority of the Jewish population of Israel would soon be non-Ashkenazi until the doors of the Soviet Union opened and Jews started pouring out. It is true that among these Jews were Bukharan, Georgian and Mountain Jews, but the Ashkenazi Jews were nevertheless predominant and thus affected the balance in the country.

Given the economic and housing conditions in the Soviet Union, it is not surprising that the Jewish communities of Moscow and Kiev, of Odessa and Leningrad were static or even falling in number. Most couples—though not all—opted to have only one child. It was the most that could be acceptable in situations where two or three generations shared a single room in an apartment. More elderly Jews were dying than babies were being born. Coming to Israel, many of the younger couples who had the option, proceeded to have the second child they had always wanted. Israel meant a new life and a new opportunity for the family.

For some, the dream of a chance of a new career that would fulfill hopes that had been dashed in the Soviet Union became a reality. In Israel they would be able to pursue a degree or obtain a job in a field that had previously been closed to them. On the other hand, at least as many of the newcomers—even those only in their forties or fifties—would probably never be able to attain the same high degree of specialization and responsibility that they had had in their Soviet jobs. Immigration would be a time of disappointment as well as of elation and opportunity.

During the nineteen seventies, it became common to refer to the immigrating adults from the Soviet Union as the "desert generation." It was quite clear that most of the adults would never make the country entirely their own. They would continue to speak in Russian at home, read the Russian-language press, value Russian literature above others and, in many ways, think in the mode of someone brought up in the Soviet Union. Many of them realized that they would never again find work at the level of their achievements back home in Kiev or Moscow. They had largely decided to move to Israel for the sake of their children. Their children, at least, would live their lives in freedom, able to express themselves as they wished, develop their future without the limitations of the Soviet system, feel comfortable and proud to be Jews. They were the ones who would become true Israelis, speak Hebrew fluently, serve in the army of their own people, study at the university without any kind of *numerus clausus*. It had all been done for them.

The new immigrants were helped in the beginning by official departments of the Ministry of Absorption and the quasi-governmental Jewish Agency, both of which had been caught by surprise. Who would have dreamed that the flood gates would suddenly open and Jews come pouring out to Israel? Where could they live? In the beginning the new immigrants were placed, after a possible initial stay in an absorption center, in apartments that were rented out to them. In order to find sufficient numbers of places, the government urged owners of more than one property to rent out the second one if it was sitting empty. They would receive a dispensation: no taxes had to be paid on income from rent received. Although this encouragement produced a goodly number of apartments, it was insufficient and the government then started to build new housing, specifically for the large influx of immigrants, mainly from the Soviet Union. Some of this construction was scattered around the country—in Upper Nazareth, in Carmiel in the Galilee, in Beer Sheva in the south. In Jerusalem, four large neighborhoods were constructed on land that had belonged to Jordan before the Six Day War: in East Talpiot looking towards Bethlehem, in Gilo in the area off the Hebron Road, and to the north of the city in Ramot and in Neve Yaakov, not far from the Arab town of Ramallah. Here new immigrant families could live in roomy apartments with all the utilities that they had dreamed of in the Soviet Union and at a decent cost with a reasonable payment structure. Those who could not buy an apartment were given the opportunity, at some later point, to enjoy the credit of all the rent they had thus far paid and apply it towards the purchase of the apartment.

The question of work was another source of difficulty. How could jobs be found for so many people in so small a country? How many teachers of Russian—or gym teachers, or engineers, or coal mining experts or musicians—could Israel absorb quickly? The joke at the time was that everyone coming down the stairs from an arriving airplane was carrying a violin case. If their hands were empty, they were probably pianists. All this indicates what an initial burden—and what an eventual treasure—these arrivals brought with them.

Israel at that time—in the nineteen seventies—did not have a strong or widespread tradition of volunteerism. There were economic reasons, of course. In most Israeli families both husband and wife had to work in order to make a decent living. Offering help for free—whether in organizations dealing with a variety of social problems or at the museum or for the orchestra—is a luxury. So many Jewish and public charities in countries like the United States were, in the post war years, organized and staffed by women whose husbands were the sole breadwinners. This was far less prevalent in Israel and at the Israel Museum, for instance, in the nineteen seventies, most of the women who served as docents or other kinds of volunteers came from the United States, Great Britain, South Africa and Canada and the other Israeli women involved tended to be from quite well-to-do backgrounds. This meant that there was no really effective framework on the non-governmental side to welcome and help new immigrants from the Soviet Union at that time. Subsequently—in the late eighties and into the post-Soviet period of the nineties—serious volunteer organizations developed. Moreover, by the end of the century the new immigrants were also helped by friends and relatives who had themselves arrived in Israel in the seventies and understood their problems. But there had been much less of a cushion for that earlier group.

The framework was there, to be sure: help was given on the part of the government and NGOs in finding housing, locating work, learning the language, getting access to money for a mortgage, establishing professional qualifications and so on. But the kind of community help that their fellow Soviet Jews were receiving at the same time in the United States was less known in Israel.

The new Soviet immigrants, in retrospect, made very impressive contributions to Israeli society and to their own Russian-speaking community. Within a relatively short time of their arrival, there were activities at the universities of Israel encompassing the intellectual interests of the newcomers: conferences, lectures, and discussion groups in Russian were held. The more impressive academics of this group found their way onto the university faculties, often helped with grants from the Ministry of Absorption. Doctors and nurses were given courses to re-qualify in their new country. Not only did the string sections of the main orchestras find themselves augmented by Russian Jewish talents, but new orchestras and chamber groups began to appear. There were more talented musicians of all kinds than the country could absorb. A new generation of musicians was also trained, though this time in Israel. The children of the Soviet immigrants eventually made up a good percentage of the scientific graduate students, though many found other academic outlets, as in the teaching professions.

The older immigrants—those of the desert generation—tried to adapt the Israeli situation to their own needs. Russian-language newspapers were established, some daily, some weekly. Serious Russian journals containing both fiction and long articles on a wide variety of themes were published. Popular magazines of different types appeared. It is no exaggeration to say that the Russian-language press was highly enterprising and dozens of periodicals were appearing regularly. Chess clubs were set up in schools, often with Russian coaches. Some of the Soviet immigrants continued as athletes in international competitions, but now wearing the Israeli colors. More and more Russian was heard in the lobby at concerts. The immigrants became great users of public parks and forests. Mushroom-picking became popular in Israel on a hitherto unknown scale. Little by little shops were opened by new immigrants featuring food products that were particularly attractive to Russians. In general, more kinds of better bread appeared in the Israeli market.

Generally, the new immigrants also expressed a need to maintain the language and culture of Russia within their families. This didn't just mean continuing to speak in Russian because it was convenient; they saw it as a cultural necessity. Many expressed the importance, to them, of making Russian literature—in the original—available to their children. This was true of those who immigrated to Israel or to the United States. However the Soviet state had treated them, they appreciated the pre-Soviet culture of Tolstoy and Dostoevsky, of Tchaikovsky and Rimsky-Korsakov, feeling that they came from a superior background and wanted their children and grandchildren to enjoy it fully.

Politically these newcomers tended to be nationalistic and economically conservative, though this was not universally true. But they carried with them attitudes and concerns developed in Soviet conditions. Much of their political behavior in Israel (and in the United States) was informed by attitudes cultivated in their home country or, on the contrary, as a direct reaction against them. These characteristics included a distrust of socialism and an admiration for capitalism and free enterprise. They tended to fear the Soviet Union, respect its strength and to back a strong defense against their former homeland and its client Arab states. This was combined with a sensitivity about the very small size of their new homeland—perfectly understandable in people coming from a country that stretched over eleven time zones. But the feeling resonated in a political attitude that opposed relinquishing any land that had been acquired in the Six Day War. They felt insecure within narrow borders and were distrustful of Arabs, even those living inside Israel. In Israeli politics this all translated into a right-wing political bias in this particular group of immigrants of the nineteen seventies.

An Israeli saying goes, "All beginnings are difficult," and this could certainly have been said for the Soviet influx in the early nineteen seventies. Israel was a small country that applauded—even relied on—immigration but it was ill prepared for the great numbers pouring in. Unlike the situation in the early years after the War of Independence, newcomers could not be put in makeshift housing—or even tents—and left to accept whatever fate had in store. This was an immigration of people with high standards, regardless of the personal domestic hardships that they had endured in their country of origin. They had lived lives that were in many ways fully protected: the state took care of a multitude of their needs, from health care to housing to work. Ultimately, despite all the help provided by the state and the philanthropies, the new immigrants found themselves on their own once they had left the protected environment of Soviet life. Each case was different. Each person experienced his own traumas or good fortune. Much depended upon personal character and attitude, as well as on skills and, of course, luck.

LEV

Lev's father had preceded the rest of the family in arriving in Israel. He left Russia at the age of seventy-one, abandoning a lovely apartment, an excellent pension, the respect of his colleagues and—something that he was very proud of—a personal season ticket at the Lenin Library in Moscow. For fifty years he had been registered in the Lenin Library and permitted to take home the rarest of books. This was a unique privilege. But he gave it all up: "Without wavering—on the contrary. He left earlier than we did."

In 1972, while the family was still living in the absorption center outside Jerusalem, Lev received a visit from some Georgian Jews. They knew about his work in the Soviet Union and, among other things, were aware of the fact that he had decorated some restaurants in Moscow: for example the Pakistan restaurant on the seventh floor of the Moskva Hotel. They wanted to discuss with him painting and decorating a new Georgian restaurant—the only one in Jerusalem—that they were planning. Within a week he had a contract. Instead of learning Hebrew in an ulpan he started work on the restaurant. The theme of the décor was the story of the Jews of Georgia.

It was not easy, however, to find other commissions and, as Lev says, he never had such a hard time earning a living as he did after arriving in Israel. "At no time had I in my life lived in such a desperate material situation, simply in poverty. For a whole year I lived on my wife's salary (my family has five people). In order to do this work, I sold all my treasured pictures. I sold a mosaic that I had prepared for the Swedish Museum of Monumental Art. . . And so on . . .They know me better abroad than they do here in Israel!"

Lev did receive other assignments later on and his work started to appear in various parts of Israel. "I left there. I'm happy. I'm terribly glad that I came to Israel. I'm happy that I dreamed of decorating Israel." One large wall of the Telephone Exchange Building in Jerusalem is covered with colorful painted tiles, Lev's work called "The Rainbow." Swirling patterns of multi-colored glazed tiles intersect and blend into a rainbow that spans almost the entire width of the fifty foot picture, set onto a grey stone wall. It brightens up a busy road where cars speed by scarce taking in the intricate work that must have required enormous time and patience to complete. It is a welcome artistic landmark. Did he receive adequate remuneration for his work? This is debatable: by international standards it was a small amount, then cut to less than half by taxes and the cost of materials. In Lev's view, he was receiving a lower salary than an ordinary engineer.

Transferring a profession can be very difficult. Lev felt that he was one of the only established Soviet artists who did manage to continue his work in Israel. Monumental art is particularly problematic, specifically because of its size, the public nature of the work and the cost of creation.

Other ornamental walls created by Lev, either in relief or in glazed tiles, can be found in public institutions around the country: soldiers' memorials, synagogues, colleges. Surely the people passing by these colorful and often fanciful constructs have no idea that they were created by the scion of a Russian Jewish rabbinical family and a relative of a famous early Zionist. In an album of his works, Lev is quoted in a characteristic statement: "I am wary of the rare days when I am completely satisfied with myself. On these days it's better not to start working at all. Nothing good will come out of it anyway."

Lev is just as outspoken about his environment as he is about his art. Dissatisfied with life in the Soviet Union he did not settle into complacency in Israel. He does not feel, for example, that there is true democracy in Israel, not as he understands the word. Democracy is based on the idea that all citizens have equal rights and equal obligations. But, he says, his two daughters (that's the first sort of citizen) have to serve in the army, but religious girls (the second sort) don't have to. Why should his daughters serve for two years? If everyone did their part, then every girl would have to be in the army for only one year. "Here's a simple arithmetical calculation: I pay taxes for a person who is not at all a believer. Believers—those are people of the first sort—fight for their homeland with an automatic in their hands—in the name of God—they're the [real] believers. The rest, they are disgusting parasites on the body of society! And in this sense that religious person who doesn't serve his country and doesn't let his children serve in the army is no better, in my eyes, than the careerist communist who uses his position and his [Communist] Party card to his advantage."

For Lev, the people with whom he identifies are the intelligentsia. There is an intelligentsia in Israel, he said, but we are isolated. "As far as I'm concerned, there are two nationalities on this earth: the intelligentsia and all the rest. Sometimes I have a feeling that surprises me. I have a lot of acquaintances who are Arabs. The Arab intellectual is sometimes closer to me than some coarse cheat in some market or shop who is a Jew."

EVA

Interviewed first in June, 1980, Lev's daughter Eva was twenty-one years old, trim, lovely, bright, articulate—and speaking good English. It was good enough for her to have passed the demanding requirements of the prestigious English Department of the Hebrew University of Jerusalem, where she studied both English literature and art history. Life was good at that time. But it had been difficult a number of years before, when the family first arrived in Israel.

Adjusting to the new situation was far from easy, and Eva was very candid about that. In Moscow she had been studying at a highly privileged school. Going from that to an ordinary Israeli high school was a challenge. "I suffered a lot there." The problem was not only in the attitude of her classmates, but also in herself. In the beginning, she was comparing the youth she met in Israel with those she had known in Russia and the Russians came out better. They were the children of the privileged, knew languages, went to exhibitions. But with the Israelis: "First of all, I didn't accept them . . . They were just silly kids to me, and they didn't accept me. They mocked me because I came from Russia. . . The situation has changed. . . I know because when my sister [two and a half years younger] went to the school she was accepted and respected." Things improved in Eva's last year of high school: she knew good English and her classmates appreciated her for that and wanted her to help them.

But for a long time, even in the army, Eva felt like an outsider. "When I was in high school, I was thinking of them, not as my classmates, but as Israelis, legendary Israelis, whom I have to help and who I have to love."

At some point Eva stopped idealizing Israelis. "Now it's gone completely
. . . the feeling of being an outsider, of still loving *the* Israeli, because now I
feel *myself* an Israeli; I want to be loved." This shift from idealizing Israelis
did not impact badly on her feeling for Israel. On the contrary, "I don't like
Israel less. I like Israel more, because it's my country. . . You don't idealize
it, you love it. You live here. I feel it's my place. I feel it stronger, especially
in front of the tape recorder [!]. I had certain possibilities to go to England,
and I never accepted that because I wanted to be *here*."

Her feelings towards Israelis changed with time and "I started to appreciate
something else they had. They had open minds. They were frank. They spoke
things they thought. They didn't lie. . . What I liked the most, they had this
unprisoned mind. They were not taught to think in a special way. They were
just the way they chose."

This comment of Eva's brings up a problem peculiar to many people who
were brought up in the Soviet Union of Stalin, Khrushchev and Brezhnev.
It was noted repeatedly by the academic community in Israel (and other
countries) in the nineteen seventies, when Soviet or formerly Soviet colleagues worked with them: the necessity, hammered into Soviet students, of
having to toe the Party line, of having to reassure themselves that what they
were saying or writing was in consonance with the accepted thinking of the
regime. There was a concern, when working in Israeli institutions, that what
an immigrant scholar was writing might intentionally be designed to match
the thinking of the head of his institute. It was difficult to convince such a
scholar that whatever he or she wrote, whatever the point of view, would be
judged on its merits and that good academic work had to be accomplished
with an independent mind.

Eva expressed this problem in describing her high school experiences in
Israel. In the beginning she had trouble in formulating her own opinion in a
particular class. "Because I wasn't taught to think in that way . . . I learned
to do it gradually. . . It was a very good thing that we left Russia because I'd
already begun—even being an outsider—I'd begun to be a Soviet product of
Soviet education, to think in such a way, to censor myself, to restrain myself,
and to mark the borders, in my speech."

In Israel, compulsory military service—two years for girls and three for
boys—is begun immediately after high school. When she entered the army,
Eva was lucky: she met her own kind of people, compatible with her. "And
they are my great friends. And what mattered is that one of my closest friends
comes from England and the other is Israeli, and we never even think about
that, who comes from where." Eva makes the impression of a happy, adjusted
young woman, doing well in her studies, traveling abroad for short stays,
looking forward toward a good future.

LIUBA AND SIMON

High in the hills of Western Galilee, on a spot overlooking rolling acres of olive orchards, pasture land, orange groves that descend, in the far distance, to the Mediterranean, where views of Haifa and the bay can be seen, Liuba and Simon were living in a mobile home at the time of the first interview, at the end of the year 1980. It had taken them a number of years to arrive at this place, but they were looking forward to a future there.

When they first arrived from Leningrad, they had been sent to Carmiel, also in the Galilee, where they spent a few months studying Hebrew in an *ulpan*. It was a difficult time for them. As Simon put it, it was hard on their morale: "You understand that a Soviet person, having grown up in Russia, is used to working all the time. And then if at a mature age he suddenly finds himself studying and doesn't know what tomorrow will bring, if he'll find a job, a home, this can be depressing." They found that it wasn't as easy as in Leningrad to find suitable work and they had to start from scratch. It was all a great letdown. They had never really had to take the initiative like this before. The Soviet socialist system had provided a protective cocoon in many ways.

In the beginning, Simon worked for a small private firm and then, after a few years, he transferred to the public sector, where he has had very interesting work on a very high professional level. He also started, after his arrival, to serve in the army reserves, which he does not find a burden. It isn't, he says, a reason for not coming to Israel. What was bad, though, was for an adult, as he was, to have to cut off his roots. Using the metaphor of a tree, Simon explained that once it is uprooted and planted in a new place, it either adapts or it doesn't; it could take a longer or shorter time and till it happens, the tree is suffering. Fortunately, Simon eventually put down those roots.

Liuba has had a harder time. First, the departure from her home and family was much more difficult. She couldn't come to her senses in Israel and didn't really shake off her depression probably until she went back to working as an engineer some time after Simon. Then things came a little easier. But that had taken seven months. During that time, their little boy had taken ill numerous times because, Liuba felt, he was confronted with a new set of germs. So altogether it wasn't easy.

They eventually bought an apartment in Tivon, not far from Haifa. It was a good place, an eighty-two square meter (882.6 square feet) flat with three bedrooms in a pleasant neighborhood. They hadn't taken any of their furniture with them from the Soviet Union, just their books and smaller possessions and thus had to buy new items in Israel. (Special tax breaks lowering the price of cars, electrical goods and so on are available to new Israeli immigrants.)

While Liuba was lucky in finding a job that was very convivial—fellow workers with whom she gets along well and who have been very supportive of their Russian-speaking and (only) female colleague—she has recently encountered serious health problems which have required more than one operation on her leg. She has ended up spending a lot of time in the hospital and recuperation, though she hopes that she will be able to get back to work after the long period of sick leave.

A few years before the interview, Liuba and Simon had decided to look for an attractive place to buy or build a home for themselves. They liked the idea of a new settlement, somewhere away from the established cities. For them, after all, Simon explains, as a city Leningrad is first and last, so they were not drawn to the Israeli cities for their home. They also liked the idea of being latter-day pioneers. They investigated various possibilities, talked to a number of building groups that had formed and were looking for land on which they could develop a community. Eventually they got together with some like-minded friends from Leningrad. Some of them were very energetic and together they formed a *garin*, an initiative group, and approached the Jewish Agency to see if they could help them find a place where they could form a settlement. A number of sites were offered and they chose this spot in the Western Galilee. Their house will not be on the precise plot of land where their temporary home now stands and, in fact, they have not yet planned the exact shape and size of the house. One of their friends, an architect and a former Prisoner of Zion, is a candidate for membership in the *garin* and he has been giving them some advice. At present, there are fifteen families in the project, twelve of which came from the Soviet Union. It is clear that they will be expanding and taking in many more families, as the area set aside for their settlement is quite large. While they have had little to do with the Arabs living in the neighborhood, local kibbutzim and moshavim have made connections with them and been helpful.

Almost no one in the group is expecting to actually work in the village that is to be constructed. Of their small group, one person is a draughtsman who plans to work out of her home, as will, perhaps, an engineer. But Simon's place of work, for example, is on the way to Haifa. He and three others who work there receive daily transport from their employer. Simon and Liuba have their own car, purchased a few years ago. Liuba says that they really economized in order to buy it: "We've been used to economizing our whole life!"

For immigrants from the Soviet Union, the Israeli political system—the ability to vote freely with a wide choice of candidates and parties—was a new experience. While there were some who claimed not to be interested, to be apolitical, or to have no faith in any of the parties, most did have an opinion about politics and many exercised their right to vote. Indeed, the "Russian" vote would eventually have a serious impact on Israeli politics.

Simon and Liuba acquire their information from the radio and television, mostly, but find it hard to make out just what is going on in the parties and how to discover the kernel of truth in the mass of information available to them. Three years before, in 1977, they had voted for Menachem Begin and his Likud party, but Simon says that he wasn't pleased with him. Liuba, too, voted for him, hoping for an improvement in the economy, but she would like a change now. With elections a year off, Shimon Perez and Yitzhak Rabin seem to be a better choice, but it is a long way off until the vote. She certainly is not interested in any of the smaller parties. Simon feels perhaps closer to what he refers to as the liberal party of Amnon Rubinstein, but, again, smaller parties can be problematic, unless they can form a bloc. Simon summarized his comparison of his former and present countries: "The difference between Russia and Israel, I think, is that there, in general, the country is standing on its own feet. People may not be living all that well there, but the country is strong. Here, on the contrary, all the people somehow or other live pretty well, or at least most do . . . but the country's economy . . ."

Their son is studying in the local school and they feel strongly that Israel is the best place for him. Good, not good, says Simon, there's no choice—"*ain brera!*" he says in Hebrew. Liuba adds: "We came from the *galut* [Diaspora]. Here there's no *galut*. He's free and his behavior is definitely different from that of young Jews in Russia, in Leningrad. It's totally different, absolutely! He would be first in his class [there]; all Jews—first! Here there are simply not those demands . . . Here everyone's Jewish."

Simon goes on: "You understand that this consciousness that this is your country, that this is your place . . . means something. Everyone feels this. When we were growing up, we always felt like the Other. They let us understand that."

ZAKHARIA

In the end, Zakharia, his wife and son and his mother-in-law all arrived in Israel and settled down in Jerusalem. His brother-in-law and his wife said that they would not come: that was a final decision.

Zakharia was very lucky, as he actually managed to land a job in Israel that was in his field and one that he has enjoyed very much. He works for Kol Yisrael, the Israel Broadcasting Authority and his voice, in Russian, is heard abroad. With this position he earns a decent wage and he and his wife are able to live in conditions which are far better than those they enjoyed in the Soviet Union, even though he had been a Party member there and very well connected. They find that they can buy significantly more on their Israeli salary than they could have in the Soviet Union. In Lithuania they had no car: in Israel they own one. They bought a color television set (which they could not have had there). They have a larger refrigerator, more clothes. More importantly, they have managed to travel abroad during the nineteen seventies, something they could never have done there. Zakharia and Bella visited London and Paris. She was also sent by the Jewish Agency to the United States on a trip.

In 1972, Zakharia was contacted by someone in Radio Liberty, an emigré radio station located in Germany and broadcasting to the Soviet Union. They were offering him a two-year contract with such a good salary and generous conditions, that he would be able to save money while working there. The man told Zakharia that he would be able, at the end of the two years, to return to Israel with a hundred thousand German marks in his pocket. Zakharia, who had no private funds and was still working in Jerusalem without any job security, was tempted by the offer. But Bella argued against it. You're on the point of getting tenure, she said, so do you really want to throw everything aside and start again? You'll even forget the Hebrew that you've learned. In the end, he decided not to take the job and has not regretted it. He did receive his tenure in good time.

Zakharia did not want to talk much about politics, but he did point out that a hundred years ago there had been early settlements—Petah Tikvah, Hadera, Zihron Yaakov, Rishon le Zion—that existed in a sea of Arabs and today there are Bet El, Ofra and so on also in a sea of Arabs. What's the difference, he asks? Comparing this with his experience in Lithuania, he sees the same general situation: two nations living in one country, hating each other. He avoids dealing with the fact that the latter settlements are in occupied territory.

They were planning a trip, at the time of the interview in May, 1982, to Berlin. Zakharia still remembers the address of his family home on Hamburgerstrasse in Berlin where his family lived when he was a child. He has been asked to speak on German radio during his visit. Perhaps they will also visit Holland and Switzerland at the same time. A friend of his, who had originally come to live in Israel, now lives in Switzerland and, with his Swiss passport, he has returned to Lithuania a number of times. As an Israeli, Zakharia would not be able to. He would love to go back as a tourist, but would be afraid to. "Even now I sometimes have a nightmare that I'm there, you understand? I think in the dream: Oh my God, it's all starting again! . . . and to give in documents, and they won't give permission, and again the factory and again to learn Hebrew from the beginning and to get a job, and to get *kviut*! [Hebrew for tenure] And an apartment! *Bozhe moi!* [Russian: My God!] Everything from the start!"

AARON

Aaron and his little family left Vienna at twilight and arrived in Israel in the middle of the night. A rather humble man, this accountant had no great expectations of a perfect reception at Ben Gurion Airport and was, likewise, not disappointed with the way that they were greeted. That same night, they were put into a vehicle together with their luggage and sent straight to Netanya, a Mediterranean town that lies to the north of Tel Aviv. There they spent about five months at an *ulpan* so that they could gain a basis in Hebrew. This was done according to the accepted Israeli immigration practice that intellectuals—people who needed a high level of language for their profession—were sent to an *ulpan* and supported for the duration of the basic course.

Following this, Aaron, Bella and Frima were brought to Jerusalem to see a possible apartment that they would be able to rent. The flat, in an upper middle class neighborhood, surrounded by gardens, was not expensive, as they would be receiving it from a quasi-governmental body (Amidar) that handled property. In the pressure to provide housing for the relatively large number of immigrants now arriving, Amidar acquired rental properties and made them available at a reasonable cost. The family immediately accepted the offer and moved in. By now the furniture and other goods that they had shipped had arrived in Israel.

The three now settled down to their new lives in Jerusalem. Bella, who had worked as a cardiologist in Kiev, had to abandon her specialization and found employment with one of the health services as a general practitioner. She was satisfied with this work and grateful that she could remain in her general field. Aaron, advised by one of his new neighbors to take an accountancy review course that would equip him for employment in Israel, was afterwards taken on by the Ministry of Treasury to work in a department that dealt with the war-wounded.

Frima had been a teacher in Kiev, awaiting the opportunity to return to the university and work on her PhD in linguistics. She now applied for entry into the Hebrew University, where she studied for a while, though she never did complete her doctorate. She also perfected her translation skills and started to translate Hebrew poetry (and other texts) into Russian. She became part of the entourage of the Hebrew poet Zelda and, though there was a great disparity in age, she felt very close to her and began translating her poetry into Russian.

During their early years in Israel, the family started moving towards Jewish orthodoxy. Both Aaron and Bella had come from religiously devout families that had maintained many of the religious precepts even in the harshest of Soviet conditions. They themselves, though, had not done so in their own home, not because of a lack of interest, but because of the Soviet regime. It was too complicated (kosher-slaughtered meat was not easily obtained for example) and too dangerous (the future of either of their jobs or their daughter's education might be jeopardized). But here in Israel they gradually returned to the faith of their ancestors, keeping a kosher home, maintaining the Sabbath, fulfilling the *mitzvot* (precepts) of their religion. It wasn't necessarily easy: one didn't remember all the traditions of the childhood home, how and when things were done, what was permitted or forbidden. One evening, after a holiday had begun—a holiday when it was permitted to cook, but not to light a fire—Aaron came upstairs to the neighbors and asked if they had a lit fire so that he could borrow a flame from it. He then took it downstairs to light the fire in his own kitchen, so that they could make their evening meal. Little by little they were making their dream come true—living their religion in the State of Israel.

ESTHER

Esther and Volt arrived in Israel some time after her father and son had done so, and settled down in Jerusalem. Volt, linguistically very gifted, found himself work as a translator. Esther has made money in various ways, largely typing. She is very much appreciated—friendly, helpful, cheerful—and one client gladly recommends her to the next. Her son was living his own life by the time they arrived, had started studying at the university, then changed his mind and entered the army. He had learned Hebrew quickly, served in the armed forces during the Yom Kippur War and after his release went on to develop his own career. He eventually married a Scandinavian woman and Esther has gradually become the grandmother of two.

Esther's son and her second husband have never really managed to tolerate each other. Iz'ka was already seventeen years old when she married Volt and they had more or less never lived together in the same house. In later years in Israel when they were in each other's company there were serious problems. Perhaps each wanted more than his just share of Esther. Iz'ka, endearing but annoying, demanded his mother's attention; he wanted her to help look after his children and she on her side very much wanted to enjoy her grandchildren. Volt felt that his step-son was rude to him and treated him shabbily, even in his own home. He grew very resentful and began to oppose Iz'ka coming to his apartment at all. Iz'ka, on his part, threatened his mother that she had to get rid of her husband or risk not being allowed to see her grandchildren. She was in a dilemma: husband on the one hand and son and grandchildren on the other, were pulling in opposite directions. She admits that her son is a difficult person, but was terrified that she would lose him. She wasn't sure of where her true interests lay and not too long after her first interview at the end of 1980, she decided to leave Volt. It was a difficult decision and would lead to lives of loneliness for both of them.

". . . when we parted, we wept like the devil. Both of us cried, because we were parting for no reason, not that we were fed up with each other, but that we couldn't live together. It was impossible, impossible because—what could be done? Iz'ka, Iz'ka was going mad."

ANATOLII AND SVETLANA

Anatolii and Svetlana were very happy to move, at last, to Jerusalem, a city that they both love. There were many peregrinations along the way, unfortunate places of residence, difficulties of all kinds. The absolutely worst thing from the beginning, says Anatolii, was the language: it's a nightmare, particularly for a person having to learn a new language after the age of thirty-five.

In the first years, they were helped by the Jewish Agency, although Svetlana is very critical, saying that she wishes that they hadn't had any involvement with the organization at all. What she really wanted was help in finding work. Anatolii points out that without the Jewish Agency they couldn't have existed at all, but he asserts that they and other immigrants had such a bitter experience with the Agency that eventually it became an enemy as far as they were concerned. "Regardless of the fact that without its activity, no process of absorption would have been possible, its activity was still very unsatisfactory and was accompanied by such a mass of every kind of mistake, of stupidity, created, probably . . . so as to make the absorption of the new arrivals more difficult," Anatolii says wryly. He goes on to say that people criticize both the Jewish Agency and the Ministry of Absorption and, in any case, "people heave a sigh of relief when they no longer have to have anything to do with either of these institutions."

Anatolii took the opportunity, once in Jerusalem, to go on with his studies and work on a doctorate, which he completed in 1977, quite an accomplishment for someone learning a new language, adjusting to a different culture and dealing with all the day to day problems of a recent immigrant. As a graduate student he was helped with stipends, including one from the President's Fund at the Hebrew University, for which he was very grateful.

In the 1970s and 80s, the University was blessed with a president, Abraham Harman—a former Israeli ambassador to the United States—who was very sympathetic to the situation of incoming Soviet academics. He saw to it that many of the deserving scientists and scholars found at least a temporary home—and often a permanent one—at the Hebrew University, that grants were provided to people who needed them and that the institution had a responsible and respected committee for dealing with problems related to Soviet Jewry. It was, indeed, felicitous timing to have a man like Abe Harman serving as president of the Hebrew University of Jerusalem during the years of the great influx of Soviet Jewish academics and intellectuals.

Anatolii and Svetlana express mixed feelings about their move to Israel. Among their friends who live abroad—and at this point they themselves had not traveled outside Israel—some are satisfied and some not. Svetlana feels, from what she has heard, that she wouldn't like America though she does think that she might have more positive feelings about Europe. Anatolii had been more fixated on Israel from the start, though he certainly realizes that the country has its problems. In practice, he says, there is endless war here. He hopes very much that this can be changed, but he's not sure. Besides that, the economic situation in Israel has recently (in 1980) been bad and life becomes harder and harder. He also questions whether it is so good that men have to serve constantly in the military. He is certainly not pleased about the conscription of girls and regrets that his own daughter will be entering the ranks of the army in seven months.

Anatolii could, on the other hand, name some very good aspects of life in Israel. "Above all, I'm satisfied that I live in a free country and in a Jewish country, in a country where opportunities have opened up for me that I couldn't have had in another country—although I'm also not sure about that . . ."

As for the political framework, Anatolii is very glad that he lives in a democratic country—though it does have a number of undemocratic elements in its political system. "In general, I'm obviously an old-fashioned person among the Russian emigrants, because I'm still not disenchanted with democracy and I consider that with all its indisputable shortcomings this form of governing is still the best by far, and for Jews, undoubtedly. It's the only possible one. Besides the basically western democratic political structure which is present in Israel, there of course exist a great number of strange phenomena, deeply contradictory to the spirit of democracy—clericalism, pressure of groups such as Gush Emunim, and so on." If you take into account, he says, that Israel is sort of an island among undemocratic countries which will not become democratic for a long time, then these inadequacies are less important. To him, the greatest danger is the occupation of the West Bank and dominion over the Arab population, which threatens to undermine the democratic Jewish character of the State of Israel. He is worried about the future of the country, the future of the next generation and their own future.

ZHENIA AND SERYOZHA

The story of Zhenia and Seryozha became more and more complicated as time went on. In the beginning, they were interviewed in 1980, less than two years after their emigration. At that point, they were still involved with first impressions, looking for the right job, making important decisions. They saw things from somewhat different vantage points and each was seeking his or her own place in Israeli society. They were already living in Gilo, an area in the north of Jerusalem that had been annexed after the Six Day War and housed a large Russian-speaking immigrant population.

Zhenia, still the mother of a young child, had not managed to enter a doctoral program of her choosing. She was still finding her way. What she missed was Yalta. She wasn't homesick for Russia, just her Yalta. Even when she was away from Yalta, living elsewhere in the Soviet Union, Zhenia had cherished it. "When I lived in Chernovtsy, I saw the sea in my dreams. I'm a geographic patriot! I love my 'little piece.' I love Crimea. I know it well. I know the writers living in Crimea. I know all the marvelous places. I know it like a geologist, a geographer." Other than that, she missed those who were close to her: her grandmother and her cousin—the young man who was older than she but had shared many experiences with her at home and at the university. If only she could just see him once a year, or even once every three years! All they have is letters, but one can't write everything in a letter.

The issue of friends is an important one for Russians. In a country where so much was lacking, the great resource was friendship. It was this more than almost everything else that Russian émigrés missed abroad. For Zhenia, too, this was a qualitative part of her life that she longed for once she had left. In the Soviet Union she hadn't had to look for a circle of friends: she had one for all time. They were strongly connected, shared a similar point of view, literary taste. "Strange as it may seem, living in Jerusalem we are more isolated. Some are studying, some are teaching, someone's got a new baby."

On the whole, though, Zhenia was satisfied. Their standard of living, even with the minimal pay that they were receiving, nevertheless was far higher than what they had attained in Kiev, or Yalta. Zhenia was learning Hebrew, though not really enough yet. She could get around on the bus or in a store, "But I can't talk on a literary theme." She was anxious that her little daughter not lose her Russian. A great culture had developed in Russia over the past hundred and fifty years and she would like her to be able to read Russian literature in the original when she grows up. "I'd very much like [her] to feel this culture, and not know it the way they teach it here. A man, a sabra, for example, comes to the university and begins to learn Russian and literature. He knows it, but he cannot feel it. I'd want her to feel it from inside."

Seryozha had worried that there would be a strong national spirit, not a religious national spirit, not that of the chosen people, but a purely material nationalism. On the whole Israel had turned out much better than he had expected. Israel, he felt, was a country of ideals and that was a good thing. Although all kinds of things go wrong, when there's an emergency, a trying situation, everyone works together and cares.

He loves Jerusalem. Sometimes at night, he says, the sky is so close that you feel you could reach out and touch it. In Jerusalem "there's always a feeling of the presence of God." He can't explain why he loves it, but he simply feels good in Jerusalem. He doesn't feel the same when he is in Tel Aviv. Whenever he's there, he wants to return to Jerusalem and to the mountains that he loves.

The work that Seryozha was doing at the time of the interview was not of a particularly satisfying kind. He had been going from one low level job to another, first delivering mail within the university system and then getting a job as a mechanic at a hospital. However, after some six months at this job, staff cuts were made and he ended up in what he called "fruit and vegetables," cleaning potatoes in the kitchen. According to him the pay was perfectly acceptable, but the work was uninspiring and the hours long. Working from six in the morning till four in the afternoon, he was coming home exhausted, without the strength even to read.

Seryozha started to wear a *kippa* [skull cap] recently. Was he religious? He'd like to be religious and sometimes he prays. He keeps the Sabbath, keeps kosher. He had embraced Tolstoyanism while in Kiev and is afraid to go full speed ahead with Judaism without thinking it all through. He'd like to do it gradually. He doesn't go to synagogue on the Sabbath and doesn't know how to pray in Hebrew. He has a Russian-language prayer book. But every morning he puts on his tefilin (phylacteries); he feels that he should. On Saturday, he walks the long distance to the Old City and back.

Like Zhenia, he too would very much like his daughter to know Russian, although he can't explain why. "You know, I love Israel very much today. I very much love my Jewishness and I very much love Russia." He feels that today there are two places where a real person can exist—in Russia and in Israel.

Although he was an active dissident, Seryozha doesn't see himself as a political person. He never voted in the Soviet Union, but that was a form of protest. He doesn't think that he will vote in the upcoming Israeli elections either, but for different reasons. He hasn't yet formed an understanding of what is going on in Israel. As he puts it, he loves Israel as a country a great deal, more than Israel as a state. Even at this stage, however, Seryozha seems to be more in sympathy with the right-wing camp. He says that he empathizes more with Begin, finds him more "sympathetic." As for the peace with Egypt (the interview followed Sadat's historic visit to Israel in 1977 and the Camp David Peace Accord a year and a half later), Seryozha feels that on the one hand that would be good, although who knows how it will work out. But from the purely practical point of view, the peace with Egypt was not good, as it deprived Israel of access to the oil in Sinai. When speaking on this, Seryozha quoted a right-wing politician, Yuval Ne'eman. And what about the settlements? "I think that they have a right to exist, just as Tel Aviv does."

Three and a half years later, in a second round of interviews, the lives of Seryozha and Zhenia had changed sharply. She, for example, after trying her luck with a few jobs, has finally settled into some very interesting and agreeable work at a major library. Just three days before, she had received tenure and was marveling at her good fortune. She does not yet have the official status of a librarian and has started taking courses to correct that. It should take about two years until she qualifies as a librarian. There is another notable change: Zhenia is pregnant with their second child and is planning the birth and her upcoming maternity leave.

Zhenia's mother, an enthusiastic communist when living in Crimea, has made an impressive adjustment in Israel. As strange as it may seem, says Zhenia, she is satisfied and has been successful in settling down. A teacher all her life, and very creative, Zhenia's mother—who was unable to get a regular job as a teacher in the Jerusalem area—started working at a mental institution instead, in the field of occupational therapy. She's marvelous with her hands, says Zhenia: there's nothing that she can't make, sew, construct. She was so successful and admired in this new profession that she received tenure. When she moved to Haifa, she was able to retain her status and has continued her work there, taking various enrichment courses. Now fifty-five, she still enjoys a satisfying career.

Seryozha's father, also in Israel, continues to live in the absorption center. Zhenia feels that this is not a satisfactory situation. He has not succeeded in finding work in his field (as a dental technician) and has been living on a pension as a war invalid. Zhenia sees life at an absorption center as very difficult, with the inhabitants closely scrutinizing one another jealously. The longer people live there, the worse they become. It is much better, she says, to get out of that atmosphere and live independently. People lose faith in themselves and their ability to manage on their own. She feels that this is one of the biggest problems of *aliyah* (immigration to Israel) and it would be much better to place people in rented apartments from the start.

For his part, Seryozha has moved back and forth between hospital kitchen work and his own profession as a mechanic. Working in his specialization— sewing machines—he has alternated between work at a factory and doing freelance repairs. Now that they are both earning a living, their material situation has indeed improved, not that it is easy. Zhenia gets up very early, clocking in at about seven in the morning. She enjoys starting the day early, doing her work, and then finishing so that by two in the afternoon she can be on her way. The ride home is long—two buses—and takes time. They do not have a car.

Religiously they remain apart, with even a greater difference than before, perhaps. While still at the absorption center, they had started to keep a kosher kitchen for Seryozha. He has been engaged in Jewish study, whether at the Shamir Institute (which was set up by a well-known Soviet scientist now living in Israel to teach religious subjects to immigrant scientists) or at Dvar Yerushalaim yeshiva (a Jerusalem institution for adult students returning to the fold of orthodox Judaism). He even joined a study group in Hebron. This was quite an extreme step, as Hebron is an Arab town deep in the West Bank, with only a small group of extremist Jewish settlers living in an outpost. It indicates how far Seryozha has moved to the right religiously and politically since his immigration five years before.

In fact, he has gone even further. Since the previous interview, Seryozha had spent about a year living in Hebron. He lived in various places, depending, as he says, on no one, working either in Hebron or in Jerusalem, traveling back and forth. He didn't sleep regularly anywhere. Sometime he would leave He- bron at eleven at night on the last bus to Jerusalem. At one point he had shared a room in Hebron with a young American—Aaron Gross—who was killed in one of the many incidents in that very inflammatory part of the region. During the interview, Seryozha kept switching back and forth between Russian and Hebrew, while Zhenia carried on her part of the interview in Russian.

Although there were clear political implications to his move to Hebron, Seryozha suggested that there seemed to be a good business rationale for it as well. As in other comparisons that he has made, he said that as far as he was concerned, wherever Jews live there are Jewish businesses and it's just as natural to open a business in Hebron as in the Carmel Market (in Tel Aviv). After all, he averred, if he had said that he wanted to open a business in Gilo (a recently constructed Jerusalem suburb located on land taken from Jordan) someone would ask, why not in Rehavia (in the heart of Jewish Jerusalem). And Hebron, after all, was the first Jewish city, historically linked to Abraham.

Seryozha's plan was to open a shop in Hebron for his sewing machine repair business, but it never materialized. He seems to have run up against various Jewish groups in Hebron and its outskirts that opposed this idea. In general, Seryozha clashed with some of the leaders, specifically Rabbi Lev- inger, and tended to keep himself independent. In the course of his Hebron experiences, he befriended the great grandson of Leon Trotsky. At the time of the interview he was serving in the Israeli army, according to Seryozha, and was about twenty-two years old. He had emigrated from Russia to the United States, then left his parents there and come alone to Israel "without a kopeck." This member of the Trotsky family was known in Israel as a fanatical young man, roaming the Hebron area with his rifle. An interesting feature of Israel is that a variety of descendants of famous historical figures (Trotsky, Tolstoy, and so on), not necessarily Jewish, who often had conflicting views of the country, have ended up living within its borders.

As in the interview a few years before, Seryozha insists that he is not planning to vote, that he has no one to vote for. If he votes, it will probably be for Kahane. (Here Seryozha is referring to the right-wing American rabbi who settled in Israel. Starting with the theme of self-defense in New York City, he reformulated his credo to one of aggressive action against Arabs once he lived in the Middle East). Seryozha says that he knows him and that "of all of them . . . he's the only more or less decent person." Seryozha likes him as a person, not as a party leader. He certainly wouldn't vote for the Tehiya party or for Rabbi Valdman's party (other groups on the extreme right). Nor would he consider Navon, Shamir, Peres, or Burg. He cannot forgive Yitzhak Shamir (of the right-wing Likud party) for what happened to the Jewish underground. The whole treatment of the case, shadowing people, listening to telephone conversations, is very upsetting to him. Nor does he approve of Begin (also of Likud) having given back Sinai.

Seryozha's father has come with him to Hebron a few times and, according to Seryozha, likes the life there. This one-time fervent member of the Soviet communist party, who is still not religious, now does not ride on the Sabbath on principle. On the Sabbath, Seryozha will not listen to music; he reads. Actually, he says that they read, referring to his wife. A person, he says, has to know that he's a human being, that there's not just work and television—that he's a person.

Zhenia's sister lives in Haifa and has found a good job in a hospital. During the military campaign of Shlom ha Galil (the first Lebanese war) she was working very hard with injured soldiers. Fortunately, she loves her work and has settled in well. The sisters are close and until she was so heavily pregnant Zhenia used to visit Haifa quite often, at least every other week. "She went to Haifa for Shabbat," says Seryozha, "and I went to Hebron!"

ISAAC

Isaac and Clara settled into their apartment in Nazareth. Both of them had jobs: he as a welder and she in a plastics factory. They had arrived in Israel in March, in the middle of the school year. Sophia's younger sister, Mila, two years younger than she, was registered for school. When they left the Soviet

Union, Sophia had been seventeen and just a month or so short of graduation from high school. Rather than stay with her family, Sophia went to a kibbutz in the Western Galilee, where she studied Hebrew intensively and worked for a year. Her goal was to master the language and gain admission to a university. She was, in fact, very happy there. "I absolutely loved it. There were students from all over the world," she said in retrospect. After a morning of studying Hebrew she would then work in the kitchen. She found Israel a wonderful place to live.

The truth is that Sophia's experience was, proportionately, less common among the Russian-speaking immigrants. Most of the people brought up in the Soviet Union shied away from kibbutzim, which they saw as akin to the collective farms, or kolkhozy, that they were familiar with from home. They associated the kibbutz with the socialist agricultural system that had been developed in the Soviet Union starting in 1928 and tended to prefer the world of free enterprise of the cities of Israel. There was, though, a relatively small number of immigrants who found happiness on the kibbutz, whether as a transitional home, or as permanent members or even, in the later immigration, as retirees.

Isaac succeeded in his work and, with a grant from the Jewish Agency, even opened up his own welding business, with a Romanian-immigrant partner. While it seemed promising at first, his partner turned out to be dishonest and Isaac broke off his partnership with him.

At some point during the year, Sophia took the university entrance examination. Her father paid forty lira for this—not a large sum but considerable for a new immigrant—and he did so with some resentment. He was thus very upset when they received notice that Sophia had been turned down. It was felt that she was too young and should come back when she was a bit older and knew more Hebrew. (Most students enter the university after serving in the army.)

There were other forces at work during this time of disappointments. A number of Isaac and Clara's friends decided to leave Israel and try their luck in America. Clara was caught up in their idea. "You know," explained Isaac. "This is like an epidemic . . . People are going: let's go to the United States." Their friends felt that they would have more opportunities, that life would be easier in America or Australia. Although they were in a minority of Russian-speaking immigrants to Israel to do so, they decided, after all the difficulties of getting out of the Soviet Union, and all the problems of starting a new life in Israel, that they would once again try their luck in a new place. As Sophia explained it years later, "My parents wanted to see if they could improve their lives even more . . . it's kind of 'join the band wagon.' Everybody was leaving [*sic*] and you can't pass it up—here was an opportunity."

Sophia was dismayed when her father and mother came to see her at the kibbutz and said that they were leaving. "I said, 'Wait a minute!' . . . It came as an absolute shock to me. I was in shock." Sophia, after only a year in Israel, was more regretful than when she had left her native Odessa at age seventeen. "Yes, that I was. Odessa, I was not upset, not even a little bit . . . up to this day, Odessa means nothing to me . . . I never felt close to anything there . . . I don't like the Russian language to this day."

TANIA AND PERETZ

Unexpectedly, Tania turned out to be very pleased that she had ended up in Israel. Unlike most Soviet emigrants, she was fluent in a foreign language, in her case, English. Talking at the end of 1979, she was certainly very glad that they had left the Soviet Union: "I think that now when I see Russia's policies all the time and with the Arabs and with everything, so of course I think it's awful." She goes on: "And also at that time, when I was there, I felt it because . . . first of all, they had chucked me out of the Party . . . so I can't be pro-Soviet after that. Secondly, during my life with Peretz and he was suffering and was always so terribly anti-Soviet, so of course it made an impression on me."

Life was different in Israel, but much better than in the Soviet Union. They arrived relatively late in life: "We wasted our life there . . . Perhaps not all, but part of it." Of course there are aspects of Russian life that she likes: from the ice skaters to the great musicians, to the various achievements of the country. These are all positive aspects of life there. "As to Israel, I know it much better now than when I came here. I was more idealistic when I came . . . I don't know. If I didn't arrange my life well, it was no one's fault. I have already lived my life. It's too late to come here at [nearly] sixty."

What does she think about having chosen Israel over America? She is not sure. "I've never been there, but I think that at the moment they are very weak, perhaps because they are democratic. For example, what's going on with Ayatollah Khomeini? To my mind, America should have interfered a long time ago [militarily]. But the people, they vote for Jimmy Carter." She wonders if democracy isn't over-rated. "I personally think it is the best, but when a democracy can't stand up against a dictatorship, I don't know which is stronger."

She has a problem with Soviet Jews emigrating to America, or even to Germany. They don't have such an easy life either, she feels, but she is uneasy about their leaving the Soviet Union for a destination other than Israel. "I think that Russia should allow only those Jews to go away who want to settle

in Israel. That is my opinion. . . It is not right, perhaps, but I think so. Because
it is not just; it isn't fair, if they go there and we come here. Do you see? It's
not the same life that opens up; it's quite different." Tania never considered
any other country when she left Russia. "No, even if it is bad, well if you have
to perish, you have to perish, but here is our homeland. The second point is:
Jews have no other countries. . . Maybe I'll change my opinion by the time
you publish your book because, no—you're not going to publish it today?"

As far as Israel is concerned, she has various perceptions. On the one hand,
she is disappointed that people are so materialistic in Israel, although the Russians are no better. But she does appreciate the positive aspects. "I didn't have
such great expectations regarding Israel. You see, that's the point. I didn't
want to go for a long time because I was afraid of Israel . . . I hadn't been
such an ardent Zionist and I've become more here than I was because I see
very many good points here."

Tania is baffled by Israeli politics, disappointed in the financial scandals
and isn't sure who could offer a better government. "Begin's government is
still good because another one could be worse." About the recent treaty with
Egypt, she says, "It's a very good thing in general, I think. It's correct. But
what is to come of it? And now the way the Arabs behave. Well, of course,
they want their rights. . . I understand it. But it's really difficult for Israel to
give away everything, and Jerusalem, part of Jerusalem too?"

Socially she finds that it is much more pleasant in Israel than in Russia. She
has many good neighbors—though not all—and she says that she has "never
lived among such intelligent people as I do here." In Riga she had never been
friendly with the Latvians. She had never had a personal encounter with antisemitism but had always been aware of it. On the other hand, she doesn't
know proper *ivrit* (Hebrew) and in many ways remains a foreigner in Israel.
"I knew beforehand it would be difficult. It's a new life, isn't it?"

Peretz, ever the dreamer, is also a realist. Living in Israel is the culmination
of his lifelong hopes. Living in Jerusalem also brings him down to earth, to a
real country, not just a heavenly city.

From one point of view, he says, he would have been better off in the
States: he could have made a better career there. "I am a gifted man. I have
not learned so much, but my experience is very broad in all directions."
There were more limited opportunities in Israel for him. "I cannot say that
I am happy, two hundred percent . . . I've got a position. It was not what I
expected. . . . And when I began, I was not so young. . . but I have my bread
now; I have my position. My work is not so bad. I'd like to do greater things:
I wish to be a minister—no good!" he added, with his endearing brand of humor. "But my place is Palestine [among] Jews. Why not? Why did the *halut-
zim* [pioneers] or friends of mine, the soldiers, go here and live in tents? No, I

had no question, never. It was no problem for me. And also today [although] I know that I can make a better career in the States, maybe."

For Peretz, though, the single most significant thing is that he is here, in Jerusalem and that is what he has always wanted. "Here Shabbes [the Sabbath] is Shabbes! Here is the Kotel! [the Western Wall] Here is Jerusalem! What do I need?" He goes on almost lyrically, "My life is not so bad, you know. I am here. My friends are here. I come home in the evening. Comes Shabbat, you see, it is so quiet and all . . . and you are able to pray. Maybe you'd rather go to a football match. For me it is better to go to pray, to go to the Kotel."

The impression was certainly one of contentment. Peretz and Tania had even managed to take trips to Europe, sometimes "camping out" in their car. They are no strangers to economizing, to carefully scrimping in order to eke out life's pleasures. In explaining his feelings about being in Israel, Peretz recalls the night that they arrived here, a few years ago. "When I came to Israel, when I saw at the airport it was written 'Israel' I began to cry. . . We came in the evening, maybe at night, I don't know. We came from London . . . And I began to cry and a little girl looked: why are you crying? And I didn't cry with my voice, without a voice, but it was so . . . and it went on for ten minutes . . . Israel, ours! And now, when I am telling you this story, you see, I also have tears."

Chapter Seven

America

BACKGROUND

The United States has been a magnet for immigration since its colonial beginnings. This was true not only for settlers from the British Isles, but also gradually from across Europe and, later, Asia, regardless of ethnic, social or cultural background. People were motivated for a wide variety of reasons, whether through a longing for religious or political freedom, or a need to escape a situation of economic distress or, perhaps, simply a sense of adventure and an eye for opportunity.

The Jews of the Russian empire were not the first to reach America's shores. They had been preceded long before by Sephardic Jews from Holland and England and, later, by Jews leaving German-speaking lands in the middle of the nineteenth century. At first, Sephardic Jews had come over in relatively small numbers and settled in New York and New England, but also in the South and as far as the Louisiana Territory. Later came the German-speaking Jews, many of whom left the east coast and headed inland, where they often started out as peddlers, but eventually built up businesses all over the mid-West. So there was already a nucleus of Jews in the United States when the early immigrants from the Russian empire started to arrive in the 1880s.

It was in the aftermath of the assassination of Alexander II in March 1881 that a series of pogroms shocked the Jewish communities of the empire, destroying their fragile sense of security and their faith in a better future. From the towns and townlets of New Russia in the vast region north of the Black Sea all the way to Warsaw, that most European of cities, the "storms in the south" raised havoc in the generally quiet lives of the Jewish communities. Pondering the question of how to ensure their own safety and that of future generations, members of the great Jewish population that spread out into every corner of the Russian Pale of Settlement came up with various possible solutions to their dilemma. Some of the Jews of the empire espoused post-liberal ideologies and considered participating in political activity to bring about needed changes in the governing structure. Others were inspired by nationalist dreams which might lead them to Palestine or to some combination of nationalism and socialism to be developed within Russia itself. And some turned their thoughts towards America.

In the autumn of 1881 Charles Netter, sent by the Alliance Israélite Universelle in Paris, came to the Galician town of Brody to help organize the transport of thousands of Russian Jews who were flowing over the border into Austria-Hungary. From Brody they were put on trains that took them via Lemberg, Cracow and Berlin to Hamburg, where they boarded ships to take them to America. Jewish communities in the States galvanized their resources to help their fellow Jews out of their distress. An organization was founded for this purpose, HEAS, the Hebrew Emigrant Aid Society. But it eventually had to call for a stop to the immigration: the local Jewish communities found it too difficult to bear the burden of so many destitute people arriving at once.

This brought about only a temporary lull and by the 1890s, impressive numbers of "Russian" Jews were leaving the Pale of Settlement and heading for the "Promised Land" which, in their understanding was the *goldene medina*: America. By the end of the eighteen nineties, the number of Jews who had left during that decade was well over a quarter of a million. In the first decade of the twentieth century an even larger number—over 700,000—sought their future in the United States. The great influx was only slowed by the First World War and, later, by American legislation, which sought to stem the flow of immigration. By this time, Jews still managing to leave Eastern Europe had to seek other destinations.

For those who reached the American shores life was demanding, but gradually an infrastructure was put in place to help the new immigrant on his or her way to a better future. This largely took the form of a set of non-governmental institutions that, in some ways, mirrored the world of the *kehillot* that the emigrants had recently abandoned. In the various cities and towns where the Jews had formed a significant part of the population in the Russian empire the Jews, over time—and going well back to the Polish-Lithuanian state that had preceded Russian domination over the area—had developed an intricate umbrella of institutions that satisfied their multilayered needs. The *kehillah* had looked after community issues as diverse as the building of a new synagogue or the hiring of a rabbi to charities for poor brides or the establishment of a clinic or hospital.

In the American model, the web of community organizations was less intricate and covered fewer facets of life. Their funding also came from more limited sources and was less universally levied. However, the importance of the early support groups established by new immigrants from the Pale should not be underestimated. People from the same *shtetl* would form a *landsmanschaft*, a kind of mutual-help association. New immigrants who were *landsleit*—originally from the same place in Europe—would thus be helped upon arrival, given a small amount of money, or directed to a place where they could live. Perhaps a *landsman* would offer the newcomer a job or knew someone looking for an employee. Each group of new immigrants from the Russian empire also set up its own *khevra kadisha*, or burial society, and purchased plots in the vast cemeteries of Brooklyn or Queens for their membership. Indeed, a visit to some of these plots would show, in time, an entire *shtetl* buried side by side, as they had been together in life.

Earlier, the new arrivals received help from fellow Jews who had originated in the German-speaking countries and had already assimilated. These "uptown" Jews would come down to the Lower East Side where the Russian Jews were crowded into tenements and provide social and financial help of various kinds. Coming from a different geographical and linguistic background, they nevertheless felt it their duty to help their fellow-Jews. But there was often a feeling of differentiation between "them" and "us." Once the East European Jews got their own organizations in place they felt more comfortable dealing with each other.

Eventually, the Jewish immigrants who had arrived before the First World War found their places in American society, moved out of the Lower East Side whether uptown, to Brooklyn, to the suburbs or even further. They and their children and grandchildren proved to be one of the great success stories of the United States as an immigrant country.

The next large Jewish group—and the last one before the immigration of the 1970s—to reach America was the one that left war-torn Europe at the end of the Second World War. Suddenly there appeared in New York (and other places) a new cluster of immigrants, this time the remnants of the great Jewish communities of Europe, people who had, miraculously, survived the Holocaust. These were individuals who had gone through the terrible years of the war, the bombings, incarceration, fleeing, hiding, doing anything possible if only to survive.

In comparison to the previous waves, the immigrants of the 1970s, leaving the Soviet Union by train or plane, first selling their apartments or cars—if they owned them—before departure, packing family possessions, often furniture and photographs, books and pianos, were a completely new phenomenon. These people were neither penniless and unworldly folk trying to start a new life nor fragmented individuals seeking peace and quiet, a refuge. On the contrary: the new group often represented well-educated and highly qualified members of their former society. While not all of them had lived privileged lives, and certainly not materially satisfying lives on a Western model, many had indeed been in the upper economic and professional echelons of Soviet society. Their expectations and demands were higher than those of the people who had arrived at the end of the nineteenth century or in the middle of the twentieth. The level of life that they had lived—if not in all its facets—was on a par with colleagues in the United States.

This does not obviate the fact that most of the new immigrants arrived at their destination with little or no money and would have to endure a precarious economic situation until they could organize decent jobs—if they could. Coming from the comparatively protective social environment of the Soviet Union, they had never had to compete in the market place for work. They lacked the sophistication and skills known to any American who had ever had to make a living, even a high school or college student who sought a summer job. The process of looking for employment that involved the composition and presentation of a well-organized resumé, going through the interview process or simply chasing down a good job advertised in the newspapers was a skill to be learned.

America might be the land of plenty, with no waiting lines and everything you might possibly desire readily available in the shops, but it could also have its drawbacks. All those wonderful things cost money. Medical care was on a very high standard, but it wasn't free. Medical insurance cost a fortune. Cars might be cheap, but insurance wasn't. Gas was very inexpensive, but repairs could cost plenty.

Furthermore, the new immigrants lacked language. Few of the people emigrating from the Soviet Union spoke fluent—if any—English. Few—if any—of the people in the various Jewish organizations, government offices, employment companies or social services could speak to them in Russian. It might be the Golden Land, but it wasn't going to be easy. They may have been grateful that the gates were open, but they would have to deal with the difficulties of a new life largely on their own.

After a lifetime of being told what to do, which direction to take, what was permitted and what was not, the Soviet emigrants found that now they had many decisions to make on their own between the time of their initial decision—to leave—and over the months or years when they were finally settled in their new homes. Should they settle in New York or would another, less populated city, give them more opportunities or a better environment for the family? Should they look up relatives and see if they could help, perhaps try to live near them? Rumors were rampant. Letters and information went back and forth feverishly with friends and family who had already made the leap. Often what those letters said was the decisive factor. At other times, the new immigrants were gently nudged toward a city whose name they only vaguely knew, but where there was a promise of a supportive community and the possibility of making a livelihood. Sometimes successfully settling into the right community was a matter of pure luck.

SERAFIMA

Serafima and Tamara ended up in the United States—which had not been their first choice—and in Buffalo, because Tamara was afraid of living in New York City. Serafima was happy to let her daughter make the decision. They were faced with a number of problems upon arrival. First, they knew no English. Second, while Tamara had a few Soviet certificates in health care, none of her diplomas were recognized in New York State and she could thus not be hired as a nurse. It is probable that had they realized in Italy that she would not be able to pursue her profession in America they would have held out for another country.

For Serafima, her professional life had not worked out either. There seemed to be no opportunities for her to play her keyboard instrument with an orchestra as she had in Leningrad. She might have tried to teach, had she known English. She thus ended up with no professional life. But, once in Buffalo, Serafima did not consider another move. She simply settled in. Mother and daughter were placed in a residential hotel on a pleasant shady street. English lessons were offered to both, but Serafima, in the beginning, did not take them. "I felt that I was no one . . . a feeling that my life was over. That's not just me; it's like that for all Soviets."

In the beginning, the Jewish Federation of Buffalo helped the two women with services and financial aid. Afterward, Serafima was on Welfare. She devoted herself to running their little household, thus helping Tamara to establish herself in her field. One day, Serafima went out shopping for food. She was very careful to budget their tiny income frugally and was pleased to find an inexpensive package of food, which she brought home. They ate it, not realizing that she had bought cat food. "I can tell you that food for animals is better here than what [people] ate there."

Their luck changed with the appearance of two people. First, the Davis family came to their help, having heard that Serafima and Tamara were new immigrants in their midst. They provided material help when it was needed— clothing, shoes—and also friendship. The family continued to remain in touch with the two women over the years. They were real friends.

The second person to play an important role in their lives was an architect who had designed Roswell Park, the local cancer hospital. He had come in from New York and heard that there were recent arrivals from the Soviet Union in Buffalo. He himself had immigrated to the United States at the time of the Second World War and—wonder of wonders!—he spoke Russian. Through his hospital connections he helped Tamara to find work, at last. Although her qualifications were not recognized and she could not work as a nurse, she did succeed in finding part-time laboratory work in General Hospital. Needless to say, her pay was low, but this was a beginning.

In the middle of the nineteen seventies, Serafima and Tamara traveled to Israel, to see their family there. Her nephew—the one who had seen to their receiving official invitations back when they were trying to leave the Soviet Union—had been a champion wrestler in the USSR. Now he was a gym teacher in Tel Aviv. He loved Israel and felt very positive about living there. But by this time, Serafima and Tamara gave no thought to coming to settle in Israel. They had already made friends in Buffalo, learned English and couldn't imagine moving and making another start.

Back in Buffalo, however, Tamara continued to have difficulty finding a good full-time job. The truth is that the economic situation in Buffalo had, over the years, been somewhat depressed and the city had never really recovered from the closing down or re-location of some of its big industries. So Tamara started to send out far-flung applications to various hospitals and received a number of invitations. She decided to take her chances in Seattle and, leaving her mother in Buffalo, set off for the Pacific area. She wouldn't be alone there, as she had at least two first cousins who had moved to Seattle from the Soviet Union. Tamara was delighted with her new career, which involved working with children. According to Serafima, Tamara was living in a comfortable apartment and had her own car and she lived very much "*po-amerikanski.* "

As for Serafima, she prefers to remain in Buffalo, in the residential hotel where she was originally placed. By the time of the interview, in 1981, she could talk with pleasure about the number of friends she has. Not all of them are originally from the Soviet Union. One, Carmen, is from Peru; another, Mrs. Davis, one of the first Buffalonians to befriend her in the early seventies was going to take her to see a ballet the next day at Art Park, a large cultural center outside of Buffalo. In addition, Serafima, as would be hoped, attends many concerts and musical performances and knows various members of the Buffalo Philharmonic Orchestra.

Even in her sixties Serafima is working, if not in the field of music. She is involved in caring for patients at night, bathing them, changing their bandages—know-how that she acquired at the front, in Leningrad, during the

Second World War. Who would have believed, she says, that these skills would be useful again? The work she does enables her to send occasional packages to her family back in the Soviet Union.

Serafima has tried to keep in touch with her twin daughters, inside the USSR, but it is complicated. One of her daughters works at a secret aviation factory and she is afraid of jeopardizing her job. There is no privacy on the phone lines and everything has to be done indirectly, or by innuendo. Once, when she asked her daughter Zinochka if she would be coming to the United States, she answered, "Mama: I can't." And then the phone was disconnected. Serafima hadn't even been able to go to Bashkiria to say good-bye to her daughters: she didn't have enough money for the trip out there.

Serafima also does volunteer work, helping out newcomers in Buffalo, people who are starting out as she and her daughter did eight years before. She helps them to orient themselves, telling them where the local school is, helping them with shopping, seeing what the prices are, explaining about pounds versus kilos and, above all, making sure that they don't accidentally buy cat food for themselves.

When asked about her income—received from SSI—Serafima commented that this was not a question usually asked in America. However, she happily communicated that she got regular payments into her bank account of about $347 a month. The sum is increased from time to time. Her rent was recently raised to eighty-one dollars per month, which still leaves her, she says, ample money for her expenses. "I live like a princess," she declares. "Who would have thought that I would have an old age like this?"

ISAAC

A year after arriving in Israel, Isaac and his wife Clara changed their minds and, together with their two daughters, Sophia and Mila, packed their bags and came to the United States. At the time they did so, they were among the first—perhaps the very first—of the new wave of immigrants to settle in Buffalo. They were directed to an apartment hotel and looked after by the local Jewish community.

As a welder, Isaac was far better off than many of his university-educated or professional fellow immigrants. He easily found decent employment, just as he had in Haifa. Work was never a problem for him. Mila was still in high school and Sophia—with her eye towards studying for a B.A.—enrolled in a language institute for foreign students at the university and took evening courses. She first had to finish up certain high school requirements and only then could proceed to her B.A., gradually increasing the number of courses she was taking. She would eventually become the first person in her family with a university degree.

Mila was not oriented towards education. She and Sophia form a contrast, though the sisters are close. Sophia says that she herself was never very good at making friends: "I have friends, but a few friends, and I have a lot of acquaintances, but I'm not a party kind." Mila, on the other hand, is very outgoing and sociable. She was only twenty years old when she got married, in Buffalo, in 1977. Her husband was a tailor, also originally from the Soviet Union, and made a decent living. A few years later he decided to sell his business and the couple moved down to Florida with their son. He had an occupation that was easily transferable.

The family soon became a magnet to newcomers as the number of Soviet immigrants in Buffalo grew in the mid-1970s. Isaac helped out in every way he could, especially if the new family came from Odessa. He was a source of great strength to them and helped them over the first difficult period of settling in. They formed life-long friendships with many of the people who were arriving in Buffalo in those years.

At the time of the interview, in the summer of 1981, the family was living in a very comfortable, decently furnished house. Isaac remained the principal breadwinner and Clara continued to suffer from chronic health problems. Isaac and his older daughter Sophia—who were the two actually interviewed—both seemed pleased with their present lives and the direction they had taken. Then the conversation turned to their departure from Israel. Did his wife feel any better in the United States than in Israel? "She didn't feel very good [there] and now she doesn't feel good here, just the same," Isaac replied. Part of their rationale for leaving was Clara's health: she had pushed for it. There had also been the factor of their friends' decision to leave. Isaac, when asked if he would have preferred to stay, replies, "I would go [back there] now." He goes on: "For almost nine years I am asking a question—why I am here?"

"But you've got a beautiful home."

"I don't care for this. I would leave today."

"Do you think that there are a lot of Russians like you?"

Sophia: "Only those that came from Israel to the United States. . . Only those that were in Israel already and came to the United States ask themselves the question why they left. . . It's just a feeling that you have . . . that you're at home, that you belong there and you're home."

LUNA

Of all the people interviewed, Luna was, perhaps, the spunkiest, the most energetic, the most ambitious of the new immigrants. She was enterprising and innovative, goal-oriented and capable of achieving her aims. That said, her goals were modest and within her grasp. She had a realistic understanding of her abilities and adapted well to the demands of the market. This was something that she had understood in the Soviet Union and knew, too, in America: how to survive.

When they arrived in Buffalo, Luna and Sam (his American name) and their twelve year old son were put up in the same residential hotel where Serafima and Tamara were staying. Within only a month they had managed to move, having found a pleasant three-bedroom apartment. They were given furniture, towels, bedding, everything by the community. "I still use everything they gave me; I still have all the furniture in my house."

In discussing their first days in Buffalo, during the first interview in the summer of 1982, Luna singled out one family of recent immigrants who were an enormous source of help. She talked about the kindness of Isaac and his family: "I'll never forget the goodness of [that] family. Never, because they were the first ones who called us when we were in the hotel . . . They heard about a new family, from Odessa, and they gave us a call, just like that." Isaac's family helped with "the first steps, they just helped us to make those first steps. That . . . will never be forgotten, never."

Both Clara and Isaac helped, but so did Sophia. She helped with the "language, translating, and all these letters. You know, now we understand it's a lot of junk there, but [in the beginning] anything you get in your mail you just go crazy: 'what's this, what's that' and you think it's very important." In the Soviet Union they hadn't received the kind of advertisements and junk mail that arrived daily in America. "Then you start to run all over the place, to find someone who can explain it to you. . . it's a cemetery lot for sale and you don't know [until someone tells you] 'Oh, throw it in the garbage!'"

Both Sam and Luna are very down to earth. They had marketable skills and neither was choosy in the beginning about work conditions or pay. The main thing was to be employed and to start bringing home a pay check. After about two and a half months Sam found a job. He was the first to succeed. Until that time, the Jewish Federation was helping out economically: they paid the rent, the utility and telephone bills, and gave them money for food. No limit had been placed on the length of time Luna and Sam would receive support, and the couple did not feel pressured.

With the help of his English teacher, Sam had found his first job, at a knitting mill, through the newspaper. Until this, both husband and wife had been studying English at an adult education center in the morning. The job lasted for six months and then Sam was laid off, but he received unemployment checks for a couple of months after that. Then he managed to find another job, more permanent, again through the newspaper. He knew machines well and, after all, "a sewing machine is a sewing machine."

Luna decided to look first for a modest job and, instead of demanding a starting salary of five dollars per hour, she began as an alteration girl at a small, well-established department store away from the downtown shops at $2.35 an hour, for only two days a week. An excellent seamstress, she was promoted and was soon working four days a week. She worked with a woman whose husband was director of the training center at the company where Sam now worked. Sam mentioned Luna to this man and explained that his wife was a talented engineer/designer and had worked as a technology engineer at a Soviet fashion house before emigrating, with one hundred twenty people working under her.

The director of training then offered Luna a job, so she left her seamstress work and moved to the company where Sam was employed. She soon mastered eleven different operations at the clothing factory and worked as a utility operator, substituting for various people when they were out sick or on leave. By now she was doing well, knowing many of the jobs at the factory, and was then offered a job as an instructor at the training center. She succeeded in passing the requisite tests in English and math and was second highest among some dozen women who were tested. For almost three years she worked as an instructor.

The trouble began in 1979 when the new director of training discovered that she was an engineer and encouraged her to be tested for an engineering job. Luna was only too happy to do that. But while she passed the tests, she was somehow never given the new job. They kept promising, but never came through and she became impatient. In the meantime, a fellow Soviet immigrant whom she knew—a tailor by profession—decided to move to Florida and offered her the opportunity to buy his shop. (This was Isaac's son-in-law.) Luna checked into the economics of the enterprise and realized that the engineering position, while a better job, would potentially give her less money than a tailoring business. Still, Luna felt convinced that she would rather work as an engineer: it was something that she loved. The tailor, who was about to leave, pressured her—he had to arrange things before he left in a month or so. Luna went to her immediate boss, Judy, and said, "Let me talk to the plant manager to see what the chances are that I can get that engineering job." Judy replied, "Luna, I have very bad news for you. We just hired a boy for an engineer." Luna couldn't understand it. "That hurt me so bad. And was I happy when I could [say] at the same minute: I have worse news for you—I'm quitting."

Luna found it hard to accept that only men (or boys, as she put it) were given engineering jobs. She felt that it could certainly not have happened in Russia. "You're absolutely sexless there. You can take any position you want. Really."

It was this policy of the management that resolved Luna to go into business for herself, a decision that she does not regret. Buying the tailoring business meant that she was purchasing his equipment and hoping to keep his clientele. Having no ready cash, they had to borrow money, and Luna's very closest friends—who lived over the border in Canada—came to their aid. It was an informal arrangement. Her friend's husband told her to return the money— interest free—whenever she felt comfortable doing so. "That's what you call friends," Luna says. It took her a little less than a year to repay the entire loan.

When she first took over the shop, Luna saw a man walk in, look around, and start to walk out again. He was looking for a man tailor. To encourage him, she suggested that she would mend his garment but that if he wasn't satisfied, he wouldn't have to pay for the work. She wanted to prove that she was a good tailor. (She calls herself a tailorette, as, she says, a seamstress is thought of as working on women's clothing.) He and his family became very good customers after that.

Financially, opening her own tailoring business was a good move. She and Sam, within six years of arriving in Buffalo, bought their first house. Without her work, it would have taken much longer. She's very proud of that house.

Luna closes her shop for Jewish holidays and attends a synagogue (though they are not members). Their son, eighteen at the time of the interview in the summer of 1982, stays home from school for the holidays. "He is more of a Jew than we are," says Luna. ". . . In feeling a Jew. He's more devoted to that. He knows more than us."

While their son Jerry did not have a bar mitzvah (which would have been quite soon after their arrival in America), he was circumcised when he was twelve. This was his choice. At the time, he was attending a Jewish day school in Buffalo. He went to the hospital for the procedure, with a Jewish doctor and a rabbi participating. The next day he went home, still in pain. Luckily, Isaac—who was always happy to help—came to pick him up in his car, pulling up as close to the hospital as he could so that the boy wouldn't have far to walk.

Luna worries about the prospect of having a daughter-in-law who isn't Jewish some day. Jerry has already had a non-Jewish girlfriend, and it hurt her. Recently, they went to a beautiful Jewish wedding in Toronto and everyone, she says, was so relaxed and happy. A year before they had attended a mixed wedding, with a rabbi, but the groom wasn't Jewish. "I tell you, it was very tense."

Jerry has become very Americanized and speaks English without an accent. In fact, he doesn't tell people that he's from Russia, although that is still the language of the household. Luna and Sam brought a large Russian library with them, all the classics. "That's all I had in my luggage." But her son doesn't read them. He does his reading in English. "He doesn't even eat with us anymore. He eats all American food." Luna's mother does a lot of the cooking and she prepares traditional Russian food. But Jerry prefers chicken wings, hamburgers, pizza. He just graduated from a public suburban high school and has a mix of Jewish and Christian friends. He has been accepted to study architecture at RPI in the fall and has received a good scholarship as well as $4,500 in student loans. Sam and Luna will have to make up the difference of $2,500 every year, but they think that they can manage it. Perhaps Jerry will get a student job as well.

Jerry will be coming home for Thanksgiving and Christmas, of course. "But first he says he's going to be home for Yom Kippur." They will buy tickets for the services. Luna had never heard a shofar blown before coming to America. "That's why it's so hard for me to pretend that I am an all-Jewish girl, you know, because I don't know. I don't know Jewish history. I'm picking it up right now."

One year after Luna arrived in America her mother came. She had found it very hard to be so far from her only daughter and grandson. Her husband suggested that she go and that he would follow when he reached age sixty-five. He wanted to continue to work as a barber until then. It was clear to him that if he came to the States in his sixties he would never find employment there. As it happened, Luna's mother, who arrived in her early sixties, immediately found work as a manicurist and was thus able to earn money and not be too much of a burden. She was very happy—and still is—to be with her daughter and see her grandson grow up. Unfortunately, her husband reached retirement age two years ago, but still has not received permission to leave. This was something that they had not foreseen.

The emigration from the Soviet Union came to an abrupt diminution at the end of 1979. There was a diplomatic crisis as a result of the December Soviet invasion of Afghanistan: the SALT II talks ended without an agreement; the United States and other countries refused to participate in the Moscow Olympic Games in the summer of 1980; in a word, the period of détente with the West had come to an end. Concomitantly, Soviet emigration policy changed and the number of people permitted to leave was reduced to half and then by half again the following year.

Luna's father had been caught up in all of this. "It's very heartbreaking; very hard. . . she's crying and it's very heartbreaking. . . I think we all . . . we all made a mistake. . . We shouldn't have separated them." The plans are that when he finally does arrive, the older couple will move into their own place together. Luna's mother is on a waiting list for an apartment through the Jewish Federation. The building is under construction now.

All in all, the impression is that Luna was happy with her work, her family, and with Buffalo. She has visited other places—Toronto, New York, San Francisco—"We went there, lovely, beautiful, but, I don't know—you'll probably laugh at me, but I love Buffalo."

VALENTINA

Valentina and Roman came straight to Buffalo with their children. It was quite clear during the interview in the early 1980s that he was far more upbeat than she about the immigration experience. While Valentina says that she can't believe it, Roman insists that in the four years since they left he hasn't once thought about his former life in the Soviet Union. Valya says that it is impossible simply to cross out your whole past life.

As might have been expected, she misses the house in Belaia Tserkov that her grandfather built. With time some of the pain has receded. Oddly, she misses her mother as well. This is somewhat surprising, given that she and her mother had never had a close relationship. She cannot explain it, but there it is.

Throughout the interview, Roman energetically interposes, takes over the conversation, corrects or amends what Valentina has said. While Roman enthusiastically explains how busy they are—work, children—Valentina returns to the subject of her sadness. "Sadness, all the same. When I said in the beginning that nevertheless half of a life, more than half, was spent in Russia. . . But time is already continually smoothing out, and already events that have happened here are taking over so that—it's not that you forget [the old events], but somehow they are distanced, a little secondary."

Roman agrees that not everything has been easy, but they had been prepared for this. There have been problems in finding work, for example. They have had to contend with the difficulties of a new language, which were far greater than they would have imagined. Four years after emigrating, the interview was still necessarily carried on in Russian. On the other hand, Roman points out, in no other country would they have received the help that they have here. The Jewish Federation has been outstanding. The government paid for Valentina's course in English. During their first six months in Buffalo they received a great deal of help, including food stamps and whatever household utensils they needed.

According to Soviet law, it was impossible to take money out of the country or exchange it for another currency. As they had a large quantity of cash after selling the house in Belaia Tserkov, they spent it on furniture, which was then shipped. They had also bought various souvenirs and other items that might be marketable and sold them in Italy during their stay near Rome. That permitted them to buy other goods there which they would be able to use in whatever home they would have in the future. Most of the furniture and dishes in their house come from the Soviet Union (or Italy). While they had a comfortable home in America, they, of all the emigrants interviewed, did not feel that they had improved their domicile by leaving the Soviet Union.

There was also a mixed picture in their present employment. Roman had, luckily, started working in his field as a dental technician within two months of their arrival. But the situation was much more complicated for Valentina. In order to work as a dentist in New York State, she would have to pass a set of examinations to re-qualify. In the meantime, her English is nowhere close to a level that would enable her to do this and language isn't the only problem in taking a test. Beyond that, she is the mother of a small child. Whether she will ever manage is a question. Valentina herself says that she fears she lacks the determination to go through with such a laborious process. In the beginning, just to help the family income, she even did babysitting. Now she works in a laboratory, full time, earning five dollars an hour, forty hours a week. Together with this salary, she has the usual rights accruing to a regular job—a pension, vacations and sick leave.

As far as Roman in concerned, things are going very well and they manage adequately on their salaries. They have already bought themselves a new car, a washing machine, a television set—their standard of living, he says, is clearly higher. They pay one hundred eighty dollars a month for rent for their two-bedroom apartment. Occasionally they manage to go out to a restaurant or to a movie, something they had little opportunity to do in Russia because Roman worked so hard and everything there was so much more complicated.

The couple agrees that life in Buffalo has less tension, that they have a calmer existence. To illustrate the difference in her life as a housewife in America and in the Soviet Union, Valentina explains that when she leaves work in Buffalo she can easily pick up whatever she needs on the way home and prepare dinner in a short time. Back in Belaia Tserkov it might take hours to collect the various products necessary for the household. She could find herself waiting in long lines at a number of stalls or shops—one for bread, another for cheese, yet another selling fresh fruits and vegetables (of which there would be only a meager choice).

They have managed to travel a bit, of course visiting Canada, which is just on the other side of the border. They have also been to Baltimore, where an old and dear friend of Valentina's moved to after they had left the Soviet Union.

Their daughter, Marina, is already a university student in Buffalo. Their little boy, Sasha, is in a Kadima school, a Jewish day school. They are very pleased with it. As it is a private school, they do have to pay, but not fully: the tuition is subsidized. According to them, as the Buffalo Jewish community is relatively small, it cannot afford to cover the costs completely as some communities do in other cities, but the subsidy helps. Valentina disagrees with Roman that they can manage on the two salaries they now receive and feels that paying for the children's education is—or will become—a problem.

For Roman, his chief goal is: "We want to make our children good people, give them a good education. I want her to have eight years of school, then four, then more. I want him to go to a good school." His mother has left the Soviet Union and is also living in Buffalo. She receives a pension, has an apartment. "Only in America! Only because I loved this country. I understand: it's difficult. Everywhere it's like that. And I love it and want my children to be patriots of this country. Freedom: it's a great thing!" And is he free here? "Yes, of course! . . . I can leave tomorrow and go to another city. I can say what I want. Do you understand?"

MARK AND BRONIA

Mark and Bronia had only arrived in the States six months before their interview in July, 1980. Mark already had a job and Bronia was still at home, looking after their two daughters. But she assumed that she would look for work soon: she had worked all her life and was used to it.

Mark and Bronia received a lot of help from the community when they arrived. For the first half year Jewish Community Services paid for the rent on their three-bedroom apartment, for example. During that first half year, the couple also took advantage of the opportunity to take English lessons. He studied in a school in downtown Buffalo together with Russians and Poles, Vietnamese and Chinese. Everything in their apartment was given by the community, free. Mark and Bronia hadn't expected this. They had assumed that they would be provided with things that they would then slowly have to pay for.

In leaving the Soviet Union they had been very limited in what they could bring, for various reasons. They felt that the furniture that they already had would probably be unsuitable for an American home. Buying new furniture would have been difficult in Soviet conditions. Given the chronic shortages of many consumer products, items were not readily available in Soviet stores. Everything on display requires a waiting list and they did not have time. Limited in what they could send, they shipped their piano. Tanya is ten years old and has been taking piano lessons for the past two years. Their piano just arrived a month ago.

For the rest, they brought with them only what they could pack into their suitcases—clothing, linens, cutlery. They brought no books, hoping that Bronia's parents would send them afterwards. And they brought almost no photographs.

Only a month before the interview, Mark had started to work. He was aided in his search for a job by an extraordinary man, Joe Malek, who was extremely kind and helpful to the new immigrant community. They had met him through another family. These people had a house that had burned down and he had come to their aid. They suggested that Mark turn to him for help in locating a job. Mr. Malek's parents had left Russia around the time of the First World War and he himself had been born in the United States. At sixty, and comfortably off, he was able to spare the time to help others. He knew the owner of the factory where Mark started to work. They manufactured hospital beds and Mark is working as an engineer there, though his work is less demanding and creative than what he had done in Minsk. On the other hand, he is receiving a much higher salary in Buffalo and is enjoying a higher standard of living. It would have been impossible in Minsk for the family to exist on his salary alone. Though they are managing that now, Bronia assumes that their needs will rise and that an extra salary—from her—will become necessary.

Mark finds the system of locating a job very difficult and complex in America. You have to send in a resumé and then wait, often for some time, to be contacted, interviewed and informed of the decision. He complains that this is a long process. In fact, it was because Mark had sent in his resumé to various places of employment and received no positive responses that in desperation he finally turned to Mr. Malek. "It was his concern, his energy, his understanding of our immigrant problems" that resulted in a successful outcome to Mark's job search. In the Soviet Union, things are much simpler. You are more or less told immediately if you've been accepted.

Mark feels that it is very important, as a new immigrant, to get on your feet as soon as possible. Not only is it good for you, but once you have work, you also free up the community money so that it can be spent on others in need. He wishes that American enterprises understood immigrants better and offered them jobs more readily.

The family joined a synagogue in Buffalo quite soon—the reform temple, Beth Zion. They were the first to invite the family and so that is where they went. One of the affiliated families befriended them and has been very helpful as problems and questions arise. Community and friends are very important for this family and they are extremely appreciative of the help that has been proffered. Already, in this short time, they have made friendships and visited people's homes. Of course, there is a language barrier, but they somehow manage.

When asked of his initial impressions of the democratic system, Mark is at a loss. He has not yet participated in an American election and those in the Soviet Union "are an empty formality." But in America there is a major difference. "Though I have to say that it's more that I have the impression of what I had known earlier . . . but I'd like to know, now that I'm here, it's natural to understand, but I still can't understand in the deepest sense what it's all about. Do you understand? For me it's difficult—that people themselves elect the president and have the ability to choose him directly without any preliminary selection [by the authorities]. . ." It was simply impossible for Mark to conceive of voters choosing a representative, even a president (ignoring here the niceties of the electoral college system) by themselves, based on whether that person directly corresponds to their own set of priorities.

He recalls how difficult it had been earlier in the Soviet Union to obtain any kind of reliable information about life abroad. "People listened to the BBC . . . the Voice of America. But earlier they only had one-sided information, because there was no" possibility of foreign travel, of obtaining outside information, of going abroad or writing to one's relatives there. Only the most privileged were permitted travel outside the borders of the U.S.S.R. With their present language limitations, it will be some time before the couple becomes adequately informed in their own new country.

Mark, however, is very upbeat about the choice that they made. "Here in the States there's the possibility of realizing your desires. There, if you want to fulfill your desires, it's a dark path. Here, it's a light, direct path." He recognizes the irony of the situation. "The paradox here is that you know what all the possibilities are. You may want to improve your situation, live in a better place, travel. You need money for all that."

What about the quality of life here? Is this a good place to bring up your daughters? "For me, the big thing always was—if my daughters asked me, living in the Soviet Union, what I asked my grandmother: why am I a Jew?" Mark wanted to get his children out of a situation where they would be second-class citizens. Excluded from celebrating your own holidays and customs you became alienated from the national holidays. "You cease to be a person. . . .[you are] gnawed by the feeling that you are not a complete human being. Do you understand? . . . in my view, nothing has improved in the [Soviet] attitude toward Jews; the situation has only deteriorated." He says that the Soviet denial that there is any antisemitism in itself presents a difficulty. "If they don't recognize that there's a problem, they can't do anything about correcting it." The biggest thing, for Mark, is that the weight of his national heritage has been lifted and he feels now that it is not so bad to be a Jew. "A Jew can do and be whatever he wants here."

It may be that migration was much harder on women for a variety of reasons. A woman had to get used to new living conditions and achieve in her new home an approximation of the familial and familiar comfort the family experienced in its former existence. She had to get used to new products, make use of different ingredients in her cooking, adjust herself to what is acceptable in child-rearing, diet, style in the new country. Her husband was most likely to be the first one back in the labor force and making his own adjustments. If she stayed at home, the woman probably had less social intercourse, made fewer contacts and might be slower at mastering the new language. If she did find employment, it was probably on a lower level than what her husband had managed to find and also on a lower pay scale. This was certainly the case for many of the women interviewed here.

It may also be that emigration is a more painful experience for women, who are, perhaps, more attached to home and family. Leaving their loved ones—people whom they may never again see—is the source of great and often lasting sorrow, even if the migration brings them to a far better life, materially, politically or religiously.

Bronia, too, explained how sad it had been for her to leave. "Now, it's nothing. I've gotten used to it. Half a year has passed; I've calmed down a bit." Would she go through with the move again, knowing what she does now? Would she leave? "No, of course, I couldn't. Just one time, not more. To repeat all this would be very difficult. To part again, the difficult journey—it's hard to get used to things."

YAN

Yan says that he did not decide to leave the Soviet Union—he had wanted to live there but could not. He had been given the ultimatum that he could either be imprisoned or leave the Soviet Union. He thus left unwillingly and came to the United States without the clear motivation that others had. As a result, his entire outlook in the early period of his life as an émigré is in contrast with that of many of his fellow new immigrants.

At the time of the interview, in August, 1980, Yan had been out of the Soviet Union for a little over a year, including the two and a half months that he and his wife and son had waited near Rome for an entry visa. After starting out in Oakland, California, he had soon found a good position with a company in Silicon Valley and his family moved there. Yan is clearly a highly qualified physicist (specializing in semiconductors) and is earning a very satisfactory starting salary of $27,000. His present job is very interesting and he is satisfied with it—although he had also had a very good job in Kiev. Because his place of work is very security conscious—a visitor may not even enter the front office to speak to a receptionist—the interview took place sitting outside on the grass in the shade of a tree.

Yan has nothing to complain of in the reception that his family received in Oakland. The community was very warm and friendly and his son was enrolled in a Jewish school there. (Where they live now there is no Jewish school nearby.) Yan himself is not a believer, although he is thinking of going to synagogue for the High Holidays this year, just to see what a service is like. He has never been to one.

He finds it very difficult to get used to San Francisco. "Rome very quickly became my city. Yes, I could live there for years with pleasure. Not San Francisco. It doesn't look like a city. (I imagine that Jerusalem is like that too . . .) There are no courtyards. There are no passageways, no squares. In San Francisco I keep feeling I'm walking along a fence, someone's fence. . . It's hard after a city like Kiev."

The departure from the Soviet Union was so difficult for Yan that for the first half year after immigrating he didn't want to see anyone; he just wanted to rest from the ordeal that he had recently undergone in the Soviet Union. He has been satisfied to sit at home, read books, watch television, just to recover. He and his wife have no relatives in the United States, no friends. He did have a connection at Berkeley who had suggested some time before that there be cooperation between Yan's institute in Kiev and his own in California. This was the opening gambit by which Yan originally sought help. Through him and HIAS (the Hebrew Immigrant Aid Society) he arranged to find his first employment upon arrival in America.

Yan speaks to his son in Russian and hopes that the boy will grow up knowing Russian literature and reading the books that Yan had loved in his teens. He hopes that he will eventually be bi-lingual:

[Classical] Russian literature is good in that it allows the reader to look at a person honestly. It's bad in that . . . it is very much under the influence of Christianity. Christianity tries all the time to bring people nearer to the ideal. My personal point of view is that in general this is a flawed path, that it's simpler on the whole to form an understanding of the real person and say: yes, a human being is deceitful; yes, he doesn't like to work, yes, he likes money; yes, he likes many women! And to accept this as a starting premise and to live, only trying to understand others. But on one side of this understanding, I think, this is better expressed in Russian literature. And the other side is expressed in *other* literature. And I simply want [my son] to have his own, independent, view of things, independent of me too . . .

Yan's wife, Natasha is not satisfied with her life here so far. While she could not paint during the last three years of her life in the Soviet Union, she is at least now painting again. But, he says, she has a relatively empty life. She has no ties. They don't have any close friends. There is no feeling of satisfaction. Obviously, he says, if they were just interested in material goods, they'd be happy.

As an only child, Yan feels very responsible for his mother and stepfather. He is also concerned about his wife's parents. His mother has only one desire now, which blocks out everything else: to be near her son. He has written very honest letters to her, warning her of the difficulties. "I'm thirty and you're sixty. I work and you will not work. You don't speak English. You'll lose everything and find only me!" He wants them to think this over very carefully, because of all the inherent difficulties of emigration. His mother, he says, would like nothing better than to sit together with him all evening. The case of his parents-in-law is more complicated because they can't actually make up their minds about what they want.

He doesn't know yet what to make of the political process. He says that he has become quite conservative recently. Yan believes that capitalist society is for the person, much more than socialist society is. Capitalism is certainly the better system to live in. He feels that it is good that society is divided into classes, that there are rich and poor. "I think that the government has to help the rich and in this way help itself." He came to the conclusion, perhaps four years ago, while still in Kiev, that capitalist society is much more natural for human beings than is socialist society. Men are not created equal:

> Society has become divided: some became poor, other became wealthy. In capitalistic society—and we can't call it perfect because man is not perfect—in this society there are certain key factors which hold up society, natural linchpins. Why do I think they are natural? First, if you do not work here, you'll be in a bad way. Financially, that's the truth. In the beginning, I was terribly surprised that the chief executive of a big company works so hard. Why? He's so rich. He can travel, do everything that I can't do now! Why does he hang around work every day for ten hours? The company president—I've been working here half a year: he's never once taken off a weekend. . .I couldn't understand why. And the Americans explained it to me. It's very simple. If you yourself aren't going to work, then the business will go under.

Yan, in spite of the distress of the past few years, would like to make a go of it in America. He'd like to make the country his own, though he doesn't know yet how. While many people, especially former intelligentsia from the Soviet Union, criticize the United States for being a petty-bourgeois, philistine country, he disagrees. America, he says, has its own great artistic achievements. Europe has produced its music, literature and art out of suffering. America doesn't suffer from the past as Europe does. The average Americans, he says, don't want to sit around talking about the fate of man. They want to go to a restaurant, go to work. They don't know anything about geography. "They don't know what Ukraine is, even though it's home to fifty-six million people. That's normal! I want to say that it's good! They don't have to be interested in that!"

As in his other ideas, Yan's viewpoint is unique. While he feels great love for the place he came from he is very particular about what he means: "I very much love Russia, its nature. I love the city where I was born. I love my friends. I have a very local feeling in terms of my native land. It is a very little piece of Kiev and, maybe, fifteen people who live there. That is my whole native land! And all the rest—I don't love. Once, Bunin said 'I like a person, but I don't like people.' Now I know that I don't like these people, that I don't understand them and they certainly don't understand me." He wishes that he could see Russia as just some other country, like Hungary or Switzerland. Russia "was the source of anxiety and torment and I would be happy if that anxiety and torment were over. In general, of course, the best part of my life was spent there, but it's a very high price."

The people with whom he was close have had disparate fates. Three friends were arrested and are still in jail. One went to Israel, another to Germany. They had all been forced into political activity in the Soviet Union because of the exigencies of the time, and then everything followed from that. "And here we all are now, scattered, and not one of us can call himself happy, but this is not a reason to feel oneself happy here. What can one do?"

Part Four

TWENTY-FIVE YEARS LATER

Twenty-five years! So much can happen in such a time span. People are born, grow up, finish university, enter a profession, marry. All in twenty-five years. People can move, change their address, their career. They can meet and fall in love; they can divorce. People can die in that period, the rest of their story buried with them. All of this happened during the twenty-five years between the first interviews in the late 1970s and early 80s and the second interviews in the early twenty-first century.

In the two concluding chapters we will re-visit most of the people first seen residing in the Soviet Union, living their lives and ultimately deciding whether they should leave. Most of them remained in the countries to which they initially immigrated, but not all.

In this section, the stories of all of these immigrants continue, although for many they are far from complete. But the long-range results of that early decision to leave what was once home can now be seen. How did it all work out? Was the aim of making a better life for one's children successfully accomplished? Are there any regrets?

Here we are, like a twenty-first century Rip van Winkle, waking up after a quarter of a century and seeing what life has brought, what changes have come about.

Chapter Eight

In America,
Twenty-Five Years Later

BACKGROUND

Vast changes have taken place since the first set of interviews. The decades of the nineteen eighties and nineties witnessed unimaginable political developments in the Soviet Union and the socialist bloc, all of them influencing political, military, and economic policies in the rest of the world. Beginning with the reign of Mikhail Gorbachev in the mid-eighties, there was an increasing receptiveness to openness and new ideas in the Soviet Union. This included everything from suggestions for the improvement of the economy or the bureaucracy, to a re-interpretation of some aspects of Soviet history, the easing of censorship, and the plethora of new publications that now swamped the Soviet bookstalls and kiosks. By the autumn of 1989, the Berlin Wall had been brought down and the Soviet bloc was dissolving. Within two years, the Soviet Union itself had ceased to exist. The various republics gradually claimed independence until all of the component parts of the U.S.S.R. had become eponymous states, with Russia the largest and most powerful.

The impact of these developments was enormous, both in international relations and on the level of individual lives, whether the people affected now lived in Russia or Ukraine or in the emigration. What had never been thought attainable had become very much within the realm of possibility. The mail started to get through without complications. International phone calls gradually became relatively routine. Previously, making a phone call to or from the Soviet Union had involved a huge effort. If the person did not have a telephone in his home—and most did not—an appointment had to be made and he would be told that a call would be coming through on a particular day and hour. The conversation would then be carried out in a relatively public area of the post office. Connections were fuzzy and conversations were often interrupted and not resumed. This would all become a thing of the past.

People who had left the Soviet Union in the seventies, knowing that they would never again see their family and friends, suddenly discovered in the nineteen nineties that they could obtain a visa, hop on a plane and visit their old home town. And the reverse was also true: friends and relatives could come over for visits to their dear ones in the United States, or Israel or wherever else they lived. A kind of normality in familial relations was achieved which had been unthinkable in the previous decades. There was no longer a feeling of finality attached to the emigration process.

Russians and Ukrainians, Lithuanians and Latvians all found that Europe was on their doorstep. They could take a cheap organized tour to Paris or Berlin, to London or Istanbul or travel on their own. Younger Russians or Moldavians or Poles looked for work elsewhere if they couldn't find anything suitable at home. They could go abroad and work, sending money back to the family, and then return when they'd had enough. Their fellow countrymen who had emigrated had been able to travel and see the world from the moment they reached Israel or the United States, Canada or Australia. Now they too could travel.

During the nineteen eighties, very few Jews (or others) had been able to emigrate from the Soviet Union and there was a large backlog of "refuseniks." While there were always a few who were permitted to leave, there was no large exodus as there had been in the seventies. Now, suddenly at the end of the eighties, the gates were open and in a way different from previously. Now vast numbers were suddenly finding it possible to leave, and to direct themselves to either Israel or the United States (or Germany, or elsewhere). Instead of being forced to leave on Israeli documents, it was possible for potential emigrants to approach the United States Embassy directly for their travel documents.

In the beginning of this new period, the United States allowed very large numbers of Jews from the Soviet Union to enter with the status of refugee. It became clear quite quickly, though, that a huge expense would be incurred by the government and to the charitable organizations that were helping if unlimited numbers of refugees were allowed to enter the Land of the Free. Combined with this, pressure was mounting from Israel to place a limit on how many could immigrate to America: it was uncomfortable for the country billing itself as the Jewish homeland to have more Jews making their way to the United States than to Israel. As a result, although American Jews had always fought for a generous policy toward Jewish refugees—rooted in the tragedy of the Second World War and earlier experiences—a numerical limit on the entry of Soviet Jews into the U.S. was agreed upon between the two countries, Israel and America. Without the opportunity of entering the United States with refugee status, more of the émigrés opted for Israel and other destinations.

Those who had arrived in the United States in the nineteen seventies had had ample time to settle in by the time their fellow countrymen began their own migration in the nineties. They had gone through their own vicissitudes, whether economic or political, social or religious. From the presidencies of Nixon and Ford, they passed to those of Jimmy Carter, then Ronald Reagan, followed by George Bush and then Bill Clinton and a second Bush. They became familiar with the political scene, began to participate in free elections, discovered the advantages and disadvantages of the democratic system of government.

The détente was over by the end of the seventies, but within a few years, with the implosion of the Soviet system and the Soviet bloc, new feelers went out. The Cold War was over and new trading partners—if not new political partners—were forming relationships. The two decades at the end of the twentieth century turned out to be fairly congenial for people seeking jobs and buying houses and getting absorbed into their new country. By the Clinton presidency, the national debt was being cut and new jobs were being created on a large scale. Did America turn out to be the land of opportunity for our immigrants?

How do you estimate the success of someone's life? How do you judge if he or she made the correct decisions, took the right chances? Surely professional success and financial stability are not the only indicators, though they are certainly significant. Did the person learn the language of his new country well, adapt herself to the new culture, blend in with the local population? How much do personal relations count, family closeness, friendships? How do you define someone's happiness? Who is the best judge of that happiness?

One question, needless to say, is how do you even locate people after twenty-five years? The United States is a vast country. Mobility is common. Indeed, of all those interviewed for this chapter, only one person had remained in the same town after all that time, if not at the same address. But, following her marriage, her name was no longer the same.

Now, after twenty-five years, the ensuing stories have unfolded. There are bound to be changes: moves, new houses and jobs, additions to the family, illness, marriage. Much was predictable, but, as in every human story, there are always unexpected developments.

SOPHIA

Sophia should have been the easiest person to locate after a quarter of a century: she had remained in the same city, if not at the same address. All that had to be discovered was her new family name. As expected, time had witnessed changes in the life of a girl in her twenties and a woman in her early fifties. She remains the same lively, intelligent, articulate person, whose English had already been good in the nineteen seventies. Sophia, who is relatively small with a neat figure, looks diminutive when her husband walks in. Mark is a very tall man and looms large over anyone else in the room.

Sophia and Mark have one child, an irrepressible, pretty little girl of seven, with dark straight hair, who keeps popping into the kitchen. All sorts of goodies have been put out for the guest, and Faith keeps coming in to grab another cream puff or cookie and run off again.

The family lives in a beautiful suburb of Buffalo in a fine-looking, two storey house on the edge of a wood. All of the trees in the area are protected by law, even the many tall ones in their own back yard. The kitchen windows look out onto this lush sight, now filled with the colors of autumn. A trail behind the house joins up with a bicycle path that extends through parkland for miles.

Sophia is clearly a person satisfied with life and is happy to go over the developments that have taken place since the last interview. After completing her undergraduate degree in 1979, she continued with her studies, this time for an M.A. in social work. During the early 1980s she worked at Jewish Family Services, as a resettlement case manager for Russian immigrants. This was something that Sophia knew first-hand, having gone through the process with her own family just a few years earlier. But in 1984, she left that job in order to complete an internship in her field. It was through this that she was to meet her future husband, who was a social worker at the same hospital. However it was a long way from their meeting to their eventual marriage in 1992.

In December of 1984, by which time she had finished her schooling, Sophia finally moved out of her family's apartment. By this time she was nearly thirty. She first moved in with a friend and then three years later into her own apartment.

Sophia has been working for the same employer since she finished her internship. This is a non-profit consulting agency that has a number of locations. She supervises a psychiatric clinic that services the mentally ill as well as alcohol and drug abuse clients. She also has her own case load. Most of her patients are of the most high risk, complex kind: mainly sex offenders, mentally ill drug abusing sex offenders. It takes a tough person to deal with them. "I have a very high tolerance for it," Sophia explains. "I'm not a judgmental person . . . You have to have a certain type of personality. You have to be empathetic because if you're not and you're so judgmental, people are not going to be able to improve. And," she adds, laughing, "I have hope for everybody."

In 1988, Isaac and Clara, Sophia's parents, decided to move to Florida and hoped that Sophia would come too. But she already had her present job and was in her thirties and decided not to go with them. "I loved it here, so I had roots here. I was very comfortable. I did not see any reason to go at that point." There was probably another reason as well: she and Mark were already a couple. They waited another four years and married in 1992.

Their relationship and eventual marriage were considered a catastrophe within the family. Mark is not Jewish. Brought up Catholic, he does not practice his religion but neither is he Jewish. Sophia must have known what an explosive issue this would be from the moment she started dating him. It was her uncle—her mother's only brother—after all, who married a non-Jewish woman in the Soviet Union when Sophia was a child. In the first interview, Isaac had approvingly recalled that his brother-in-law had been ostracized by his own mother, never permitted back into house. So this was not a family that was open to intrusion by "outsiders." Like many Jews, they had a serious fear that once someone "married out" it would be the end of their normal participation in the Jewish community and their children would most likely be lost to the religion entirely. Even with a Jewish mother—and this is the definition of a Jew, technically—the children would still be involved in the Christian side of the family and would, possibly, in the long run veer in that direction.

But Isaac's fears were less related to the theological complexities. They were elemental. This has been a Jewish tradition from time immemorial: when a family member married a non-Jew he—or she—would literally be mourned as if he had died. The family would sit *shiva* for that person for the required seven days. It is only when you see the enormous affection that Sophia has for her husband—whom she has been married to for fourteen years, but has been a companion to for over twenty—that you can understand how this small plucky girl had the courage to face the wrath of her family.

Isaac disowned his daughter after her marriage, but her mother and sister came to the wedding. They were married by a justice of the peace. Mark's parents were still alive and "to be respectful to both families . . . we decided to have a civil ceremony." After the marriage, which took place in 1992, Sophia continued to go down to Florida to visit the family. "I still continued to travel back and forth but my father would not sit in the same room with me. He wouldn't speak with me; he wouldn't answer the phone." Isaac could not deal with the fact of his daughter's marriage. "He didn't want anything to do with me, because I hurt him so badly . . . my father thought that something had happened to me . . . that there was something mentally wrong with me." He simply could not understand how this could have happened and this went on for many years. "It was not about the fact that he did not like my husband; it was the fact that he wasn't Jewish."

Things started to change, very gradually, after Faith was born in 1998. When she was nearly a year old, Sophia flew with her to New York for a family emergency involving her sister. Isaac and Clara also came, as well as Isaac's brother and sister-in-law, who were now living in California. "My aunt and uncle thought that it was a terrible thing that my father wouldn't acknowledge Faith." He refused to be in the same room with her. "I think the day I was leaving, my aunt took Faith and kind of forced my father to hold her, so he was sending messages back and forth: 'tell her she's a beautiful child.' He wouldn't communicate with me directly." Sophia continued to visit her parents, and Isaac started to tolerate having Sophia and Faith with him. "He adored her." But he wanted nothing to do with Sophia's husband.

The situation was resolved in 2003. That was the year of Isaac and Clara's fiftieth wedding anniversary. A large celebration was planned—black tie—and many friends and family members were invited. Mark and Sophia had received an invitation in the mail and Sophia planned to go to Florida with Faith. But Mark said that he wouldn't go, as he wasn't sure that Isaac wanted him there. "I'm not going to go to this big affair and have your father treat me disrespectfully. So unless your father, unless I know that he wants me there, I'm not going to go." Sophia recalls her surprise when the phone rang: "Suddenly, out of the blue, my father called and wanted to speak to him . . . my mother was very upset with my father . . . the family was coming . . . all his friends were coming, people they hadn't seen in twenty years . . . and they kind of shamed him into it . . . My father called and wanted to ask my husband if he would come. . . at that point it was almost too late because we [Faith and I] already had plane reservations, but I said to my husband, you know, you better go." It was too late for Mark to arrange more than two days off from work. "He called to invite my husband. I said, I don't care if you're there for twenty-four hours, but you really should be going because this was a very big step for him. So he did."

Sophia had never considered giving up Mark because of her parents' opposition. "I was very tolerant with my father for many years because I understood what he felt, so regardless of whether he wanted to talk to me or not I . . . never argued with him over that. I knew it was just a matter of time. . . . I never judged him and I always tried to have a very positive relationship with him." They had to get an expensive last-minute ticket for Mark. "At that point, we didn't care how much money it cost. We didn't care . . . My parents made a beautiful dinner. I brought my husband over to their house and my father loves him. So now we [both] go visit him; my father just loves him."

Mark's parents were very loving towards Sophia from the beginning, with none of the prejudices that might plague a mixed marriage. In fact, they had a positive stereotype of a Jewish woman and were glad that their son—a long-time bachelor—was marrying one. A Jewish woman, as they understood it, can cook, is responsible, has a career. Unfortunately, his mother died before Faith was born, and by now his father and brother have also passed away. The three of them are a tightly-knit, loving, supportive family unit.

Sophia enjoys much more of a social life now than when she was younger and they often have friends over in the summertime, when Mark takes care of the outdoor cooking on their grill. But they don't manage to go out a great deal because their working day is long and, as a psychiatric nurse, Mark is often on duty on the weekend in the emergency room at the hospital.

Sophia's friends come from all kinds of backgrounds: only one is Jewish. But she is now making friends with Faith's friends' mothers. Faith goes to religious instruction twice a week, on Thursday and Sunday, at the reform temple, where they study Hebrew and Jewish religion and customs. The household tends to be more Jewish than Catholic—there is a menorah but not a Christmas tree, for example. Faith has been brought up in English, though she has some passive knowledge of Russian from the visits to her grandparents in Florida. Sophia and Faith are involved in activities at the temple and sometimes attend services (though without Mark). Sophia gives money to Jewish charities through the temple. When Faith goes to her class on Sunday morning, Sophia also attends her own adult class once a month. The class deals with Jewish parenting, parental values, and what makes a good Jewish home. While Sophia does not light candles on Friday night, nor serve challah, she does host a Hanukah party every year, preparing potato latkes for her guests. She and Faith attend High Holiday services and, since her arrival in America, Sophia has regularly fasted on Yom Kippur. Faith will celebrate her bat mitzvah in a few years.

Far more assimilated than many of the older immigrants, Sophia watches CNN for information on currents events and reads the local paper, the Buffalo News. The important issues for her are the war in Iraq and also health-related matters, and the political solutions to these problems. While she has always been a Republican, her husband is a Democrat. She started out as a Republican because her degree was in economics and she favored their policies. "But as I became a social worker that has kind of changed . . . so it's not so much the politicians but what laws are proposed and how the laws are followed. . . I don't know that I so much believe in politicians or trust them." Neither she nor Mark voted for Bush in the 2004 election and she is quite certain that she won't vote for a Republican president next time either.

While she follows the news out of Israel, she is not overly involved. Israel is not really "on the agenda" today. Even when they travel, it is either to Canada, or to Mexico, where Mark can enjoy the snorkeling. Most of their trips are to resorts rather than sight-seeing. They don't even visit Europe.

Twenty-five years ago Sophia had said, in the first interview, that Israel had given her the feeling that she was home. How does she feel about home now? "Buffalo's home. I feel very comfortable in this environment. I mean, look how beautiful that is," she says, pointing out the window at the autumnal trees.

ISAAC AND CLARA

Isaac seems smaller and thinner than at the time of the first interview. He's been through a great deal since then—work accidents that affected his back and knee, to the extent that he has to walk with a cane, and two strokes. He has a goatee now on his intelligent face. This time, the interview—in October 2006—is taking place in Isaac and Clara's home in Miami Beach. He insists on doing it in English, though he has none of the fluency of his daughter. But this is part of his proudly adopted Americanization. Their apartment house, which probably looked quite smart when first built, has a rundown air about it. Both black and white residents appear in the rather bleak lobby, sometimes greeting one another. Isaac's apartment is at the top, on the tenth floor.

Clara is in the apartment too and floats in and out of the interview, spending some of her time with another visitor. It is clear in looking at her that she has weathered a huge number of health problems which must have worn her down. ("My mother," her daughter, Sophia, had said, "is a medical miracle.") However, in the photograph of their fiftieth wedding anniversary celebration three years before when she was sixty-eight, she looks quite handsome and distinguished.

Despite a certain physical infirmity, Isaac still drives. His memory remains extremely clear and dates come easily in a discussion of past events. There is a lot of catching up to do. They left Buffalo in 1988, largely because it was felt that Florida, with its warmer climate, would be better for Clara. By the time they left, Isaac was no longer working. He had been injured on the job, in two accidents—one affecting his back, the other his knee—and had had surgery. He doesn't feel that he was well compensated: one hundred dollars a week plus social security. Since their move to Florida, he hasn't worked. Altogether, with everything he and Clara receive, they have an income of about $1,400 a month and they manage on that, without having to take any money from their daughters. They sold their house in Buffalo and bought the little apartment in Florida for $28,000, so their housing costs just $210 a month for maintenance plus electricity. They seem satisfied with their life in Florida.

Isaac and his younger brother—the one who remained on the train with his mother during World War Two, when Isaac went in search of milk for his cousin—have a close relationship. They are just two years apart in age. Isaac waited for Alexander to leave the Soviet Union for nine years. First, their mother had a stroke and he could not leave her. After that, he and his wife and daughter had to wait a long time for an exit visa. This was during the post-détente period, when all emigration was very low. At present, they live in a beautiful house in San Francisco and are very happy there. Alexander, now retired, was a house painter and did very well, economically, both in the Soviet Union and in America. Altogether, that branch of the family has been highly successful. The brothers—Isaac and Alexander—see each other at least once every two years and are in constant touch. They have just one daughter, Sophia's age, and she is already a grandmother. While she and her husband do well, their son has become an extraordinarily successful entrepreneur, owning a number of construction distribution warehouses as well as having business interests back in Russia. This is an intriguing phenomenon in recent years: many Jews, former Soviet citizens, have returned, at least partially, to the place of their birth to take advantage of the business opportunities available in the newly capitalistic economy there. They bring with them the polish and know-how of their new home countries. With their fluent knowledge of both Russian and English (or Hebrew) and their contacts in both Russia and the West, these new investors feel at home in both worlds.

The story of Isaac's younger daughter, Mila, has been tragic. She was sixteen when the family emigrated from Russia and only twenty when she married in Buffalo. She never had any advanced education, unlike her older sister. Like many children of Soviet emigrants, Mila married someone who was also originally from the Soviet Union. They were the first to move to Florida, where they lived for a number of years together with their little boy. However, the marriage was not successful and the couple divorced. Because of his father's behavior to him in childhood, their son, now twenty-eight, has nothing to do with him.

But Mila was lucky and met a wonderful young man—also originally from the Soviet Union, though he had lived in Israel most of his life. His family, too, had immigrated to Israel and he had served in the army there, eventually fighting and getting injured in Lebanon in the early nineteen eighties. Sometime after this, he came to live in New York and once, on a visit to Florida, he met Mila and they fell in love. They married in 1994 and she went to live with him in Brooklyn. He was a wonderful man—everyone in Mila's family loved him. As an auto mechanic, he owned his own business and did well. In 1996, when Mila was well into her pregnancy, her husband was hit by a car while crossing the street and suffered a serious head injury. He lay in a coma for three months. After that, he was severely disabled, physically and mentally.

When it was time for her to give birth, Mila's parents and sister came to New York to help, but there was a limit to how long they could stay there. By this time Mila's husband was in a nursing home. She continued working, as the only breadwinner (for some reason he was not eligible for insurance, except for the hospital bills). Isaac and Clara took the baby grandson back to Florida with them and brought him up, speaking to him in Russian. When the little boy started to call them Mama and Papa, Isaac told Mila that she'd better return to Florida and be close to her child.

During the time that she had been living in New York, she had kept the condominium that she had owned in Miami Beach—about half a mile from her parents' place—so she returned to it, bringing her ailing husband with her. He could walk and watch TV, and smoke, but not much else. She got herself a job at a medical center, where she still works, doing billing, and looked after her husband and little boy, with a great deal of help from her parents. Mila's husband died in 2004, in his forties. Her parents are still very important in her younger son's life and he is the apple of their eye. Every day Isaac picks up Michael from school and brings him to his and Clara's apartment until his mother comes to get him. That is, every day except Tuesday and Thursday, when he stays after school to play chess for two hours. Michael arrived at around 4:30 in the afternoon, during the interview, brought home this time by his older (half) brother, a sweet roly-poly ten year old, clearly very fond of his grandparents. Clara immediately busied herself getting some food ready for him.

History takes strange turns. Clara's brother, who married a non-Jewish woman and was ostracized by the family (though Clara did keep in touch), has a daughter, now living in the United States, in Florida. She married a Jewish man, while still in the Soviet Union, and so that whole branch of the family has returned to their Jewish roots. Her son, also very successful, is the vice-president of a shipping company. Almost all of Clara's family, except a cousin, has left Russia by now.

Unlike many of the immigrants interviewed, Isaac is a supporter of the Democratic Party in the United States and also a proponent of the left wing of Israeli politics. He has voted ever since arriving in America and speaks bitterly of the elections in 2000 in which Florida was mired in an election scandal involving voting machines, "hanging chads," and so on. He criticizes Kathleen Harris who, he says, helped George W. Bush become president. "This election was stolen," he says, "and the Supreme Court went along with it."

Isaac wasn't originally a Democrat—he admired Nixon because he was a very strong politician—but he gradually changed his position. While he criticized Bill Clinton for the scandals involving women, he feels that Clinton supported the right positions politically. George W. Bush, he says, wants to make permanent tax cuts: the oil companies make billions of dollars and the worker, the middle class, pay for everything. Isaac is also opposed to getting rid of social security, one of Bush's stated goals at the time.

Isaac watches the news on CNN every day and once a week they buy the local Jewish newspaper, published in Palm Beach. He never reads the Russian press, nor does he watch Russian TV. All his news is in English. While a staunch supporter of Israel, he feels that Israel really botched up the war in Lebanon in the summer of 2006. He is a great admirer of Barak who, he says, is "very smart," and doesn't think much of Olmert ("like a lamb") or of Netanyahu.

The month before the interview, Isaac marked thirty-three years since his arrival in the United States. He had been forty-five. So, at this point, where is home? Isaac replies very simply, "Here is home." He is happy with his decision. He had wanted to live in Israel but "they" had messed things up. He again cites his dismay over Sophia not being permitted to enter the University because of the level of her Hebrew. But he has gone beyond that now and seems to have no regrets. He has some unfulfilled desires, but he is not sure that he will ever see them come to fruition. If he and Clara were in better health, he would still like to travel. There is so much to see—in Europe, in South America—but there doesn't seem too much likelihood of that. And, most of all, he would like to return to Russia to see his mother's grave.

LUNA

The first interview had been held in Luna's little tailoring shop in Buffalo. The second one took place in her dazzling home in a suburb of Baltimore. Located on a little street that ends in a circle, the house looks externally like the others on the street, but each one has a different internal design. In the case of Luna's house, there is a high, vaulted ceiling over the living room, which gives a feeling of grandeur to the interior. Beautiful polished wooden floors add to the luxurious atmosphere. This is a house that is well looked after. There are Chinese-style furnishings: black lacquer display cabinets that house Russian cut glass and a variety of teacups and ornaments. The master bedroom is grandiose, with a Roman-style "marble' bust on a pillar stand, large green leafy plants, and wide flat television screen on one wall. There are a number of rooms and the house turns out to be twice as large as perceived, because there is a full complement of rooms in the extensive finished basement as well.

The first person to meet before the interview could begin was Luna's mother, now ninety years old and largely bedridden. But this cheerful, rosy-cheeked elderly lady rests in a lovely, airy bedroom, with its own television set (showing a Russian-language program). Luna had asked her first cousin over to look after her mother's needs during the interview, as she has to be fed at frequent intervals. Luna and this cousin, Ella, grew up like sisters. After the war, returning to the ruins of their area of Odessa and facing a serious housing shortage, Luna's mother and aunt decided to share a two-room apartment. Both little girls had been born in Batumi, in Georgia, during the war. Ella's father returned from the navy, while Luna grew up without hers.

Luna sometimes asks her mother about her birth-father. What was he like? Why didn't you keep in touch with his family? But her mother says that it was such a horrible time that she shouldn't be judged for not maintaining any connection. Luna knows that her father had three sisters, but doesn't know who they are. She doesn't even have a picture of him. When they were on their way from Batumi to Odessa in 1945, they were robbed on the train and all their possessions were taken from them—all of their documents, birth certificates, everything. So, aside from knowing that her father was a Georgian Jew, she has little to go by. "You know, as you get older, you get so sentimental. You want to know. I just want to know . . . my damn DNA."

While her mother had joined the family in Buffalo shortly after their own arrival, Luna's step-father (or her father, as she refers to him) only arrived in the United States after a ten-year wait. Unfortunately, their reunion did not turn out to be successful. It was hard for him to learn English. He was already seventy-two. After living together with Luna's family for two years, they finally took possession of the apartment that Luna's mother had been on a waiting list for. Things then took a turn for the worse. Her mother was diagnosed with a hyperactive thyroid gland, which necessitated surgery. The surgery resulted in complications, her mother had a strep infection and she ended up in a coma for six months.

Before this latest development, Luna's son, Jerry, had graduated from college. He had changed from his initial major of architecture to business after the first year. Not finding any employment in Buffalo, he went to New York and succeeded in landing a good job. Luna and Sam felt so far away from him that they decided that they would leave Buffalo too. At first they thought of living in New York themselves, but found that what they wanted was too expensive and what they could afford wasn't attractive to them. In the end, they found another solution to their desire to be near their son: they moved to Baltimore, just three hours away. This was in 1986. Luna now feels that this was a mistake, but at the time, they were influenced by the need to be nearer to Jerry and it seemed to make sense to settle there. When they first arrived in Baltimore, they went to Inner Harbor and Luna loved it. It reminded her of Odessa. It was also affordable. There were jobs, too, and Sam found something in Frederick, some forty minutes away from Baltimore, with a good salary. Two months later, he lost his job. Luna hadn't yet found work for herself. They had just bought themselves a house and had no idea how they would pay the mortgage the next month. This, says Luna, was real immigration. What they had experienced in their early period in Buffalo cannot even compare with what they went through in Baltimore. Furthermore, they had now been in the country for ten years and could not turn to Jewish Family Services for help.

Within three weeks they had both found jobs, but in Pennsylvania, an hour and a half away. Later, Sam found work in Baltimore, but Luna kept driving to Pennsylvania for another year. Then she decided that she had had enough of long-distance commuting and decided to open a tailoring shop again. "This time I didn't buy it from anybody. I started from scratch. I started to, you know, put little ads in the paper and the supermarkets, doing tailoring from home, and I accumulated enough customers to get started. So I went out and rented a place, bought some sewing equipment . . . So I started from scratch and built it beautifully, nicely. For seventeen years I had a wonderful tailor shop." This time she had both men and women customers. When she had too many alterations, she would farm out the work. She had just retired six months before the interview, in May, 2006.

Luna's mother eventually recovered, but only after Luna had spent some six months living at the hospital back in Buffalo to be near her. She even showered and dressed there. She wondered many times during that period whether she should have the plug pulled out, but rejected the idea. "I didn't give her life," Luna explains, "I'm not taking it from her." Suddenly, after half a year, her mother woke up, confused and unable to speak. The tube had destroyed one of her vocal chords. She could not eat for a year and a half after. Luna brought her parents to Baltimore, providing her mother with constant care and, after she had regained her strength, surgeons at Johns Hopkins Hospital managed to reconstruct her throat. Luna's parents finally split up, living separate lives in Baltimore. He never truly settled down in America. He died in 1999.

In July, 1999 Luna and Sam moved into their present house and a year later her mother moved in with them. Luna describes the neighborhood as upper middle class. Their neighbors are ethnically of various backgrounds: Greek, German, Russian-Jewish, Phillipino, American Jewish. For a while, they found it difficult to make their mortgage payments. Now, when they are considering selling the house in order to move to the New York area, they are faced with a new problem. Real estate, in 2006, is in the doldrums. There are seventy-seven houses for sale in their area and none are being sold.

With Luna at home with her mother, Sam is technically retired and collecting social security (but no pension). But because of the mortgage payments he has had to continue to work as a cab driver to make ends meet. When he returned to Baltimore after working in Pennsylvania he discovered that he had not made a good choice and he was now in a dead-end job that did not pay well. So he took up taxi driving in 1989. He drives the cab six days a week; five days a week didn't bring in enough money to cover expenses. For Sam, at least, Buffalo was a better place for employment: at least he was working in his field then. Luna says, "If you ever talk to my husband, don't even start him on that, because till this day he regrets that we ever moved. He doesn't like Baltimore. . . We've lived here for twenty years and he still hates it. It's too cliquey . . . It was difficult for us to make friends because we always were treated as newcomers."

To everyone's amazement, Sam's family all left Russia at various times. His father, it will be remembered, had been a high level bureaucrat. Sam, a middle child among five brothers and a sister, had been very sad at leaving in the mid nineteen-seventies, knowing that he would never see his close family again. One brother had actually worked in a secret factory making communication equipment for the army, so it had been clear at the time that he would never be allowed to leave the Soviet Union. By now, most of that large family lives in San Francisco, many having done very well. One of Sam's nephews, having immigrated to America, is now back Russia, "being a big shot," as Luna puts it. While his wife and children are there with him, they are all registered at the American Embassy in Moscow, "just in case."

Luna has remained close to her childhood friend, who lives in Canada, who lent her the first small sum so that she could purchase the tailoring business that she started with in Buffalo. And Luna and Sam have retained a number of the friendships that they made in Buffalo, keeping in touch and occasionally visiting them.

Like her mother, Luna married very young and already had a baby at twenty. It turns out that this was by a previous husband, whom she divorced. Sam took over the role of father when he married Luna when Jerry was a little boy. So there is a close parallel between Luna and her mother, Luna and her son. Sam has no natural children, but is very close to Jerry.

Jerry, when he was twelve, had himself circumcised in Buffalo and identified strongly as a Jew. His goal, when he was eighteen, had been to become an architect. In the course of years one would expect changes in a young man's views in various spheres and this has been the case with him. He is now vice-president of a Wall Street firm, earning a six-digit salary plus a bonus that alone exceeds what Luna and Sam earn. While his mother did not keep in touch, Jerry did maintain a connection with his birth father, who also immigrated to the States and lived in Brooklyn. When he died, he left his son some money.

Jerry is married to an American Hindu girl of Indian origin. They had a Jewish wedding, with a rabbi officiating. Says Luna, "You can find rabbis who will marry a man and a dog." This is no reflection on Jerry's wife, whom Luna is very fond of. About Jerry's Jewishness, Luna says, "You know, it all changes when you fall in love." A beautiful picture of the wedding, in 1993, is on display in the living room. Jerry and his wife have no children, but are in the process of adopting a baby. He is already eight months old, living in a foster home in Guatemala. They have visited him and can't wait until they can bring him home. They plan to bring up their son as a Jew, though it will be a multi-cultural home, which will include the Hinduism of his mother and the Catholicism into which he was born.

Luna did attempt, in the beginning, to object to Jerry marrying someone who was not of Jewish background, but he warned her that he would not feel comfortable in her house if she is not comfortable with his wife. "It's not worth it for me to lose my only child for that reason. . . It happens with . . . people who are more religiously oriented than we are. You know, for us it's a big stretch . . . being born and raised as atheists [in the Soviet Union] and come to terms with who we are and learn so much [about] Jewishness . . . It wasn't worth it for me."

Over the years, Luna and Sam have traveled to Europe several times and have visited Switzerland, France, England, Italy and also Germany, where they have friends. They go to the West Coast at least once a year to see the family and have visited Isaac and Clara in Florida twice. They haven't been to Israel yet, though they would like to. They finally decided that it was time to return to Russia for a visit and had made plans to go there the previous summer, but Luna's mother took ill and they had to cancel their trip at the last minute. They would like to see Odessa again and also to visit Sam's nephew in Moscow, but Luna's mother is a diabetic (among other problems), and she cannot leave her for so long.

Asked if she follows what is going on in the former Soviet Union, Luna says that she sometimes watches television with her mother in Russian, but that it doesn't affect her the way that the news on Israel does. Her source of information on Israel is largely the daily one hour Russian-language television program that comes straight from Jerusalem. She won't watch CNN: it is "not my kind of channel." She prefers Fox, which, she says, offers a lot of reports on Israel and is "respectful."

Luna identifies herself as a "rabid Republican." She voted for George W. Bush twice, "although he was somewhat of a disappointment." As for the Iraq war, she feels that it went totally wrong. They weren't properly prepared. "Mission" wasn't accomplished. In the upcoming congressional elections she plans to vote Republican because she prefers their platform, which she defines as "you provide for yourself; you don't wait for a hand-out; you don't wait for big government to give it to you."

Luna feels very strongly about making it on your own. Coming from a country that had very strong centrally-organized control over so many aspects of human life, she tends, like many Soviet émigrés, to seek the opposite in her new country and she thus opposes "big government." (Note that, like many citizens of the Soviet Union, she distinguishes between one's country and one's homeland.) As she explains her position,

> I have a very strong backup: I came here with two hundred and forty dollars and I got it made where I am now. I got it made against all odds . . . I didn't speak a word of English and if we overcame and if we got it made, I have no reason to excuse anyone who doesn't want to make it in this country, period. . . I never waited for somebody to give me [anything]—You know, I'm very grateful to Jewish Family Service. They took us in and they helped us for the first three months. I will never forget that and I'm still very involved in charity for, you know, the Jewish National Fund. This is a must. I give to the Jewish National Fund. I'm very much into, you know, like the trees for Israel program . . . This is the least I can do for my homeland, because this is my homeland. Israel is my homeland, not Russia. . . When I speak of Russia I speak of something different. You know, America is my country . . . for better or worse.

VALENTINA

Valentina's thirteen-year-old granddaughter, Julie, was so excited that some-one was coming to interview her grandmother for a book that she asked if she could leave school early and listen. Her fond grandmother was all too happy to oblige. Valentina had been living in the little complex of low, wooden apart-ment houses for only a couple of weeks, having just moved out of the house that she and her daughter, Marina, and Julie and her brother had been sharing. There were three locks to be opened, then a chain released—in the style of some of the old New York films—before entrance to the flat was gained.

The apartment interior is very attractive, carpeted from wall to wall, tastefully, but not over- furnished, with a large, airy, light living room, a good-sized dining room table at the far end, near the kitchen, and two bed-rooms. Valentina had prepared a delicious lunch, consumed during part of the interview, which was carried on in English. Julie, slim, sweet, medium height and blond, sat attentively, occasionally adding a comment or asking a question. Grandmother and granddaughter are clearly close and affectionate. Valentina has a broad face, with close-cropped hair—what was once called a pixie cut—and an ample figure. She has remained lively and knows her mind.

Her story of the last twenty-five years is not a happy one. Their daughter, Marina, was studying at Buffalo State, just three months short of her degree, when she went down to visit a friend in Baltimore, a girl who had been in elementary school with her in the Soviet Union. At the time, she was twenty-three. Once in Baltimore, Marina decided that she did not want to return to Buffalo and promised that she would complete her B.A. in Baltimore (which she never did). Her parents, in a quandary, decided to follow her and start a new life in Baltimore so that the family could stay together. The truth is that their marriage had been in trouble for some time, and they may have felt that moving might help things. In fact, it didn't. Furthermore, Valentina, thanks to cuts made in research funds during the Reagan administration, had lost her laboratory job at Roswell Park and was actually out of work when the family was faced with Marina's decision. Upon arrival in Baltimore, Roman managed to locate another job as a dental technician, though he eventually ended up as a taxi driver.

Valentina, in looking back on that period, feels that she made a mistake: she should have tried to find a laboratory job at Johns Hopkins once she settled in Baltimore. But at the time, with their marriage at the point of breaking down and the threat of divorce looming, she simply took what she thought was an easier option: she became a manicurist. For her, it made sense. She found work near her home, could make her own hours, and be with her son when she wanted to. She managed to earn four hundred dollars a month in the beginning, just enough to cover the rent. At the time Alex was well under ten years old. He entered a Kadima school in Baltimore and received a rich Jewish background there, much more than was available at home.

Roman and Valentina were divorced in 1986, not long after reaching Baltimore. He has since re-married. Valentina, too, was married again at some point, this time to an Italian-American. But the marriage didn't last for long. Marina, their daughter, had also married—a Jewish boy of Russian extraction—and was divorced early in the new century, after fourteen years of marriage. They had found themselves unable to have children and had adopted a boy and a girl in the former Soviet Union. Julie has an older brother, adopted around the same time. These children are, for Valentina, the positive elements of her daughter's life. Marina has been plagued with health problems. Like a number of immigrants, Valentina feels that inept diagnosis and faulty medical treatment have caused even worse problems. Not long after the family arrived in Buffalo, Marina was diagnosed with a peptic ulcer, at the age of sixteen. Since then, there has been a long series of botched operations and questionable medical treatment which have left the unfortunate young woman with a serious digestive problem and a very pessimistic prognosis. When she was taken to the Mayo Clinic some nine years ago, the comment was, "Who did this to you?"

Valentina holds herself partly to blame. She had, after all, been in the medical profession, having practiced dentistry in Russia for years. "I will take this guilt to my grave. . . Having this knowledge of medicine I forgot about everything when it comes to my kids . . ." She feels, though perhaps not correctly, that she failed her daughter, that she might have interfered and questioned some of the medical procedures that were performed and thus changed the outcome. An attempt to sue for malpractice did not succeed in the courts.

Eventually, Marina and her children moved in with Valentina and for years they all lived together. Recently, however, it became very difficult for the older woman and her daughter to co-exist under the circumstances and Valentina had thus moved out, though she is still in close touch with the family. The rather tenuous connection that the family had with Jewish traditions has become even weaker. The neighborhood where Marina and her children live has a very poor public school. In order to assure herself that her daughter will be in a decent school environment, Marina has felt it necessary to send Julie to a private school. The affordable one is Catholic. There is a reasonable doubt that the girl will grow to maturity and still feel part of the Jewish community. She writes poetry and eagerly read a poem of her own composition after the interview was over. It was a diatribe against abortion.

In talking about Marina and her health problems, Valentina has asked Julie to leave the table and to go to another room. One of the reasons is the news that she now delivers: she has recently been diagnosed with what may be uterine cancer. She is waiting for a more specific discussion with her physician, but she is clearly very distressed by this most recent turn of events. She has not told the family yet and is very worried, not only about her own condition but that of her daughter, who may be reaching the end of what the medical profession can offer. She feels that to some extent, the move from the Soviet Union has caused needless agony for the family. "In Russia this wouldn't happen," she says. There they would not have performed the kind of operation that Marina underwent and they would surely have cleared up the old scar tissue, something that was not done in the American hospital. Life at this point looks extremely bleak.[1]

Julie comes back and sits down to dessert. Besides her grandchildren, the other bright light in Valentina's life is her son, Alexander, who is thirteen years Marina's junior. He was less than three when the family emigrated and considers himself one hundred percent American. He was a straight-A student and eventually spent seven years studying architecture at Cornell University during two different periods. By the time he finished his undergraduate and graduate studies, he was thirty thousand dollars in debt. He now works with a top architecture firm on the West Coast. When he first went out there, he realized that it would be impossible to exist in California without a car, so

Valentina managed to buy him a station wagon. He learned to drive within an impressively short time and then drove the car from Baltimore across the country to his new home. When Alex was studying in Italy many years ago, Valentina traveled to Europe, visiting a number of countries, including a three day visit with him in Rome. She is extraordinarily proud of him.

Valentina's mother, whom she never saw during all the years that she lived with her paternal grandparents in the house in Belaia Tserkov, turned up again later. The two women never had much of a relationship. She feels that her mother is cold and that her own children never felt a connection with their maternal grandmother. She did actually come to visit the family about sixteen years ago, when they were already in Baltimore, and stayed for a couple of months. There were further misunderstandings and complications between them after she went home and by now Valentina has lost track of where her mother is. If she is still alive, she would be in her mid-eighties.

Valentina has never been back to her home territory, although she has traveled to Europe. Besides the trip when she saw her son in Rome, she also flew to Prague on September 9, 2001. She was in a Czech resort when the attacks on the Twin Towers took place. About half of the tourists there, she says, were Arabs and when they saw what was happening on TV, they applauded. Afterwards, "I was sitting in the dining room with them and they were all smiling. I couldn't stand that, but I had to stay for the full two weeks because there [were no flights back]."

Valentina is not very involved in the political arena. She does not have a Russian channel on her television. She watches CNN for the news and doesn't read newspapers. She has not voted much, though she did vote in the presidential election of 2004 and was very disappointed in the outcome. She votes for Democrats, though she sees herself as an independent. The truth is that she is disillusioned with the whole process. "It's not getting better, so what's the future [for Americans]? I worry about them. My life, I would say, is over. . . What's going to change . . . if I got to vote? I voted before. What change? It gets worse and worse and worse; lie, lie. You know, most of my life I was afraid to lie." She goes on, "I taught my grandkids and my kids, I don't like it when people lie . . . The worst truth is better than a little lie . . . Those politicians, they lie all the time, whatever comes out of their mouth, it's a lie. I can't trust them. How can we go to war for them if I know I cannot trust them?"

Valentina brings out her old photographs. They are her great treasure and have been carried from Belaia Tserkov to Buffalo to Baltimore. Here is a picture of her father, whom she never knew, handsome, and, at twenty-one years old, already an officer. There is her beloved grandfather, in whose house she spent such happy years, "the best years of my life." And this picture is of his wife, her paternal grandmother, a beauty at sixteen. The wonderful stone house is in another photo. And a fine picture of Valentina at dental school. Other pictures are of Valentina's mother's family when she, as a girl, visited them from Sakhalin. They stand there, a strongly Russian-looking group, in contrast to her father's side of the family. There they lie, jumbled in a box, all the wonders and complexities, pain and joys of her early life.

EVA

A car pulls up to pick up a passenger at the arrivals door at Chicago's O'Hare Airport. Eva is at the wheel, smiling her welcome. Eva, here in America! When last seen, twenty-five years ago, she was an enthusiastic young student at the Hebrew University enjoying her life in Israel. When did this all happen?

Only months after the first interview, which took place in Jerusalem in the summer of 1980, Eva was offered an opportunity to study at Tuoro College in New York City and at the same time work at the Israeli consulate there. She arrived in October, 1980. "You see, I didn't know about my future husband. I thought I was going to America to work with the Russian community in New York," she says. "Meanwhile, little did I know, I became one of them." While she was in New York, working, Sasha turned up in the city, "so all was forgotten. We drove to Chicago. I dropped out of college. . ."

Sasha's and Eva's parents had met each other through Zionist activity in Moscow in 1970, though Eva and Sasha themselves did not meet until she arrived in Israel in 1972. By then Sasha was studying violin at the Rubin Academy. At some point he left to pursue his studies in Boston and after that, was employed by the Nova Scotia Symphony Orchestra in Halifax. Then he moved on to a full-time job with the Lyric Opera Orchestra of Chicago, where he still works today. When he dropped by to see Eva in New York, she was just twenty-two years old. By early February, 1981, they were married. At the time, Eva felt terrible "because of leaving Israel, which I was so devoted to, and I was brought up like this." But her parents, rather than being upset, "were very happy for me. My parents were much smarter than me. They said getting married for love is the best thing that can happen. Forget about all this ideology."

They knew Sasha and that he was a good man. "This is very smart; this is the wisdom of years . . . In the Soviet Union they always told us to sacrifice yourself for an idea. That's wrong."

Once in Chicago, Eva pulled herself together and, studying at night, went back to complete the B.A. that she had abandoned. She worked during the day. While she had had a double major in English and art history at the Hebrew University, she now studied for a more general psychology degree at Northwestern. But she never entered the field of psychology. She remained in the world of art. She began working in a museum, then in various galleries and now, for the past fifteen years, she has been the director of a commercial gallery. Chicago, she says, is famous as an art town, a prime place for collectors. Eva loves her work and enjoys her involvement with artists and their creations. Perhaps some of that comes from having grown up in the home of a well-known artist.

Eva's husband also teaches at a music academy. As his opera company does not go on tour, he isn't required to travel a lot, as many musicians must. He and Eva brought up their children to speak in Russian. Their son, Benjamin, who is eighteen, speaks Russian very well and their fifteen-year-old daughter, Gavrielle, understands and speaks, though less fluently. The children clearly see themselves as Americans. Once, when they were only five and two, Eva was talking to them in Russian in a Chicago supermarket when a woman, trying to be friendly, came over and asked when they had come to America. The children answered, "Only she came; we were born here—we're Americans."

Sasha's parents moved from Israel to the United States and live in Milwaukee, though Israel still remains very important to them: "The most important thing for them is Israel—the welfare of Israel, the future of Israel, and the future of the Jewish people." His father is also a violinist and played with the Milwaukee Symphony for many years, only retiring in 2005. Although they do not live very far apart, they do not see each other very often. Eva's parents have come to visit her in Chicago a number of times, but it is now, in 2006, about six years since she and her husband and children were last in Israel.

Eva and Sasha have a Jewish household, though not a religious one. Eva feels that the most significant part of their Jewish education was in their trips to Israel and in their being aware of their family in Israel. When they were small, the children thought that Russia and Israel were one and the same place, because everyone whom they knew in Israel spoke Russian!

Her Jewish identity is very important to Eva and she has tried to instill this in her children. "Yes, we drilled into them that they're Jews and they're not Jews because of the religion, because we don't believe in any God. They're Jews because they have Jewish blood in them. They're Jews by ethnicity." She goes to synagogue only rarely, but her children went to Hebrew school and had their bar-mitzvah. While she is an agnostic, Eva feels very strongly about her sense of belonging: "I'll tell you this: if I hear of a Jew who converted to Christianity, I take it as a personal affront. Because it's one thing to believe, but it's another thing to believe in something else, to defy the history of persecution for so many years. People died at the stake, you know."

She is very opposed to intermarriage and worries that it could happen in her family. She has repeatedly warned her children against it, though her son—at the time of the interview—is dating a girl who is not Jewish. Eva plans to fight it. She explains that at his university, many non-Jewish girls hang around the dorms where many of the Jewish boys live and at the Hillel House on campus, hoping to meet Jewish boys. She claims that there is a sort of reverse antisemitism, that these girls have bought into the notion that Jews are smarter and richer, more likely to succeed, will be good family men and so on. "It's like Archie Bunker," she says, "all he wants is to hire a Jewish lawyer."

Eva doesn't belong to a particular party and votes as she likes. She did not vote for Bush, nor did she vote for Kerry, and she has not been happy with Bush, particularly since Iraq. She does not like his religious agenda, or agree with his domestic policy. She loved Clinton, but after 9/11, she started thinking things over and felt that he had a lot to account for, because terrorists had first tried to blow up the Trade Center during his presidency. Conclusions should immediately have been drawn and new security policies put in place at that time.

In the most recent senatorial election in Illinois, she voted in the primaries for an African-American candidate, who eventually won the Senate seat—someone called Obama. She goes on, "In this particular case, I would like the senators to be Democrats, because the Democrats are the only hope in the Senate to stamp out Christian rightists . . . So if I cast my vote for Obama that would be because I would like him to represent those kinds of views. So, he wins the primary in Illinois and he has an acceptance speech at the hotel and his first words are, 'I'd like to invite the Bishop of the First Black Church of the black south side. Let us pray.' I threw my slipper at the television set. I hate this. The black guy from Mississippi can say that, not the candidate from Chicago. Because he's really the candidate from Chicago—he's based in Chicago and Chicago voted for him, not down-state Illinois. I hated this and guess what? He gets no slack for this, none. . . So that was the first time I didn't vote for a Senator in the elections."

Asked about her views on Israeli politics, Eva shows a clear understanding of the current situation. About Tzipi Livni she says, "You know what, she's not a dummy because when Sharon goes, she's a master politician." As for the pull-out from Gaza, she comments, "It had to be done years ago. My entire family, I'm sure, told you the same thing." She expresses diverse views on politics, eschewing a single, necessarily consistent line. When asked about her statement, years before, that her father had had leanings toward Kach—the party of the right-wing extremist, Meir Kahane—Eva explained her interpretation:

All the Russian Jews did. They felt tremendously grateful to the rabbi . . . because of what he'd done for us [playing a very supportive role in the early struggle of Soviet Jews to emigrate]. . . He would galvanize Jewish youth on campus so they would stand up to the Palestinian agitators. . . We have no figure like the rabbi today. With all his stupid politics and everything, something has to be said about his Yiddishkeit and his devotion to the Jewish people. I don't agree with his ideas but I cannot not feel grateful to him, especially now when I see how defeatist the Jewish kids are on campus. . . We now have Jewish kids voting and demonstrating together with Palestinian educators on campus, being embarrassed to say anything about Israel because it's not 'in.' I find it terrible.

When Eva was a girl living back in Moscow, she had a best friend—Zina— to whom she entrusted her diary before she left the Soviet Union. They lost touch completely when Eva and her family immigrated to Israel. Two years ago, out of the blue, Eva received an e-mail from Zina, who had managed to track her down. Since then they have corresponded with each other every few months. One of the first things that Eva asked was what had happened to her diary. Zina was very upset to tell her that after twenty years, after her first marriage had broken up and she had gone through a number of moves, she suddenly realized that she couldn't find the diary anymore. So that was the end of Eva's girlhood notes in Moscow.

Eva and her family have managed to travel to Europe, though never back to the area of what was once the Soviet Union. Now, the more time passes, the less she wants to go. Other places have risen to the top of her wish list: Sicily, India, China. In the meantime, they have had to travel to Israel whenever they could manage it and that has taken up a lot of their budget.

Eva's immigration experience has not been typical. As she says, she fell from one thing to another, not because of any rational decision. She also didn't feel like an immigrant in America, as she had married someone who was already an American, established, with a car, a job and an apartment. And she had her Israeli passport. ". . . it's a huge confidence, you know, that you have some place to go back to. Not like those poor Russians who had no place to go back to." Nor does she have anything to do with the new Russian immigrants in her area. "I find them very crass." Her father assures her, though, that those who came more recently to Israel have made a wonderful contribution to their new country. They serve in the army; many are officers. Whenever there is a terrorist attack, these new immigrants are among the victims. "They pay a heavy price for living in Israel."

In explaining her feelings about having become an American, Eva expresses a certain ambiguity. What does it mean to move from one place to another, to change cultures, to adjust one's standards and loyalties? How simple a process is it? Where is home? These are fundamental questions. Eva, when asked if she is an American, answers "supposedly." She does, of course, have citizenship. She participates in the political process. Is she happy here? "Oh, very happy. I love America. I love America because it lets you be who you are. No one bothers you. Nobody interferes and nobody rams anything down your throat."

"Look. When you travel from one country, to say the least, one continent, one culture, one political system and come to another continent, another culture, another political system, then you finally are in a completely different hemisphere, a very different political culture and a very different culture altogether . . . You become a voyeur. You belong everywhere and nowhere and you just observe."

MARK AND BRONIA

"We received your e-mail (letter) from 1/16/06," wrote Mark in an e-mail. "Thank you for remembering us. And of course we remember. Particularly, I was very impressed with your Russian. You were the first American talking to us in the [only] language which we knew at that time. . . Yes, we do remember you, and if you will decide to come to see us, in conjunction with your work or without, you will be welcome."

The drive from Detroit Airport to the beautiful neighborhood near West Bloomfield takes a good forty minutes. Mark and Bronia live in a fine, well-furnished, ranch-style house with three bedrooms and an attractive remodeled kitchen that looks out on both the front garden, at one end, and the backyard at the other. The dining room, where the interview took place in October, 2006, also faces the street, while the living room behind it looks out on the back grass. Half way through the interview, Bronia brings out lunch: delicious home-made blintzes served with good strawberry jam. The hot tea, served with cake, is made Russian-style: a dark essence is poured into the cup which is then topped up with boiling water.

In 1983, a year after Mark had started working at his first job in Buffalo (at a factory that manufactured hospital beds), he decided to move on to another and better job and went to his boss to apologize that he would not be working there any longer. He felt very bad to be leaving the first person who had given him a job in America, but the boss explained that that was the way things should be.

As she had expected, Bronia did, indeed, start to work not long after their arrival in Buffalo. She didn't even consider looking for a job as a librarian—who would need a Russian librarian? But in Minsk she had had a hobby, out of necessity, that she felt might prove useful. As it had been very difficult to acquire nice clothes in the Soviet Union, especially for petite women (neither Bronia nor Mark is tall), after finishing college Bronia had taken a two-year course in cutting, sewing and designing ladies' clothes. As she had one daughter and then another while still in Minsk, Bronia had started to sew clothes for them. At first, in Buffalo, she did alterations in a small men's shop that sold high quality clothes. She was paid by the hour. Once Julie was enrolled in kindergarten and looked after for half a day, she found work at J.C. Penney, again paid by the hour. Within half a year the family was able to move to a different apartment.

Many American Jewish communities subsidized Jewish schooling for new immigrant children from the Soviet Union. They felt that it was a significant contribution towards establishing a meaningful Jewish identity for families with tenuous links to their Judaism. But this help was not open-ended and would run out after each family had established itself to some degree. Tanya, their older daughter, had attended a Kadima school for a while, but once the scholarship funding had dried up, and they had to pay the tuition fees by themselves, they had to take her out. It was simply too much of an expenditure for their limited budget.

The family acquired a car not too long after their arrival in America. It cost seven hundred dollars and Bronia learned to drive for the first time. Eventually, she started to work full time and her salary improved. She also made clothes at home, not just for the family, but also for others, private customers. She had an electric sewing machine at home that they had bought at a garage sale in Buffalo.

Bronia's parents did come to visit them once in Buffalo and were surprised at how well Bronia and Mark lived, though by American standards their life-style was relatively modest. "They thought when I wrote a letter that it's all propaganda and they *made* us write letters like this," explains Bronia. The stores and other facets of American life impressed them, but they didn't stay. Bronia and Mark weren't that well off, their older daughter was just getting ready to go to college and Julia would be going later. Bronia's father was already in his late seventies and they were concerned that if his health, or that of her mother, deteriorated they would never be able to afford the necessary medical care. Their own economic situation was not sufficiently grounded yet. Now Bronia regrets "that I never brought my family here, that I didn't push hard enough." They might even have been able to convince her brother and sister to come at the beginning of the nineties, but Bronia had feared that if things didn't go well and they were disappointed in their lives in America she and Mark would be blamed for it.

Mark's third job was as a product engineer at a company that manufactured windshield wipers for cars. He had now, finally, found as interesting a job in the United States as he had had in the Soviet Union. In 1993, the company relocated its engineers to Detroit, where they organized a technical center and headquarters. Mark and Bronia were faced with a dilemma and ultimately decided to make the move—paid for by the company, which included a raise. Taking into account the tough employment situation in Buffalo, they felt that it was certainly worth it. By this time, Tanya had completed her B.A. as a chemistry major and Julie was a sophomore in high school. Julie made new friends in the Detroit area, but for Tanya, Detroit never really became home. It was hard for the family to leave Buffalo, where they had made many friends. In Michigan they didn't, of course, ask for help from the Jewish community, as they had when they first immigrated. In fact, they didn't connect with the Jewish community very much at all, nor did they join the local synagogue. In the beginning, one of the synagogues allowed non-members to come to services, as a means of encouraging the couple to join though that policy was dropped. But that backfired. This year, they did not go to temple at all for the High Holidays. They do give donations to Jewish charities, however. Most of their friends are Russian Jews.

When the family moved, Bronia was able to transfer her job as a tailor to a J.C.Penney in Michigan. Two or three years ago, the company closed the alterations department and they now outsource alterations. Bronia has been permitted to stay on at the store, though, as a sales person, without any change in pay. and she now has another few years until retirement. She plans to stop working at sixty-two, at which point she will also be able to start receiving Social Security. Mark had wanted to remain at his job until seventy and then take his pension at the same time as Bronia, but his company, in an effort to make cuts, has offered a good retirement package to those who want to take it soon, so he will, regretfully, be retiring earlier than he had planned.

Their daughters have done well. Tanya ended up going for a PhD in chemistry in Wyoming on a full tuition scholarship. She also helped to meet living expenses by working as a teaching assistant at the university. The little Jewish community in the university town where she studied hired her as a cantor for the High Holiday services for a good five years. Although she had not continued at the Kadima school in Buffalo, she had gone to Sunday school at the Shaarei Tsedek synagogue and can read Hebrew. She had a bat mitzvah. The cantor in Buffalo discovered that Tanya had a good voice and a good ear. Tanya was well equipped to take on cantorial duties in Wyoming when the opportunity arose. The cantor in Buffalo helped her with a recording of the melodies.

When she completed her doctorate, Tanya decided that she didn't really want to continue with a career that involved lab work and eventually found a job in sales with a company that hired people with M.A.s or PhDs for their dealings with academic customers. She seemed to like her work and, in the meantime, met and married a young man of Russian Jewish descent. Once their daughter was born it became difficult for her to do the kind of traveling needed for her job. She now works for a non-profit organization as director of education. Her husband has not had the educational background that she has and is still trying, in his mid-thirties, to work out what he wants to do, what kind of training he should have, what direction to take.

Bronia and Mark's younger daughter, Julie, only four foot ten and very attractive—actually, both girls are—is very determined and career-oriented. "She's really Scorpio," says Bronia. Mark and Bronia were in a better position to help Julie when she went to university than they had been when Tanya started out. So although it was quite a financial drain, they also coped with dorm fees for Julie. She now has an M.B.A. from the University of Chicago and works as a senior financial analyst for a large company. She has a broad circle of friends, mainly not Jewish, though she has primarily dated Jewish men. While Tanya has retained much of her inherited Russian culture, Julie has not. She sees herself as one hundred percent "American" and, while she speaks some Russian, it is heavily accented. She certainly does not see herself marrying someone of Russian Jewish background.

Mark and Bronia are interested in American politics and do vote. They see themselves as Republicans, but are not happy with George W. Bush. Bronia says that "it didn't work out in a way we thought it was going to work out." Mark, though, predicts with regard to the next elections, "In advance, I will tell you that I will stay with the Republicans." But according to Bronia, "I'm not sure about that." On the local level, they choose according to the issues and the candidates and are thus not strictly one-party voters. For information, they see the circulars that are sent out, watch television, including the debates. They do not receive a newspaper at home, though Mark sees one at work every day, at least the front page, and also scans the computer for news. At home they mainly watch Fox, and occasionally CNN. They don't feel that CNN is fair to Israel, and think that it mostly presents the Arab side. They try to watch closely what is going on in Israel. They do not express opinions on internal Israeli politics, averring that as they don't live there they can't understand the issues thoroughly. "We just stand for Israel," says Bronia. "That's it." When Julie was in college she took a trip to Israel with the local rabbi when she was eighteen. She loved the country—and also fell in love—and wanted to remain there. Mark was very anxious that she return to the States, "Because, you have to understand, with us, we don't have a big family and we want them to be together." This deep-seated need to maintain family closeness is very evident among the Russian Jewish immigrants. In fact, neither of their daughters now lives near them.

Bronia traveled back to the former Soviet Union a few times to see her family in the 1990s. On one trip, in 1996, she took Tanya along to see her grandparents. But Bronia felt distinctly uncomfortable in Minsk and, later, in St. Petersburg and decided not to go back again. There was too much criminal activity and she felt insecure walking out at night. In contrast, they tell of a trip that they made to Israel in 1998, when they saw close cousins of Bronia's for the first time in twenty years. "We felt like we came home . . . like it's our country." The two of them have also visited Spain, northern Italy, France and other countries.

The couple certainly does not regret their original decision to emigrate, even though not everything has gone easily. Bronia, particularly, found parting from her family very trying. There had been such a strong family infrastructure in Minsk, with lots of support. When they arrived in Buffalo, she had had to do everything herself. There was no one whom she could turn to for advice or help. When she returned to Belorus for the first time to see her family, her older sister had expressed her surprise at how she had matured. It's true, says Bronia, "We had to grow up."

YAN

Of all those interviewed, Yan was unique in that he had really not wanted to leave the Soviet Union, but had been pushed to do so. At the time of the first interview, in spite of his success in finding very good employment—probably better than any of his fellow immigrants interviewed—there was a sense of sadness, of homesickness, that was almost palpable. What changes might twenty-five years of living in America have wrought?

Tracking him down was not easy. He was not living in California anymore and only through a series of somewhat serendipitous discoveries was he located in Portland, Oregon. He was most gracious about a repeat interview and arrangements were made to come to his home on a Sunday morning in November, 2005. This time, the interview would not take place on the grass outside a security-conscious set of offices, nor would it be conducted in Russian.

It is clear that Yan has been extremely fortunate in his career in the United States. His first job, in Silicon Valley, had been very interesting but, while it had seemed to be a good salary in the beginning, after two years he realized that he should be receiving not just a good salary but also equities from the company. To illustrate his point, Yan recalls a Jack Nicholson film where he says, "Hey, if he was so fucking smart, why is he so fucking dead?" Laughing, Yan says, "And in my head it clicked differently: if you're so fucking smart, why are you so fucking poor?" So, in 1982, three years after starting, he switched jobs and became an engineer at a semi-conductor company. This proved to be an excellent career move and he remained there for the next three years. By now the family had been living in California for about six years and his wife, Natasha, was becoming very restless.

Natasha did not like living in California and was interested in building a new life in a different setting. For her, the California population was too transitory. There were too many people there from elsewhere. "In California your neighbor is just as far from you mentally and emotionally as anybody living in Nicaragua; you just don't know these people." As a person who had lost her own roots and culture when she left Kiev, she felt a deep need for a place that did have roots, a place with a sense of home. When Yan was offered a position in Oregon in a start-up with one of his former company managers, he was attracted to the new opportunity. He was hired as a physicist, working in optical design which, he says, he knew nothing about. But the challenging new work was just what he wanted. The family moved to Portland, where the new job was located, and found the city very much to their liking. Within a few months they had bought the property they now live in. All three of their closest neighbors had been occupying their houses for generations. "So I think that Natasha got exactly what she wanted—a place with deep roots."

Yan and his family live in a roomy old house in a spacious—at least an acre—property. Behind the house is a large, lovely garden, set out in an unconventional but very attractive style by his wife, who devotes a great deal of time to it. The house has the beauty of so many old houses—nooks and crannies, upstairs and downstairs, verandahs, more rooms than one knows what to do with. It is all comfortably and tastefully decorated. Paintings by Natasha and her older brother—a well-known artist back in what was once the Soviet Union—grace the walls. Natasha has devoted much of her time to art—whether painting or other media (she has some remarkable items in découpage)—while Yan has been the principal bread winner.

He has managed to do so very successfully. In 1987, he left the start-up (which wasn't making a financial go of it) and joined a very large international firm, where he has worked ever since. His job has made him financially independent. "I can retire any time . . . I work because I like to."

Yan and Natasha had planned that their parents would follow them to the States right after their own exit. But because their departure closely coincided with the Soviet invasion of Afghanistan, the emigration started to dry up and gradually there was hardly any permission to leave given at all. Yan decided to use his own technique to push the authorities into allowing his mother and step-father out: he would harass them. Looking through *Pravda*, he found the names of hundreds of deputies to the Supreme Soviet, the legislative body, and wrote to them. The letters contained inflammatory, anti-Soviet content. He selected particularly vulnerable deputies in rural areas or in the military, who would be especially nervous about the KGB and would rush to hand over the letters and assure them that they had nothing to do with this. Every few months his mother would be invited in to the local office and she would be told: "Please ask your son to stop sending all those letters." She would reply "He would, if you let me go." Yan feels that his idea worked, because she was among the first to leave—in 1987—when things started loosening up. The truth is, of course, that they had been prevented from emigrating for many years.

In the meantime, after their arrival in Portland, Natasha gave birth to a second child, a girl. Their son was fifteen years old when Sasha (Alexandra) was born. She is now a university student. While Yan prefers to speak to his children in English, his parents and Natasha have always spoken Russian to them. While the children are bi-lingual, Sasha does have an accent in her Russian. Both children identify themselves essentially as Americans. When Anton visited Ukraine at age twenty-two, he was amazed that he couldn't really blend in, even though he has no accent. He found that he had a different perspective from people there, clearly separating him from them.

When his parents did finally arrive in the United States, Yan found them an apartment in his neighborhood and eventually bought them a house just two blocks away from his own. They seem to have settled in very happily, both of them mastering English, and his step-father even learning to drive for the first time, in his sixties. Yan bought him a car, urging them to be independent. While they do not receive Social Security, they do get Social Security Supplement, which comes to over one thousand dollars a month. They also have twenty percent of their living expenses paid for by the state (called "assisted living" although they are in their own house). They even have a large circle of friends, though, now in their eighties, the number is diminishing.

In the end, Natasha's parents did not emigrate. They came for a four-month visit, but after two months, Yan could already see that they would not stay. Unlike his parents, Natasha's had another child, still living in Ukraine. "They had to choose to live there and have proximity to their son and [that] lifestyle or live here, and I think they made the right choice." At the time of the interview, Natasha was in Kiev, where her mother had just died. Her father had passed away three months before.

Yan and Natasha returned to Ukraine for the first time in 1994. They had left the Soviet Union in 1979 ("I was sure I would never come back") and in the interim their family members had made visits to them in Oregon. Now they finally did convince themselves to return and, after that first visit, Natasha has been there every year since. In the course of all their travels Israel has never been a destination. "It's not on top of my wish list . . . I was thinking why . . . I have worked very intensely all the time so I really look for relaxation when I go on vacation and Israel looks like a very intense place to me. It's not [a place] that allows you to put your mind at ease and just vegetate a bit." Perhaps, he says, after he retires.

Their children have lost their ties with their own background to a large extent. Where Yan and Natasha (who is only Jewish on one side) see themselves, ethnically, as Jews, while non-religious, Anton and Sasha have largely shed their connections. Yan himself, while saying twenty-five years before that he would like to attend High Holiday services, did not feel a real tie when he did so. "I went a couple of times, just because I was interested in what it was; I'd never seen it . . . I just felt out of place." Anton is now married, but not to a Jewish girl. And Yan is convinced that when his daughter finds the right person, his religion will not be a factor "just as it wasn't for me. It truly wasn't."

Yan is a man of ideas. He doesn't make judgments lightly, but probes and investigates a topic until he feels that he can form an opinion wisely. This is not just in his own field, but in any facet of life that touches him. When asked about current politics in Ukraine, he said that, by chance, his wife had been visiting her parents just at the time of the orange revolution. Everyone was so hopeful then. But now, a year later, "you can start seeing huge cynicism building in Ukraine as a result of the complete . . . implosion of forces that brought new power." He compares it with the hope, followed by disappointment, after the events of 1991 in Russia.

In American politics, Yan sees himself as a conservative, certainly fiscally. While he voted for George W. Bush the first time, he did not the second, but that was for reasons of foreign policy. He feels that going into Iraq "was a sign of great ignorance." Politicians chose the wrong way to deal with a very old culture—radical Moslem culture—"with its own way of living and doing things . . . You cannot assume that you can come in and impose your way of thinking on those people and they will accept it gladly . . . It's pure stupidity."

For him, "Republican means small government." Almost half his salary is taken away in taxes. "What I see is that people who get things from redistribution do not benefit that much from getting it, but it absolutely perverts the structure which deals with distribution. It becomes more powerful; it starts to serve its own means. It absolutely doesn't have in mind the best for people in the name of whom this distribution is [intended]. It becomes completely self-serving." There is no unity within his family on these issues. Their political views seem to span the political spectrum.

Yan accesses most of his news on the Internet, where he sees papers from Ukraine, Britain, Israel and so on and he has a generally low opinion of the

American press. While he does not watch the news on television, he does hear it on the radio, especially while driving.

Yan has kept up with a few of his old friends. Those who were imprisoned have long since been released. Some perform important functions where they live. He has managed to see his closest friends every year or so, at least. While he and Natasha have friends in Portland—most of them not speakers of Russian—they never really made the closest of friendships here. "My conclusion is that in order to have real friends you have to have a common past."

The big question, of course, is about happiness. In 1980 Yan felt that he had lost all hope of happiness. What does he see, when he looks back over the past twenty-five years? Yan, in his usual introspective way, has given much thought to the subject. "By the age of about forty-three, forty-four, I had everything going my way. I had a beautiful family. I had beautiful children. I had a beautiful house and I had beautiful work. By this time, I was pretty well-off financially and I was not happy." He was afraid that too much concern with personal achievement and how others valued him—too much vanity, in a word—were preventing him from attaining happiness on a very personal level and he made a concerted effort to focus on the "real things:" his work (but not publications), his family. He tried to do things that did not require a "pat on the back" to give him satisfaction. In the end, Yan feels that this exercise was good for him and good for his work. His brain, he says, "became much more productive" and his new way of looking at life brought a sense of happiness.

Having worked with many different companies and in many different countries, Yan says that "I think what makes the life of the immigrant in the U.S. different from any place else (and I don't know Israel) . . . but comparing to Europe and Japan, I think America gives an opportunity to everyone to rise as far as this person can . . . This person will be judged fairly." He adds that "the culture of the country allows you to be judged just on your contribution and your merit." He sees this as uniquely American.

Now, when he looks back on his life, he no longer feels that his happiest years were in Kiev. "I think I was blessed. I had a very happy life there and after about ten years of a difficult time here—the first ten years—I've been very happy."

NOTE

1. A phone call to Valentina many months later clarified that her doctor had been mistaken and that tests showed a non-malignant growth, which could probably be taken care of easily.

Chapter Nine

In Israel,
Twenty-Five Years Later

BACKGROUND

Profound changes had taken place in Israel during the twenty-five year period since the first interviews. Towards the end of the nineteen seventies, Anwar Sadat had made his dramatic visit to Israel and this was followed, a year and a half later, by the peace accord between Israel and Egypt, signed by Menahem Begin and Sadat, under the aegis of Jimmy Carter. While the agreement provided a certain feeling of security at Israel's southern border, developments in Lebanon eventually brought on Israeli military intervention in the spring of 1982. A period of enormous inflation characterized the mid-eighties, and it took a few years until the economic situation was gradually brought under control, under shared stewardship of the government. Political leadership passed from the Likud to the Labor party in the early nineties.

As the eighties drew to a close, a dramatic increase in the—until then, nearly dormant—exodus from the Soviet Union was set in motion thanks to political and policy changes there. This new influx exerted its own influence on Israeli politics. In general, the new immigrants tended to back the right-wing parties, and, as the nineties progressed, their voting power was palpable. These voters showed themselves to be highly skeptical of pressure from the center left-wing parties to embark on peace initiatives. Their Russian-language publications reinforced this position. However, the attitude of the "Russian" voters did not always remain rigidly in one camp, largely because the economy also played an important part in their calculations.

In 1986, the highly symbolic refusenik and Prisoner of Zion, Anatolii Shcharanskii, was freed from his Soviet prison and made a triumphal entry into Israel, where his wife and eager supporters awaited him. Though appearing to be a strong supporter of human rights while active in the Soviet Union,

Shcharanskii disappointed those Israelis who had high expectations that he would be a pivotal figure in the protection of human rights in Israel and, possibly, a proponent of the peace process. Instead, he gravitated towards Benjamin Netanyahu and the political right and, eventually—in 1995—set up his own political party (Yisrael baAliyah), attracting large numbers of Soviet immigrants, many of whom were new arrivals. But many people who had immigrated in the seventies and saw themselves as his former comrades in arms also joined up with him. The party won seven seats (out of the total of 120) in the Knesset in the 1996 elections.

What the Palestinians dubbed their "*intifada*" began at the end of the eighties and proved to be very intimidating and dangerous. It encouraged the Soviet immigrants both in their distrust of the Arab population and their belief in a strong right-wing government. By this time, an enormous flow of Russian-speaking immigrants was inundating Israel. Close to eight hundred thousand of them entered the country between 1989 and 1999. In terms of elections, one has to consider that for every twenty thousand votes, one member of Knesset was chosen. In casting their ballots, immigrants were influenced by various considerations, including economic ones. At least twice their pockets indicated the need for new leadership. The alternation between the Likud and Labor, giving the vote to Rabin in 1992, followed by Netanyahu, and then Barak, reflects to some extent the contribution of the "Russian" voting pattern to the political picture. Still, it is safe to say as a generalization that they did tend to lean to the right. Shcharanskii himself, now calling himself Natan Sharansky, eventually abandoned the "center-oriented" party that he had created, or, rather, joined it to the Likud party. Other Russian-speaking immigrants—including some who had arrived in the 1970s—also made political careers, again, mainly, but not only, on the right of the political spectrum.

A second intifada began at the end of September, 2000. This marked the end of the peace negotiations being carried out by the Israeli Prime Minister at the time—Ehud Barak, a member of the Labor Party—and the Palestinians, led by Yasir Arafat. A new spate of bus bombings and other terrorist attacks ensued. It was hard not to notice, in the lists of those wounded or killed, the number of clearly Russian names. They were paying the toll like every other Israeli.

In the late summer of 2005, under the leadership of Prime Minister Ariel Sharon, the Israeli government removed all Jewish settlers from the Gaza Strip, resettling them inside Israel, largely in temporary housing until permanent arrangements could be made. No Israelis were permitted to remain there and the army itself withdrew, leaving the area to the Palestinians. This was a major issue that was hotly debated in Israel for many months.

Some contrasts should be noted in the more recent immigration. First of all, the proportions were completely different. It was said that the number of new immigrants arriving in Israel from the former Soviet Union in the nineteen nineties was, relatively, as if the entire population of France had suddenly ended up in America. Clearly, in this situation solutions had to be found for this enormous influx on the macro and micro levels. One of the significant changes—connected with the immigration of the nineteen seventies—was that many of the new arrivals in the nineties were welcomed by their friends and family members, who had immigrated twenty years before. They were able to provide help and advice of a kind that they themselves had not been able to benefit from. They were now the "old-timers."

Those now coming in were, in a way, fleeing uncertainty—unseen or unpredictable problems. They were aware of the earlier emigration and knew that the doors had then been shut, leaving many "refuseniks" to wait out the decade. They weren't going to let that happen to them. Who knew what dangers for Jews lurked in the new post-Soviet Russia, Ukraine and Belarus? Why take a chance? If America didn't allow them in, then there was always Israel. They encountered a completely different situation from that of their predecessors and the attitude of many of them toward Israel was decidedly different. The ideological factor governing the actions of many of the immigrants to Israel in the nineteen seventies was largely absent from this group. Indeed, many were deeply unhappy to have to live in Israel and made their decision *faute de mieux.* Furthermore, among the many who arrived during the later period were numerous spouses and in-laws who were not Jewish, not even a little bit. Their proportion was far higher than in the earlier immigration. Furthermore, as the American door was closing, other options became apparent and the 1990s saw large numbers of (formerly) Soviet Jews emigrating to Germany, which was to become the fast growing Jewish community in Europe. But this is a different story of another kind, which will doubtless be studied with interviews by other scholars.

Unlike the later—and far larger—immigration of the 1990s, a significant part of the group that arrived in Israel in the course of the nineteen seventies had been ideologically motivated. They had seen Israel as a goal, not only a haven, as the fulfillment of dreams, not only a place to find refuge. It would therefore be expected that the satisfaction level of this group might be very high. For some, residing in Israel was living out their dream and a tremendous sense of fulfillment came from just being in Israel, participating in life there on a daily basis, serving in the army reserves, voting for the party of choice, hearing your children or grandchildren speak Hebrew. For others, things were not so simple. Dreams are funny things: you are sometimes disappointed when you wake up.

LEV

Sitting with Lev, one is caught up in a whirlwind of talk, bombarded with ideas bouncing in every direction. Lev, at seventy-six, is still capable of producing a barrage of words, of questions, opinions that are almost impossible to absorb, so great is the intensity. While he has retired from active creation of monumental works of art, he is still very much part of Israeli life and the art scene.

He and his wife live in a comfortable apartment in the French Hill neighborhood of Jerusalem. His world is the world of art. His ideology is that of Zionism. His goal was to live in Israel, where he now is. But his complaints focus on that conjunction of his art and Israel. These center on a few main points: the appreciation in Israel (or lack thereof) for his work; the number of works he has been commissioned to do since arriving in Israel; the amount he was paid for them (which he connects to appreciation and respect) and— perhaps his worst criticism—the way his works of art have been treated here.

From the point of view of his professional life, Lev does appear to be disappointed. He shows pictures of some of his works in Israel, marvelous swirls of color and shape, often pieced together from countless small bits of naturally colored stone. "This is not transparent glass in various colors. It's eternal. Forever. But here in Israel of my thirty-two works, six have already been destroyed by the people of Israel." Only one, he says, was destroyed by Arabs (in a terrorist attack in the heart of Tel Aviv). The rest were ruined by ordinary Israelis: "Our people are not hooligans. We are barbarians, not hooligans. Jews." Turning to the interviewer, he says, "You live in an ivory tower. I don't have my health, nor time and no great willingness to stand before our remnants of an intelligentsia and tell you what's going on in Israel." At the faculty of Medicine at Rambam Hospital in Haifa, where Lev has created a huge masterpiece, he claims that medical students used pocket knives to dig out the little stones.

Lev, having been a successful artist in the Soviet Union with many important works to his credit, has found it difficult to adjust to the more modest scale of opportunity and budgets in a small country like Israel. (Indeed, he even says that an important university figure told him years ago that he should really move to the United States if he is looking for large projects.) The problem is that Israel is really where he wants to be and so it has been hard to accept the lowering of options in order to live in the country that he loves above all. He complains that, "Today we are spending millions of dollars to restore a very average mosaic at Beth Shean [an important archeological site in the north of Israel]. Then we exhibit a not badly done—handcrafted, it's true—woman's head in the museum and everyone goes to see this important sight. Here lives a living artist working on mosaics who made a huge work. New—a new word in art. And no one came."

Invited to enter a competition for a tender, Lev refused. He said that he had participated in four competitions in Israel and every time there had been deceit and ugliness; every time there had been *protektskia*, bribes. And every time the resultant work by the winner of the competition had been awful. He doesn't feel that he has ever been recompensed properly in Israel—or almost never. He refers to himself—the son of a prominent Zionist family—as an *oleh* [immigrant] without trousers.

His major project in Haifa was actually composed in Italy, in Ravenna. Lev felt that Italy had more qualified people to complete the task skillfully. He went over (with his family) three times during the six months that it was being made. Then the huge panels were shipped to Israel.

Whatever his complaints, there is no doubt that Lev has made a tremendous contribution to the aesthetics of Israel, with his vibrant, colorful, moving monumental works everywhere from Sodom to Haifa, from Ashdod to Jerusalem. They are rich with Biblical references: here is the creation of the waters and all that is in them; there is day and night in the Garden of Eden; a panel elsewhere shows Zebulon the mariner; other panels are filled with birds of every kind, or the cosmos.

Lev is blessed in his private life with a lovely wife ("the best in the world"), two daughters and a son. Eva is the daughter who now lives in the Chicago area. Her younger sister is based in Israel but has an exciting job that keeps her in Europe much of the time. Lev's son—the baby whose birth delayed the family's departure from the Soviet Union for Israel—is now in his thirties and is a respected Israeli film maker. Lev and his wife have traveled a number of times to the United States, both to see Eva and to work, but they have never returned to Moscow. Lev hates the current regime.

Financially, life has been difficult. He receives no pension but only thirteen hundred shekels (about $380) a month from Bituah Leumi (a form of social security payment). His wife, who received an excellent salary as an economist, does have a good pension. It is a disgrace, he says, that the Israeli government should maintain its outstanding artists in this way. Lev, of course, grew up with a different model of treating artists: officially accepted Soviet writers, painters and people in the other arts received from the government privileges not ordinarily enjoyed by their colleagues in the West.

Asked about politics, Lev at first demurs. "I'm an artist. I've never belonged to any party." He has voted differently every time, he says. In fact, according to Lev there isn't any difference between the political parties. The religious have too much power. As far as he is concerned, the Maarach (Labor) ceased to exist after the murder of Rabin. He cannot forgive that terrible crime. "After the murder of Rabin, I spent a sleepless night. At first I regretted that I had come to Israel. Then that passed, but there's this feeling that for me, a patriot, a Zionist, the son of a Zionist family, having given my life and everything to Israel with a pure heart, all for naught."

Asked about the *hitnatkut*, the evacuation of the Jewish settlements from Gaza, which was in the offing at the time of the interview, Lev says that it should be done quickly. It's only too bad that it's being done so late. "It should have happened thirty years ago."

Lev, who has friends among the Arab population in the Jerusalem area, has also had run-ins with terrorists. When he and his brother wanted to visit their parents' graves on the Mount of Olives at the time of the second intifada, rocks and chunks of cement were hurled at his brother's new car as they made their way to the cemetery. A fifteen-year-old boy, he says, aimed at Norman's head. Had he not dodged it, he would have been killed. Lev, too, acted instinctively and raised the window at the last minute. "By chance we remained alive." The policeman who appeared on the scene couldn't believe that they were all right when he saw the car. He said to them, "Go and pray; light a candle. You should have been killed here. How are you alive?"

Much of Lev's criticism of Israel rests either on his attitude toward religion or his dismay at the state of the Israeli intelligentsia. "I live simply in this country. We have huge gaps. We are involved with nonsense: we ourselves don't know what we want . . . We're departing from the Zionist ideal and way of life. We've got hundreds of thousands of men who have a legal dispensation from army service and don't work. And they produce children whom they keep in darkness and ignorance." This is not an unimportant subject. "I myself am a person, already an old person and quite rich in life experience. By nature, I am a Zionist. Nothing in the world is of interest to me, except Israel." He points out the interconnection between this and the Biblical theme that entwines much of his creative work.

In a rambling way, Lev comes out with his thoughts on the problems of the two peoples who occupy the immediate area. "We don't have to live with them. We should have separated from them long ago. Each people has its own fate. . . . Not a single Jew on territory where the Arabs rule; not one Arab here. It's very simple. For the sake of the lives of two peoples. Otherwise we'll slaughter each other . . . and in the end one will be wiped out. . . . We live in a state that is the main, the last hope of Jews on earth." If we want a Jewish, a

Zionist, state, "let's do it, starting with having every man who can bear arms serve in the army, do reserve duty. Everybody has to work. No parasitism." Lev has more of a problem with ultra-orthodox Jews than he does with Arabs. When his son, a soldier and an officer, came home from serving in Lebanon during the first Lebanese war, his car was stoned, because he was riding on the Sabbath. "This wasn't Arabs; it was Jews."

Lev's Jewish identity is an integral part of him. "Even if I became a Buddhist, I wouldn't stop being a Jew. I would be a Jew who believes in Confucianism. I'd be a Jew who believes in Karl Marx, . . . I wouldn't stop being a Jew . . ." And then, taking a breath after all of his peregrination into politics and philosophy, Lev settles back: "Actually, I'd rather talk to you about art."

ANATOLII AND SVETLANA

While many of the immigrants interviewed came as Zionists, only Anatolii and Svetlana changed to Hebrew names when they arrived in Israel. They have enjoyed a low-key but modestly successful life in Israel, though they are not the sort of people who speak in hyperbole about achievements and happiness. Svetlana pursued her music career and taught music (and film) in various schools for many years. From the beginning, she taught in Hebrew. Since their move a few years ago, there is no piano in their new apartment.

Anatolii continued in the academic world after receiving his doctorate and taught courses at the university, mainly to Russian-speaking students in the preparatory department. He was also employed by the Russian-language Jewish encyclopedia, an enormous project that spanned many years. Working his way up through various positions, he eventually became the editor-in-chief. While it was a good job, he would have preferred a more strictly academic position. Although he is now officially on pension, he has continued to work on it. At the time of the second interview, they were preparing an electronic version of the encyclopedia.

Their daughter, Sonia, has not lived in Israel for decades. Her husband, a Soviet-born mathematician, first took an academic position in America (after she finished her B.A. and M.A. at the Hebrew University), moved from job to job, dissatisfied with life there, and eventually received an unexpected invitation from a university in Sweden, where they and their daughter now live. Anatolii and Svetlana are in frequent touch with them, both by phone and e-mail and they see each other at least once a year. Their granddaughter speaks English and Hebrew well (though she cannot read or write Hebrew), and understands Russian, though she doesn't like to speak it. She completed a B.A. in computers and was now—at the time of the interview—traveling around the world. She even worked on a kibbutz for four months as part of her adventure.

Svetlana and Anatolii moved into a lovely apartment in 2002. They did so partly to accommodate their daughter's visits. Having lived in Israel for thirty-five years, they are finally mortgage-free. Much to their relief, they managed to pay it off. The inflation helped, says Svetlana. In spite of this, they do not feel that their economic situation is better now than it was twenty-five years ago. "Perhaps," says Anatolii, "it's a bit worse . . . [in a reference to a reform made by Benjamin Netanyahu]. They even stole money from Bituah Leumi." He suggests that their finances are worse because they are now living on pensions, but he does tend in general to think in negative terms.

When Svetlana enters the room and is asked to catch up on the news since the first interview, she sums it up quickly: "I can answer precisely: this ship is sinking." Which ship? Israel. Then Anatolii adds, "It's already sunk." "Almost," she responds.

Anatolii and Svetlana, besides traveling to the United States and Sweden to see the family and taking other trips to Europe, have returned to the former Soviet Union three times. The first, before the breakup of the country, was in 1990, when they were sent to work there within the Jewish community. They were in Kiev and then in the Crimea. This was at the beginning of the tremendous exodus of Jews from the area. At the time, various Russian-speaking Israelis were sent over either to teach Hebrew, organize the community or help with the emigration process. The next visit, when they were also sent, was to Odessa in 1993 and then they went for a week on their own in 1997. While they do not have much family remaining there, they still have some close cousins whom they keep up with.

Though Anatolii may fly to the former Soviet Union again to see an ailing cousin, Svetlana fervently hopes that the 1997 visit was the last one she will have to make. She found the first trip, in particular, unbearable. She felt, among other problems, that there was a tremendous amount of dirt everywhere. Svetlana was also distressed at the amount of bribery that was prevalent for absolutely everything. She finds it reprehensible.

Anatolii was attuned politically even as a youth, so it is not surprising that he has an enormous interest in Israeli politics today and holds strong opinions. He is particularly concerned about two integral factors in the Israeli state: defense and Israel's international position. The economy is also problematic and he feels that in general the situation has become worse, not better, over the years. He and Svetlana are delighted that Gaza has been evacuated. Neither of them reads the Russian-language Israeli press and their paper of choice is a middle-of-the-road large circulation Hebrew daily called *Yediot Aharonot*. On television they tend towards the Hebrew-language channels, while also keeping an eye on the news on CNN and the BBC (and occasionally the French channel) for news.

In discussing Russia today, Anatolii says it is possible, after all the unsuccessful experiments with democratization, that perhaps what they have now is the most suitable system: enlightened absolutism, not too harsh.

Israel is different. Twenty-five years ago, he said that he was a believer in old-fashioned democracy. He says that he still feels that way. "At my age it's hard to change one's views," he says with his quiet humor. However, he feels that, certainly among Russian immigrants, he is in a minority here in Israel. And that minority lacks influence. As a member of the peace camp, he is also in a minority among his fellow Russian-speaking immigrants.

Anatolii does not regret that he chose to live in Israel. On the contrary. "It's important that this is Israel, that it's a Jewish state." They've been urged by their daughter to come and live with them in Sweden. Svetlana doesn't want to. She doesn't want to feel like a foreigner again. "How many times can I be an *oleh hadash* [new immigrant, using the Hebrew term]? While Anatolii is half tempted, he prefers, at this stage of his life, to stay put and not make changes. They both feel that they are among their own in Israel and have many friends, largely friendships of long standing.

In talking about his life in Kiev many years ago, Anatolii described himself as an internal émigré. Does he feel like one here in Israel too? The answer is a definite no. "But from the political point of view, I feel myself in the minority, without a doubt."

FRIMA

Aaron died in 1998 after a lingering illness. His wife Bella died the next year. Frima, left all alone, was the only person available to complete the family story twenty-five years after the original interview. She gladly welcomed the visit to the home in a very religious Jerusalem neighborhood that she had shared with her parents for years. She looks like any other orthodox woman: head modestly covered, a simple, well-ironed dress. The apartment is decorated in an already familiar "Russian" style with cupboards filled with all sorts of little items, memorabilia, china, books, and many many photographs, mainly of her parents or, more precisely, of her father. The apartment is clean and neat almost to the point of being sterile. It is the home of a person who lives frugally. She suggests that the interview be carried on in Hebrew.

While the lives of these three people had been low-key, Frima and her father eventually entered into quite exciting terrain and for a number of years

they were unexpectedly busy and productive. According to Frima, Aaron—
who was outwardly very quiet and lacking in forcefulness—was the dynamo
behind their new activities, although they were based on her own work. They
were related to Frima's translation skills, the overwhelming political changes
in the former Soviet Union, and their religious concerns.

Besides translating Zelda's poetry from Hebrew to Russian, Frima began
to translate from German, English and Yiddish as well. She also settled down
to her *magnum opus* of translating the Tanakh (Five Books of Moses) and
commentaries into Russian. Aaron managed to see through the publication
of this great work in Israel. Then Frima went on to translate the Prophets and
other texts. It was an enormous task. When Aaron died, Frima continued with
her translations, but these more recent ones have never been published. Her
father had been the one who had made it all possible and without him she cannot find the initiative and inner strength to see her work published. He found
the money, saw the books through the publishing process, everything. "He
was amazing. He did things that were impossible to do at all. He succeeded in
an impossible way . . . Now, after his death, I've understood what he'd done."

In 1979, Frima got married. It was not an arranged marriage, but someone
whom she had met. Unfortunately, things didn't work out. "[I wasn't mar-
ried] a long time. I received the *get* [religious divorce] in 1986 and it was
very, very hard . . . It could be that it was even harder on my parents . . . I
thought that he was religious; a friend introduced us . . . [It was all very diffi-
cult]" This was all happening at the same time as Frima's translation project.

Frima and her father were busy with another activity in the nineteen nineties as well. Starting in 1990, when the Jewish Agency sent Frima to Russia,
they started traveling to the former Soviet Union a few times a year. After
the first visit, Frima's trips were funded by various organizations that were
interested in her teaching Torah and Jewish studies, mainly to Jews living in
Moscow. But she also taught in Odessa, Kiev, Leningrad and Riga. And she
was never alone. Her father accompanied her on every trip. He insisted that
she should not go by herself. And your mother: what was she doing when you
and your father traveled to Russia? "She stayed here and worked."

It was Frima who was doing the teaching. Aaron simply accompanied her.
Did she enjoy the opportunity to see all these new cities? "I'll tell you the
truth, this was more my father's decision . . . That is, I had no curiosity; I
could have taught in Israel. It wasn't that I was missing something. But he,
davka, thought that it was important, that it had to be done, so we traveled, we
traveled." Once her father took ill, in 1994, he would not agree to her going
alone. She might go again now, but no one has asked her to since her father's
death, and she would not take the initiative.

The family were not travelers in a touristic sense. Bella never went back
to the former Soviet Union at all; she had no desire to. Her sister eventually

moved to Israel. Her brother ended up in the United States and died there. His family lives in America. Frima has cousins in Israel through her father as well. His older brother arrived in Israel with his sons and grandchildren in the 1990s. The brothers had not maintained close communication for many years when Aaron received a request for an invitation so that they could leave the Soviet Union. He gladly took care of it. By the time he arrived, his brother was already in a deteriorated mental and physical state. He died in 1996, but his family largely seems to have settled down well economically. The cousins do not maintain close contact.

Frima does not belong to a political party, but has voted in elections up until the present. "I participated in the elections because it was important to my father, very important." Aaron was not in a political party either, voting for candidates whom he could identify with. She is less motivated to vote and doesn't know what she will do in the next election. She does not agree with the right, with the Likud party, and sees no means of influencing what is going on. She is definitely against the withdrawal from the Gaza Strip, feeling that it is a catastrophe. She doesn't go out and demonstrate, but prays that everything will work out the right way:

> In terms of politics, I am on the right side of the map, of course. Why 'of course'? Because in the end the interests of my people are more important than any other consideration . . . I'd like it to be good for everyone. But when I know that we live in times of a struggle and that it's a question of them or us, I'm on the side of 'us.' And I have no doubts. That is, I have no hostility toward the Arabs, but the problem is that they have hostility towards me. I'm really sorry that they'll take down the settlements . . . and I'm very sorry that it will only increase the danger. And I'm sure that it will increase the danger but I don't fight politically because it's not my way.

Frima's view of Israeli politics is through the prism of her family's original attitudes towards emigration. They had not been Zionists in the full sense of the word. Their reasons for coming to Israel had been, she says, strictly religious. "My father loved Israel [*ha-aretz*] very much, felt a strong tie, maybe even more than I. Look, I've been in Israel for more than thirty years and it's clear that this is my place, my people without any doubt. I'm not a Zionist in a secular sense. I'm very tied to this place, very much so. This connection is, you understand, religious, a national tie of course."

ZHENIA

Zhenia turned up for the interview at an outdoor café looking distinctly different from the previous encounter over two decades before. Instead of the lovely slender young woman with neat dark brown hair, here was a woman in her mid-fifties, with a heavy figure, graying hair in an imperfectly kept bun with loose wisps. But Zhenia, with her wonderful liquid brown eyes and ready smile, still exudes warmth and humor and is as observant and articulate as before, making her a delightful interlocutor.

She has done well in her career, which she began not very long after the family arrived in Israel so many years ago, and has a highly responsible professional job. The dream of working on a PhD and becoming an academic may not have come to fruition, but Zhenia gives the impression that she is happy with her work. Hers is certainly a personal success story, professionally.

At the last encounter, she had been expecting a baby. That second daughter, Liza, is now serving in a crack unit in the army. She has had some terrifying experiences, not as a soldier, but as a civilian. One day, a few years ago, she was in Zion Square, in the middle of Jerusalem, when a terrorist bomb exploded. She was hospitalized for shock. Her denim bag was full of holes and her clothes retained such a stench of the blast that Zhenia took everything that Liza had been wearing and burned it. But the smell was so entwined with the experience of the bombing that some time later, when they were at a picnic, her daughter refused to eat meat grilled in the campfire. Her second encounter with terrorism happened when she was already in the army and had been sent to a hospital in Beer Sheba for a checkup. When she left the hospital, there were two explosions on a bus some thirty feet away. While she was not physically hurt, she went into shock again.

Zhenia's family had to deal with other violence during the second *intifada* (uprising). In the early period, the Jerusalem neighborhood of Gilo, where they live, was frequently shelled from Beit Jala, a Palestinian town on the way to Bethlehem. The situation went on for months and numerous houses suffered from damage, not to speak of the physical and emotional strain on the inhabitants from months of shooting. Once the Israeli tanks moved in and started replying to the attacks, the noise was enormous. The family couldn't even sleep at night. But it was more than just the noise. "In our place the floor was jumping. Books flew off the shelf."

Zhenia's older daughter, following a spinal problem that required surgery, went straight on to the university after high school, not qualifying for military service. She has had a number of different jobs and now seems to have settled into a good position with a public company. She is soon to be married and, following something of a pattern, her fiancé is also from a Russian-speaking family.

In Israel, there is a choice of a religious or secular state education (besides various private options). Both of Zhenia's daughters were sent through the religious stream of education. This was partly done in order to compensate for the lack of a strong Jewish tradition in the home. Seryozha, while Jewish, experienced a minimal Jewish atmosphere while growing up. Zhenia, clearly, had none. They hoped that the girls would get a strong foundation in the religion of the country that they were living in. Today, neither of their daughters is particularly religious.

Unfortunately, the romance between the girl from Yalta and the Jewish boy from Kiev did not last, though they remained married for a long time. Zhenia and Seryozha were divorced after nineteen years of marriage, some nine years before the last interview. It was probably predictable. Seryozha had been increasingly drawn to extreme religious observance and, with that, far right nationalism. He followed an eccentric life style, spending more and more time in the Hebron area, working, studying, and supporting the right of Jews to live in what he considered historic Jewish land. The couple spent less and less time together, though Seryozha continued to be a caring father to his daughters. In fact, it was he who took their older daughter for a visit to Kiev, her first after the family had left when she was a small child. Zhenia, who stayed behind with her younger daughter, says that wherever she and her father went, her older daughter kept saying the same phrase: "*U nas lushche!*" (in its time, a frequently-used Soviet expression meaning "We have it better.") Characteristically, Zhenia laughed and said "How could you have compared the Dnieper River and our Yarkon?" Well, she answered, we have three seas! Three years later, the same daughter returned to Kiev, this time for only ten days and when she came back to Israel she said that she wouldn't seek anything further there.

An illustration of the diverse paths the husband and wife eventually followed can be seen in the decision on their daughter's surgery when she was fifteen. There was a complex question—given the delicacy of the operation and potential complications—as to whether she should go through with it. The decision was left to Zhenia. What about Seryozha? Seryozha said, "If there is such danger, I'll pray." As Zhenia tells the story, "I laughed a lot, because if everything turned out all right, that meant his prayers helped; and if it turns out badly, then I'm guilty."

The divorce was ultimately Zhenia's decision, but they have both come to realize that it was the best thing to do. "He got a more interesting life for himself. He's less occupied with the family; he's freer; he started to cook. It's great: he cooks better than I do." Seryozha lives in occupied territory, in the Hebron area. He works very little. Years ago, because of a medical problem, he lost the use of a few fingers on his right hand, making it impossible to continue being a mechanic. Seryozha has been legally declared an invalid since his forties and has a small pension. Living alone, frugally, he finds that it is enough. He also receives a modest sum from the *kollel* (religious community), if he regularly joins them in study and prayer. For those days when he is ill and cannot come, there is no remuneration. His older daughter phones him every day to make sure that he is looking after himself. At the time of the interviews, Seryozha was actively busy with the groups opposing withdrawal from Gaza.

Zhenia would also prefer that Gaza remain in Israeli hands, but for security reasons. As far as she is concerned, the further the border is from the center, the less danger. (She is guided in this thinking by her own experience of being shelled at quite close range during the second *intifada*.) In the last few elections, she has voted for Likud. To her "great regret," she voted for Sharon (the architect of the Gaza pullout). She has no idea whom she would support if there were an election today. There is, she says, no one with charisma. "Besides that, I'm tired of generals at the head of the government. Politics should be handled by politicians." She is not impressed by Shcharanskii who, she feels, would have been better placed as a top official in the Jewish Agency, not in the government. "That's his place, not higher. Here," she criticizes, "you can have a minister of culture who knows nothing about culture. A person can be switched from one ministry to another without accomplishing anything anywhere."

The rest of Zhenia's family seems to have made a remarkably happy decision in following her to Israel. Her mother—that staunch communist teacher—eventually moved to Haifa and settled into a successful professional life. She even met a wonderful man, a doctor, whom she married. The twelve years of their marriage—until he died—were very happy ones. Zhenia's sister, still working as a nurse, never married. But she does have a daughter, who is about to enter the army. The three girl cousins maintain a warm relationship.

Zhenia has also gone back to the former Soviet Union, and, particularly, to Yalta. She and her sister traveled to Prague and, from there, to Chop and Lvov, re-living, in reverse, the entire exit route that Zhenia and Seryozha had followed on their way out. From Lvov, they spent three days in Chernovitz, where Zhenia had spent her university years. The city, she says, is still beautiful. The sisters stayed with two of Zhenia's professors, a husband and wife who are in literary criticism and the history of literature. They told Zhenia that they had expected her to come from Israel very thin and sun-burned and what they saw before them was someone white and not so thin. (The reason for the lack of thinness is a medication that she has to take.) For Zhenia, the meeting with these professors was very moving.

Following Chernovitz, they went on to Yalta. "I have always loved Yalta and do to this day, but the Yalta that I remember. Now it's something else." Almost thirty years had passed. There is no money in Ukraine for keeping up the scenic areas. They stayed in their father's apartment in Yalta, as he was visiting Israel at the time, living at her sister's place in Haifa. They had invited him, arranged his visit, paid for his fare and he stayed in Israel for six months, then went back. Two years later, he came back again for another visit. In all, he came three times.

Zhenia seems to have become a religious, or at least a traditional, Jew. This has been going on for some time. Years before, a small separate set of utensils had been put aside for kosher food for Seryozha and the rest of the house was non-kosher. Now she maintains a kosher home. She does not ride on the Sabbath. She does not, however, go so far as to dress "modestly" in a way demanded by the very orthodox. When and how this position evolved is difficult to explain. Religion is not something that she cares to discuss, for obvious reasons.

On the eve of Passover in 2002, twenty minutes before the holiday was to begin, Zhenia received a phone call from Yalta. As usual, she had invited lots of friends and neighbors to the seder and her younger daughter was there with her, helping. The call was to tell her that her father had passed away an hour before. Zhenia simply did not know how to handle the situation; she had so many guests, but she wanted to do the right thing. She called the rabbi and asked what to do in such a case and he said, "I am almost certain that you do not have to sit [*shiva*], but I will phone my own rabbi." He phoned back to say that she should sit for exactly five minutes, get up, and receive her guests. It was an unforgettable Pesach. Putting it in a nutshell for the guests, her daughter said, "The seder will be short."

LIUBA AND SIMON

In a scenic area of the Western Galilee, a road leads towards a small Arab town and, further on, to a number of kibbutzim. A turn to the right takes the visitor to a narrow road winding up through groves of olive trees on one side and mixed fir forest all around and, about half a mile on, to a Jewish settlement atop a hill. This is Tal El, where Simon and Liuba have built their house. The village is particularly lovely, spreading gracefully out over a hillside—a far cry from urban crowding. It has its own pool, used by the inhabitants. There is no standard style here: each family has chosen its own architectural design. In all, there are about two hundred fifty families living in the village. About sixty percent are "Israelis" and forty percent "Russians." Tal El possesses an excellent Russian-language library.

At the time of the first interview, Simon and Liuba were living in a mobile home and enjoying planning this new settlement and the home that they would build. Now, for many years, they have been proud owners of a spacious house (two hundred square meters, or over 2,000 square feet), with many bedrooms, a dining room, which doubles as a living room. Upstairs is what they call their music room, a large open space with leather-type sofa and chairs and the stereo. No television sets are to be found in the public rooms; they are probably in the bedrooms. Everything is very clean and orderly, almost sterile. Unlike many Russian homes, few decorative items are to be seen, save for some pictures on the walls. There are no rugs or carpets on the tile floors; the kitchen counter is completely clear. Even the books must be elsewhere. They fondly point out photos on the wall of their beautiful six-year granddaughter and her two-year-old twin brothers.

The interview takes place on the large balcony, which overlooks the green lawn and fruit trees of their garden, then further on, an olive grove owned by a Druse family, other houses, and the surrounding rolling countryside. In the far distance the land stretches lazily across to the Carmel, where the landmark tower of the University of Haifa can be seen. A good breeze is blowing: a relief on a warm June day. There is a constant chattering of birds.

Simon enjoyed an excellent career and retired relatively young, at age sixty, in 1996, having been offered a good early retirement package. Liuba never really worked much in Israel after the initial few years, just a few months here and there, because of her physical problems. After a series of operations, she was officially given disability status. She was just over fifty. In retrospect, she sees this very positively, as it has given her the opportunity to engage in all kinds of activities she could never have had time for otherwise: to read books on philosophy, learn English, and so on. While she is still in pain, she functions well and can walk distances, though she does need therapeutic massages, which she pays for herself.

Liuba and Simon have an active cultural life. They go down to Tel Aviv a number of times a year for the opera. They also attend a concert series of the Israel Philharmonic in Haifa and have a subscription for Hebrew theater productions in the Galilee town of Carmiel. They see their son and his family once a week, usually on a week night, as Michael and his wife like to spend time with their own friends on the weekend.

Michael, after studying in the secular school system while growing up, went on to the army for three years, as is usual in Israel. Following this, he studied mechanical engineering at the Technion, but finished his studies (after a year and a half out because of a medical problem) at a private college in Israel, which Simon had to pay for. He now has a good job as a designer at a respected international firm. His wife's family actually lived on a street parallel to theirs in Leningrad, before they left for Israel. While Simon and Liuba were active in emigration politics, their future in-laws were not. The families did not meet until they all ended up in the same absorption center in Carmiel. The children went to nursery school together. The families kept up a low-key relationship with each other after Simon and Liuba moved to Tivon and the others settled elsewhere in the center of the country and they didn't see one another often. But when Michael was drafted and stationed in the south, he sometimes broke up the trip home by stopping off at their house and thus the romance between the two youngsters began.

While both come from Russian-speaking families, the younger couple speak to each other in Hebrew. (Her Russian isn't at as high a level.) It is a great disappointment to the Liuba and Simon that their three grandchildren do not speak any Russian. Seeing their grandchildren only once a week, there is not much that they can do to alter the situation, aside from trying to teach them a few words. The younger family celebrates the Jewish holidays, usually with Michael's parents-in-law, as the grandparents live there too and have retained—or returned to—religious traditions. The Passover seder is always at their house, with Liuba and Simon attending as well.

About a year and a half after Simon and Liuba came to Israel, his parents and brother arrived. Simon's brother, a construction engineer, is a year and a half older and is also retired. While he lives on a more modest scale than Simon—an ordinary city apartment—he is satisfied. Their father was already seventy and not very enthusiastic about coming in 1973, worried that he would have nothing to do. But he settled down in one of the suburbs north of Haifa and enjoyed the last seven years of his life there. Their mother is still alive, frail but alert, and lives at home, with a carer, paid for by Simon.

To her surprise, Liuba's brother also came to settle in Israel, but only in the nineteen nineties. With the large gap in age (ten years), they had hardly been brought up together. She thought that she would never see him again, once they emigrated. She certainly never expected him to want to come, but his children insisted. He has two sons, now fifty and forty-five, and some grandchildren. In Russia, he did very well and realized that he would lose his good apartment, the dacha and the car if he emigrated. They enjoyed a high standard of living in Russia. In Israel he is subsisting on national insurance, but one of his sons helped him to buy a flat and he is satisfied. All of them are. Liuba's sister, still living in Petersburg, has visited Israel at least seven times, sometimes staying for as long as a month or more, but her residence remains in Russia.

Simon and Liuba still find politics of great interest, though their choices have gone through some metamorphosis. Their source of news is both the Hebrew and Russian press (they buy the Israeli Russian-language *Vesti* once a week), and Israeli and Russian television. They probably get more news in Hebrew than in Russian. Liuba seems to have remained more right-wing, while Simon has edged more and more to the center. Liuba has always been for the Likud party. "Today, I would vote for Liberman [in the right-wing Israel Beitenu party]. But my vote would simply fall by the wayside," she says, referring to the weakness of the smaller parties in the decision-making process. In spirit, she is against the withdrawal from Gaza, though she understands that there is no choice. But she certainly does not want to see the larger settlements—Maale Adumim, Ariel and so on—abandoned.

While Simon voted for Begin in 1977, he since seems to have moderated his views. He sees himself as in the center of the political spectrum. "You have to be realistic, not beat your head against a stone wall." A propos the elections, "Look, Israel is a country where you're never bored. The situation is changing all the time. Sharon isn't the Sharon that he was twenty years ago. But [with all that], I think that there's no alternative to him." (This was at the time that Ariel Sharon was preparing the evacuation of the Jewish settlements from Gaza.) His impression is that there's nothing to talk about with the Labor Party: they're not serious. As for leaving Gaza, "In principle, it's the correct thing. We have to get out of there." He feels that it's odd to leave without any agreement [with the Palestinians], but that's the way it is. "We tried to talk to them, but nothing came of it. So there's no choice." Simon also very much favors the security fence. "It's just too bad that they're building it so late. It should have been built earlier." And what about the Jewish settlements on the other side of the fence? The big settlements have to remain, of course. You can't uproot places like Ariel. But the small settlements and the illegal ones have to be abandoned.

They still keep up with their old group of emigration activists when they can, though now, with everyone older, it has become a bit more difficult. Last year the group held a memorial meeting for Hillel Shur, one of the activists who had been imprisoned in the Soviet Union. After coming to Israel, Shur had remained involved, trying to help other newcomers. Various old comrades in arms were there, though these people were not necessarily their best friends. Their relationship was cemented by the purpose which had once joined them together.

In the mid-nineteen nineties, Simon was sent over to the United States for additional work and study. He and Liuba spent two years there, not far from Philadelphia. He enjoyed his work there very much and they managed to travel and meet many people during their stay. Did they have any regrets about the choice they made to immigrate to Israel? Simon: "I think not." Liuba: "No, no." She has no doubt. "We spoke with those who had come there [to the United States] in 1979 . . . We didn't even have a common language. They were completely different people." She doesn't know if it was because of America or because they had been different in the Soviet Union, that is, that the types of people who had opted for Israel were not the same as those who chose America. "Maybe it was because life in America is completely different, not the same as here. It changes people. Obviously, we've also changed."

The couple has traveled a great deal, almost every year. They've been all over Europe, though it took them a long time to go back to their former homeland. The year before the interview—thirty-three years after they had left—Liuba and Simon traveled back to Russia for the first time. Liuba spent the whole two weeks in St. Petersburg, while Simon took off some time to visit Moscow. They were glad to leave at the end of their stay. "It was terrible," says Liuba. "It's terrible how the people we left are living. They live on a miserly pension, in areas that formerly were considered not at all bad. Today, everything looks ugly. The only thing that looks good is the center. Nevskii [Boulevard] is very very beautiful . . . but when you go to those districts where they live, which were considered good—good districts, three-storied buildings—now it all looks awful." She doesn't feel that this can simply be attributed to the changes in neighborhoods over a thirty-year period. Newer neighborhoods are for the very rich. That's another problem—"there is too much contrast between the rich and those who are on pensions."

Simon agrees with her. It's not just the material problems. After all, they had a very hard time after the war, but people managed. But now the level of relations between people is at a low level. Service is terrible. He talks about coarseness, rudeness. There's hooliganism, banditry. The atmosphere is somber.

Liuba sums up the contrast. "Life was different before. People could stand in line all night for a copy of Sholem Aleichem, or a book of reproductions. This was completely normal. Or travel to a different city because they could buy a book there that couldn't be bought in Peter, because only a few had been printed. People lived a completely different life, it seems to me. Now life is built on materialism."

Both seem deeply pleased about the choice that they made and are happy with their life in Israel. "Yes," says Simon, "I even have trouble now picturing how we lived there." Liuba notes that they had so little information about Israel in that closed society, so little to base a momentous decision on. "We knew that Jews live here and we wanted to go there, to where Jews live. That's all."

ESTHER

At 1:10 in the afternoon, there was Esther, waiting at the bus stop opposite her dentist's office, a little woman carrying a large handbag with a bright orange ribbon tied to it. The ribbon is a symbol of the right-wing settler movement, specifically coming into use early in the twenty-first century as a sign of opposition to the breaking up of the Jewish settlements in the Gaza Strip. She had made it clear that it was not a good idea to conduct the interview in her home on the other side of the Green Line, as the drive out there could be dangerous. So the best thing would be to wait until she had a dental appointment and then meet right after it. Luckily—or perhaps not so—she came to Jerusalem frequently to see the dentist.

Esther is now over eighty, very lively and garrulous (in Russian), as always. She still gives the impression of a plucky little bird—though plumper than before—chirping around with great interest. Without her feistiness, would she ever have survived the ordeal of her first husband in prison and his subsequent death, found another husband when she was a woman alone with a little boy, organized the family exit from the Soviet Union, survived the breakup of her second marriage?

Esther's life continued to be tumultuous in the years following the first set of interviews. She has a very complicated relationship with her son, her only child. After the divorce, Volt, though a man in his fifties, returned to live with his parents. Esther had housing problems, moving to different locations, eager to buy her own place but without sufficient money to do so. Moving in with her son was not a real option: they are diametrically opposed to each other, politically, and both are uncompromising and edgy. She clearly needed a place of her own. For a while she hung on to what she had, but then her son started to express concern, wanted to free up his own money invested in the flat.

To earn her own living, Esther, well into her fifties at the time of the divorce, finally found herself a job in a souvenir-gift shop in the Old City of Jerusalem. With her good English, she had no problem dealing with tourists and she enjoyed the social activity involved in talking and selling. As she was below pension age, it was very important to Esther that she remain in Jerusalem, near her place of work: the salary was important to her.

Esther and Volt lived their separate lives, but when his mother died, Volt phoned Esther and she came to the funeral. That was all. But in 1986, Volt phoned again, now to tell her that his father had died and this time everything started up again. Volt was in despair and Esther felt that she had to help. They remained in contact. Volt was evicted from the apartment that he had been living in because it had actually belonged to his parents and he had no rights to it. He had to find a new apartment, one which he would buy, and Esther helped him to look for one. "And then we started phoning each other on business. Well, and even without business, just to talk . . . Our relationship was improving, and we started to have conversations and we started phoning each other." Through the Russian grapevine, Esther heard about a good apartment—"a pretty apartment, a very plebian street"—which Volt immediately went to see, and bought. He couldn't believe that he could find something so nice. It cost $32,500 (prices of apartments usually being quoted in dollars in Israel) and was thus affordable.

Esther started to walk out to visit him on Shabbat, first when he was still in his late parents' flat in the German Colony and then out to his new place—a very long walk. They began to spend more time together. At some point her son pressured her to move out of the apartment that she had been living in, which belonged to him. Esther was frantic and started to investigate what options were open to her. One day, walking along King George Street in the middle of west Jerusalem, she saw a sign that encouraged joining a settlement in Judea and Samaria. She had always been in favor of the settlements, but didn't know much about them.

Politically, she says that she had always been on the right. When they first came to Israel, Volt had voted for the Liberal party and Esther had backed the religious Agudat Israel. But in the next elections, in 1977, they both voted for the Likud party. Esther's son, Izka, was already going in another direction, politically, and with time they diverged strongly. Esther and Volt continued to back Likud, but when Begin started to give back land to Egypt, they became disenchanted. "We were living in Ramat Eshkol [a Jerusalem neighborhood]. We didn't know that sometime we would be settlers. We didn't think of it, but we empathized all the same. It's Eretz Israel [the Land of Israel]. Look, it's the same people who started the struggle in Russia [sic]. . .I can say honestly and confidently that, it's true, we began the struggle and didn't know where we were going; we didn't know exactly." She names all sorts of comrades-in-arms from the emigration struggle who are still on the right in Israeli politics. After the Israeli government under Likud leadership gave back Sinai, Esther and Volt backed another right-wing party, Tehia, under the leadership of Yuval Neeman. After this, Esther, for the first time in her life, actually joined a political party, the extreme right-wing Moledet, under the leadership of Rehavam Ze'evi, known in Israel as Gandi.

After the idea of living in a settlement was planted, she (and Volt) began to look into the possibility of her moving to the occupied territories. They attended meetings and visited potential home sites. Houses there would be relatively cheap—they were priced economically to encourage people to live outside the Green Line, even if they were ideologically hesitant about it. Looking for housing in the West Bank, Esther liked what she saw in a little place called Eli, not far from the larger Ariel. The houses are small and not as solidly built as in the city, but it is a village with many of the attractions of one. The price of the house was forty-one thousand dollars, of which Esther had thirty thousand dollars to put down, paying the rest in a mortgage. Eli is growing fast: many of the families there have eight or ten children. It is a mixed community of religious and secular people. In the most recent elections, Likud received the most votes, and Moledet came in second.

Esther is delighted with her little house in Eli. It is perfect for her. She has a living room and kitchen and two other small rooms. The house is surrounded by its own garden, which she looks after. Esther is a lover of animals and has some thirty cats, one of whom lives in the house and the rest in the garden. She feeds them all out of her tiny income.

The couple are both vegetarians, though Volt has started to eat eggs recently. For a while, Esther was the head of the Jerusalem branch of the vegetarian society, though she stepped down at some point. She claims that there were many leftists in the group who were hostile to her as a right-winger. Neither Volt nor she is religious, though they respect religion. "Nu, it's hard for me to believe in God." But she does not ride on the Sabbath: "I feel it isn't proper." If they listen to the radio on Saturday, it is on very low, so as not to offend the neighbors.

Volt still maintains his apartment in Jerusalem, but makes little use of it. Some years ago, she had a medical emergency that landed her in Hadassah Hospital for two weeks. She was afraid to leave her house in Eli because of the garden and the cats, so Volt said that he would take care of it. He took her to the hospital, "and Volt started to live at my place and started to feed the cats and started to water the plants." When she came from the hospital, he worried about how she would get on by herself, and stayed on with her. It's a long way from Novosibirsk, but, after all the drama in her personal life, Esther seems to have found her stability and happiness.

ZAKHARIA

At the beginning of this volume, Zakharia set out quixotically on a bicycle to the relative freedom of Poland and from there to Palestine, where the Jews were hoping to found their own state. It is only appropriate that we should finish with him, still living in Jerusalem thirty-five years after his arrival.

Zakharia lives in a comfortable, well-furnished apartment. He is a vigorous man in his late seventies, with a good head of salt-and-pepper gray hair, a full black mustache and black eyebrows. Photographs in the flat show his wife, extremely good looking, with dark hair. Unfortunately, Bella had passed away some months before the interview, which took place early in January, 2006. It was four in the afternoon on a chilly day. As, in many Jerusalem houses, the central heating doesn't go on in the building until six, he considerately turned on an electric heater.

The interview, at Zakharia's suggestion, was in Hebrew. This is a man who started life in German, learned Yiddish, some Hebrew, Lithuanian and Russian while growing up, and then mastered Hebrew upon arrival in Israel. So what difference does it make which language one speaks! The impression is one of great satisfaction with both his work and the country where he now lives. He never expected—having been a radio journalist in Lithuanian—to find a comparable job in Israel. "Look, an engineer maybe, but a journalist, even with a higher education, an M.A., who worked for twenty-five years in Lithuanian. What can he do in Israel?" But as luck would have it, he did enjoy employment for twenty years at Israel Radio in their Russian-language service. Not only did he live in the country he loved, but he managed to work in the field that he loved.

Like most Israeli men, Zakharia served in *miluim*, the army reserves. A year and a half after arriving, he entered the Israeli army. He had already served in the Soviet army for two years, from 1949 to 1951, as an officer. Now he would be called up to the Israeli army every year, and continued until the age of fifty-five. (Nowadays, Israeli men serve in the reserves for a shorter time.)

Zakharia's beautiful wife, Bella, had been a teacher of German when they lived in Lithuania. Unfortunately, this was not a good subject for Israel, where, for historical reasons, the teaching of German is not offered in the high schools, leaving very little opportunity for teachers. So she took a job with the Jewish Agency at the absorption center at Mevasseret Zion as an education organizer, deciding which school each immigrant child should attend. She, too, picked up Hebrew well; and she also knew English. When she retired at age sixty, she proceeded to work at the Ministry of Education as a supervisor of foreign languages. Both she and Zakharia had managed very well in Israel, and retired with pensions. When asked to compare their financial situation in Israel with that in the Soviet Union, and whether it is at least on a par, Zakharia says, "And how. Ten times as good. "Who ever dreamed of a car? Who dreamed of an apartment like this?"

Zakharia and his wife, who was seven years older than he, never had children together, but Bella's son Alexander has been a son to both of them (though he goes by his birth father's family name) and his daughters call Zakharia "*Saba* [grandpa]." Alexander, who had started out studying law in Vilna, decided, when they arrived in Israel, that he wanted to join the police. He served in the Israeli police force for some twenty-five years. It was there that he met his wife-to-be, Zipporah, who was in the same field. Both of them were born in 1946. Zipporah's parents survived incarceration at Bergen Belsen and were hospitalized after the war. They married and lived in the town of Bergen Belsen, where their daughter was born, until the State of Israel was declared, at which point they immigrated. All four daughters of

Alexander and Zipporah are married, and Zakharia already has great grand-children.

Traditionally, Zakharia has always voted for the Likud party, but he is not sure how he'll vote next time. He sees himself as right of center ("if that is right"). It would really depend upon what kind of coalition might be formed. If Kadima joins up with the Likud and the religious, that would be one thing, but if they want to team up with Peretz (which is what eventually did happen, after this interview took place), that would be something else. He is certainly opposed to Amir Peretz, the head of the Labor party, who, he says, attacks capitalism. On this subject, he refers to his own experience in the orphanage those many years ago, where everything was equal—clothes, food, every-thing—but when you look at what happened afterwards, you see that different children grew up with vastly different achievements. There will always be inequality, he says, people who achieve more or less.

Zakharia isn't opposed to the withdrawal from Gaza, though he doesn't think that it was Sharon's dream to do so. He feels that Israel had to make some sort of gesture in response to President George W. Bush's demands and that Sharon decided to give up the thing that he liked the least. He does not feel that the withdrawal was executed well.

Bella and Zakharia made some exploratory trips into their past. For many years the city of Berlin has invited those of its sons and daughters who left be-cause of the rise of Hitler to return, at least for a visit. In 1993 the couple decided to take up the invitation and see the city of Zakharia's birth. They were there for a few days and were greeted by the mayor of Berlin, who spoke to them warmly. He pointed out that since 1933 until fairly recently no German had won the No-bel Prize (with one exception). His message was: we need you.

Zakharia went to visit his old house and recognized it. It was three or four storeys high and contained a number of apartments. The courtyard, which he remembered from childhood as being very large, seemed small. When he was a little boy, bringing the ball back across the courtyard had been a long way and now it wasn't. The trees seemed smaller. He photographed the building, but didn't go in. "Some people from the lower apartment came out and asked who we were. I said that we were Jerusalemites and had once lived here. They understood right away."

The couple also went to England and, while there, tried to unearth the bank account where funds had been set aside for Zakharia's father in the nineteen thirties. They went to the Midland Bank, the Bank of Scotland and the Bank of England. The clerks, he says, were not eager to help. His uncle told Zakharia that he had received five hundred pounds sterling. That was certainly not the whole amount that should have been on deposit, but that's all they got. Zakharia's uncle gave it to him.

In 1992 Bella and Zakharia went to Lithuania on a sentimental journey, to see his school, some friends and to look into any possibilities of inheritance. Zakharia's father, an excellent businessman, had increased the income in his branch of the family leather business to the extent that in 1938, he had a new building constructed, a special design with two sets of external stairs. There it stands today, occupied now by a company that had originally been next door to them. Zakharia hoped to establish his ownership of the building, with the aim of receiving some repayment for the value. First he contacted the man at the medical school who had recognized Zakharia when he came back from his wartime exile and told him that he had seen his brother being killed. He signed an affidavit that attested that Zakharia was the only living heir. But then his lawyer explained that only people who had had property taken over by the Bolsheviks, and who had Lithuanian citizenship, had any rights—unless someone he knew could make an exception. Zakharia then contacted a well-placed friend and had him arrange to meet with the president of Lithuania. Landsbergis agreed to meet with him and even recognized him from the time when Zakharia had worked at the local newspaper and Landsbergis, a student at the time, used to write reviews of concerts. (His field was musicology and, during his studies, he needed the extra money that could be earned from his articles. He would ask Zakharia to make sure that his articles were placed on page one, or, at the very least, page two, as the rate of payment there was higher than for articles at the back of the paper.) "So he received me and he recognized me and he, very openly, explained to me why the law only applies to Lithuanian citizens. He also said to me, 'We are not afraid of you Jews; only a few of you survived.' [But, he continued,] 'If we give [property] to foreigners, then three-quarters of Vilna would have to be returned to Poles.' Because Vilna was a Polish city until 1939. 'The whole of Vilna, the whole main street and all the buildings that the Poles built, we would have to give back three-quarters of Vilna.'" So, unless efforts to change this regulation are successful, Zakharia has no chance of any compensation.

Zakharia's attitude toward the ethnic Lithuanians differs in many ways from the standard Jewish (or, more accurately, Allied) view, particularly toward those Lithuanian intellectuals who left the country at the end of the Second World War together with the retreating German troops. He certainly does not condemn them. The way he sees it, is that, for the Lithuanians, the German invasion in 1941 represented the second recent one, the first having been the Soviet occupation. "I imagine that after the Russians were the first occupiers, that when the Germans came and threw them out, then the Lithuanians in the beginning saw them as their liberators." Having experienced life under Stalin for a few years, they seized their opportunity to flee at the end of the Second World War. Germany, by then, was a defeated country. These

Lithuanians did not necessarily have to remain in Germany and, in fact, many proceeded to the United States. He differentiates between those who actually helped the Nazis and those who simply did not feel that Stalinist Russia was better. Even the Lithuanians who collaborated, he says, are not always easy to define. For example, he gives the example of someone (from the family of the future first president of independent Lithuania) who greeted the Germans with bread and salt when they first entered Lithuanian territory, but—later in the war—took in a five year old Jewish child and hid her. (She now lives in a kibbutz in Israel.) Zakharia doesn't feel that everything can be seen in black and white.

When asked if he did the right thing in immigrating to Israel, Zakharia is quick to say that he doesn't consider what he did immigration. "Really, first of all, we came home." Home? "Yes, there's no doubt. This is not only my feeling. It's also the feeling of people who were very far from Jewishness." He remembers that in the Soviet Union people he knew—those who worked with him at the radio, for instance—were embarrassed that their grandfather spoke Yiddish. They didn't like to be heard speaking in Yiddish in public places. Zakharia never felt that way, never felt ill at ease with his background. It's true that people left the Soviet Union for America, or Canada, but that, he thinks, was just a matter of money. Money, he says, can make a homeland.

Are you satisfied here in Israel? "Very. Very. And I wouldn't leave it for any other place."

Afterword

The story is not over, nor will it be as long as these immigrants live and their children and grandchildren live on after them. In many ways, their experience is that of everyone who ever came to America or made their way to Israel. Every one of us who is the descendant of immigrants can empathize with them.

But, from another aspect, theirs is a uniquely late twentieth century phenomenon, where the emigrants were faced with the know-how and advanced control exercised by a regime far more totalitarian than the Russian empire that preceded it. Nor is the America of the late twentieth century the same as that of one hundred years before. And Palestine, drawing on small numbers of intrepid settlers then, has become a significant Jewish state since 1948.

Was the struggle worth it? Were those who left the Soviet Union satisfied with the results? Do they feel that they made the right choices for themselves and their families?

Emigration is, by definition, often a bittersweet experience. Leaving one's familiar surroundings, saying goodbye—perhaps forever—to beloved friends and family can never be easy. As it happened, because of political changes in the Soviet Union, these emigrants discovered that they had not cut themselves off forever from their native land or their families. But that could never have been predicted when they started the fateful step to leave back in the 1970s. A certain amount of dissatisfaction and even desperation had to have been present in most of the people who chose to leave the Soviet Union. Their desire to emigrate had to have been greater than the emotional draw of their country of origin. These factors exist in a delicate balance, which can shift with each success or disappointment. The past is always with one and with luck it can become a mellow recollection and not a gnawing pain. The present, if successful, can more than compensate for the losses encountered in the emigration process.

Were people happier in one destination rather than the other? Was America a better choice or was Israel? Nothing in the interviews indicated that there had been a "right" or "wrong" choice. Most people seemed to be happy with the lives they had chosen, though there were certain misgivings. But that is just human nature.

Very possibly, in the future, some of the people who chose to live in Israel—or their descendants—will try out life in the United States. And surely someone in the families of the American group will be attracted by life in Israel. Some will be delighted with the change and others will wish that they had never moved. Once again, it will be a very personal matter for each individual. Happiness is so ephemeral. Do we even know when we have it?

List of Immigrants and Where They Appear

CPSIA information can be obtained at www.ICGtesting.com
Printed in the USA
BVOW060106090412

287110BV00002B/3/P